THE NEW BOOK OF
MAGICAL NAMES

About the Author

Phoenix McFarland is an irreverent Renaissance woman who lives in British Columbia. She and her husband, author Kerr Cuhulain *(The Law Enforcement Guide to Wicca, Wiccan Warrior, Full Contact Magick)*, live near the sea with an assortment of cats. Phoenix has had many articles published in mundane and Pagan publications, including the column "Rainforest Echoes." An erotic short story of Phoenix's is featured in *Seductions* (Dutton). Phoenix holds a college degree in earth science (geology). Her working endeavors have included: coal mine geologist, Old West history researcher, environmental hazardous waste cleanup technician, TV newsroom secretary, and reporter. At one time she also worked with satellites to map Earth from space. She is currently working as a background performer in movies and television.

To Write to the Author

If you wish to contact the author or would like more information about this book, please write to the author in care of Llewellyn Worldwide, and we will forward your request. Both the author and publisher appreciate hearing from you and learning of your enjoyment of this book. Llewellyn Worldwide cannot guarantee that every letter written to the author will be answered, but all will be forwarded. Please write to:

Phoenix McFarland
% Llewellyn Worldwide
P.O. Box 64383, Dept. 0-7387-0395-8
St. Paul, MN 55164-0383, U.S.A.

Please enclose a self-addressed
stamped envelope for reply, or $1.00 to
cover costs. If outside U.S.A., enclose
international postal reply coupon.

THE NEW BOOK OF
MAGICAL
NAMES

PHOENIX MCFARLAND

2003
Llewellyn Publications
St. Paul, Minnesota 55164-0383, U.S.A.

SECOND EDITION, REVISED
Second printing, 2003
Previously titled *The Complete Book of Magical Names,* five printings

Book design and editing by Kimberly Nightingale
Cover design by Gavin Dayton Duffy
Interior art created by the Llewellyn Art Department

Material from *The Kalevala: An Epic Poem after Oral Tradition* by Elias Lonrot (Keith Bosley, trans.), © 1986, used by permission of Oxford University Press.

Material from *The Long, Dark Tea-Time of the Soul* by Douglas Adams reprinted with the permission of Simon & Schuster. Canadian rights granted by Reed Books, London. Copyright © 1988 by Serious Productions, Ltd.

Material from *The Morrigan* by Teara Jo Staples, used by permission. From the album *The Seeker,* Earth Tone Studios, 49 Alafaya Woods Blvd., Oviedo, FL 32165.

Material from *The Homeric Hymns* (Apostolos N. Athanassakis, ed.), © 1976, reprinted by permission of the Johns Hopkins University Press.

Material from *The Mists of Avalon* by Marion Zimmer Bradley, © 1982, reprinted by permission of the author and the author's agents, Scovil Chichak Galen Literary Agency, Inc., New York.

Material from *Firelord* by Parke Godwin, © 1980 by Parke Godwin, reprinted May 1994 by AvoNova Books. Used by permission.

Material from *Interesting Times,* © 1994; *Sourcery,* © 2001; *Maskerade,* © 1996; *Small Gods,* © 1993; and *Guards! Guards!* © 1989, all by Terry Pratchett and reprinted by permission of the author.

Library of Congress Cataloging-in-Publication Data
McFarland, Phoenix, 1955-
    The new book of magical names / Phoenix McFarland. —2nd ed., rev.
        p.   cm.
    Rev. ed. of: The complete book of magical names. 1996.
    Includes bibliographical references and index.
    ISBN 0-7387-0395-8
    1. Magic. 2. Names, Personal—Miscellanea. I. McFarland, Phoenix, 1955-Complete book of magical names. II. Title.
    BF1623.N3M37 2003
    133.4'3—dc21   2002043412

Llewellyn Publications
A Division of Llewellyn Worldwide, Ltd.
P.O. Box 64383, Dept. 0-7387-0395-8
St. Paul, MN 55164-0383
http://www.llewellyn.com
Printed in the United States of America

FOR KERR

How can I name that which means everything?
And sounds like sweet music to my ear,
is there a word for this much joy,
to speak for all the world to hear?

It is, as it has been, for all these many years
unchanging, as it is true
for all of this is known to me
in the sweet-sounding name of you.

TABLE OF CONTENTS

INTRODUCTION

So what are "magical" names?

The woman panted and clenched her lover's hand in a grip that transmitted her struggle. He wiped the sweat streaming down her face and kissed her wet hair, tears in his eyes as he helplessly watched her. A voice came from what seemed like far away, urging her to push. He helped her sit forward and whispered excited encouragement to her as she ground her teeth and held her breath and bore down with all her might. A mighty effort gave pause to a few minutes of recovery as she gulped in breath and lolled her head back. The urge was soon upon her again and with one last push she let life surge through and from her a new voice joined her cries. A new person was in the room. She sank wearily back into her lover's arms. A son. A daughter. Life.

"Do you have a name picked out?" they asked as they lay the child onto the mother's chest.

"Yes." The parents smile and murmur it in greeting to the wizened infant.

"That's your name, darling child," the mother coos.

A tiny fist grabs hold of his father's finger. "How do you do?" said the smiling man. "So, we meet at last!"

. . . The priestesses took her gently by the hands and guided her through the darkness. She stepped hesitantly, barefoot and blindfolded. They neared the fire and she was glad to feel the warmth on her skin. She passed from one person to another and secret, magical things were spoken to her. They asked her questions that she answered in a clear, strong voice. From her they took the blindfold and bid her to see herself anew.

"Leave your old name behind and step into the Lady's path bearing a new name," they said.

Did she know what that name was? Silence filled the glen. The moon peeked out from the treetops as if it, too, were curious to hear her choice. The moonlight gleamed upon the magical symbols painted on her upturned face. After drinking in the moonlight for a moment, she smiled and answered.

"I do," she declared, and whispered it to the coven of witches. Nods and smiles of acceptance circled about her as her new name was whispered by each person together with kisses and hugs of welcome.

. . . She stood by her mother, whom she numbered among her best friends. Her mom kissed her on her forehead the way she used to when she was a little girl. They both sighed. It was time to go. By the light of the new moon, they stepped out into the night. Candles burned in pretty lanterns all around the private garden. Waiting there were the women, friends of her mother, silent yet welcoming. Together they moved through the magical ritual. Each woman spoke in honest words about the secrets to being a woman. The girl nodded, slightly embarrassed, but inwardly thrilled. They welcomed her, they challenged her, they asked from her the many things that she had achieved. They made her laugh and at last, they asked her if she had her new name. The name to herald the change from girl to woman. The name spoken not as an adult to a child but as adult to adult. Yes, she nodded. She had. She had thought about it long and hard before deciding. She spoke it aloud. The women all joined hands and shouted her name into the treetops. With presents and kisses the women embraced and welcomed her to their ranks. They sank into the damp mid-summer grass singing "I am woman, hear me roar . . . " until they dissolved into laughter, deep hearty woman's laughter with not a girlish giggle among them.

These are instances of magical names. A magical name is more than a mere name-word. It is a name to which much thought has been given. Found at the end of a search of one's heart, mind, and self, it is the result of a quest for the perfect name. Magical names harken back to rituals deep in our past when we first named ourselves, when we first looked at ourselves and knew that we were sacred. So, it is more than just a pretty name. It is more than a cool-sounding name scribbled in a margin of a notebook. It can be more than a name; it can be a tool. A tool for transformation. Magical names can take us from child to adult, from woman to mother, from worker to elder, from married to single, and back again. We can use names to define the edges of these transitions, to help us visualize what we want to be in our upcoming life-stage and help us bear our goals in mind. It isn't just babies who are getting new names these days. Adults from all walks of life are turning to names to define and shape themselves. No matter what your path, anyone can utilize the magic inherent in our names and use it to live life more meaningfully, more consciously . . . more magically.

chapter one

NAMES THROUGH
HISTORY

From the dawn of humanity, from the time we began to speak, there were names. The custom of naming offspring is one every society shares. The mystique and importance of our names has grown over many thousands of years. Nomenclature (the system of naming) is a fascinating study because it clearly reflects the mores, customs, and history of a society. Because we put our names on public documents and record the births and deaths of our loved ones, we have access to some of the history of nomenclature.

Our names have changed as we as a culture have changed. Throughout Europe, traditions of naming changed after an invasion to reflect the customs of the new ruling influence. The dark specter of the medieval church dictated generations of baby names (these names were

1

often ugly, ridiculous, and oozing piety). Conformity was the order of the day and any variation from it put one at risk. In those dark times, choosing an unusual name could lead to death by burning, hanging, or being crushed under a great weight of stones.

As the influence of the church waned, other sources became the inspiration for a new generations of names. The poets waxed romantic and our babies had new names. A queen was popular and much loved by her subjects, and her name echoed on in future generations.

In the modern era, actors play beloved characters on television or in the movies and new names become popular. We are now in a time that allows great freedom. We are free to choose names for our children and even for ourselves that are not dictated to us by conquest, an oppressive ruler, the church, or any social convention.

We are in an age of seeking understanding and perspective that we achieve, in part, by looking to the past. We look to history. We look beyond the fearful fundamentalists of today, beyond the misogynistic murderers of the Middle Ages, and back to an era before traditional religions shaped our cultures. We are looking back to a time perhaps when wisdom was valued, nature was revered, and the feminine was venerated; a time before humans believed they held "dominion" over nature, before the quest for youth and beauty held sway over the culture. The ancient rites and rituals may have been lost in the mists of antiquity, but we can look back at what we do know and bring some things from that era forward. The ancient names we chose for ourselves, before we were named after martyred saints, are links to the past.

When our primitive ancestors held a new baby wrapped warmly in the skins of animals and gave the child a name, they probably used methods of naming that would seem odd to us today. Of course, we don't know what the ancients named themselves; their languages have faded from memory many thousands of years ago. The oldest names we know tell us that tribes might choose names for children based on birth order, a desired trait, deities held sacred by the tribe, totem animals, rocks, plants, or weapons. Each little village would build up stocks of name words, and as villages intermingled through trade or war, these names would be spread to new villages and the name pools expanded. Indo-European cultures combined two elements from their name stocks without caring if the name had a coherent meaning. (For example, *Wigfrith* means "war-peace.")

English names spring from an intermingling of several different cultures and languages brought to Britain by her various conquerors. Celtic tribes from Europe invaded Britain circa 1000 B.C.E (before common era). The mighty Roman legions of Julius Caesar first invaded Britain in 55 B.C.E. In 410 C.E. (of the common era), a group of Angles and Saxons began looting along her shores; 300 years later, Anglo-Saxon was the tongue of "Angle-land." Viking sea raiders also sought the tempting treasures Britain held and ravaged her shores about 750 C.E.. In 1017 C.E., the Danish King Canute sat upon the English throne. The Norman-French invaders came in 1066, and for 200 years tried to impose the French language upon the peoples of Britain, without much success. Geoffrey Chaucer's *Canterbury Tales* was published in 1400 and is evidence of a lingering French influence. By the time of Shakespeare's death (1616), Britain was undergoing a surge of English nationalism and rejected French influence. Societal, political, and religious pressures also contributed to the creation of the English language we use today. This rich history is reflected in the names our ancestors chose for their offspring and in the names we bear today.

Each culture had its own ways of choosing names for its children. Some of the ancient Germanic names include words that mean war, strife, battle, protection, rule, counsel, raven, wolf, and bear—all of these were important to the prehistoric Germanic tribes. The literary classic *Nibelungenlied* (a Germanic epic written in 1203 C.E.) is full of wonderful Germanic "warrior" names. Many of the methods of name-making that our ancestors used are still used today by native tribes in Africa.

1000 B.C.E. THE CELTIC INFLUENCE

The Celts (pronounced "kelts"), a group of warrior tribes spread across Europe, emerged as one of the continent's most powerful people in the first millennium B.C.E. They invaded England in 1000 B.C.E. and settled there, lending the Celtic tongue to the inhabitants of England. The Celtic language has two modern variants: Q-Celtic or Goedelic (Gaelic) languages, including Erse, Scottish, and Irish; and P-Celtic or Brythonic languages, including Manx, Breton, Cornish, and Welsh. The main difference between the two is that the "c" or "q" sounds in Q-Celtic are replaced with "b" or "p" sounds in P-Celtic. For example, the prefix "Mac" found in many Scottish names is the Q-Celtic word for "son." "Mac Donald" means "son of Donald." In Welsh (P-Celtic), the word becomes "map" or "mab." The influence of the Celts is strongly felt in nomenclature. A number of names in current usage are from Irish or Scottish Gaelic, or Welsh.

Marcus Tullius Marcifilius Cornelia
Tribu Cicero

—A ROMAN NAME

55 B.C.E.: THE ROMAN INFLUENCE

The Roman invasion of Britain in 55 B.C.E. had a profound effect upon life in the British Isles, from changes in nomenclature to adaptations in the ways in which the people worshiped their gods. The Romans brought with them the fashion of creating images of their deities, which the Celts hadn't developed (this is why there are so few images of Celtic deities). The influence of the Roman Empire had a binding and homogenizing effect on most of the civilized world, and language pools melded into one general vocabulary as Roman rule expanded across Europe and Britain. After the downfall of Rome, the medieval church took over as a unifying power and became a dominant force in molding nomenclature for the next 2,000 years.

In Rome, the system of names was very complicated, involving an individual having several names that indicated paternity and tribal association, as well as the name of the individual. Slaves in the Roman Empire had no individual names and were given the names of their masters, followed by the suffix *por* (meaning "boy"). Later in history, Roman slaves were given sexless Greek names followed by the name of their owners as a token of dishonor.

400 C.E.: ANGLO-SAXON OR OLD ENGLISH

"Anglo-Saxon," in a general sense, describes the Teutonic tribes (Angles and Saxons) who invaded England around 400–500 C.E.. Anglo-Saxon or Old English also describes the language of those peoples. By 700 C.E., the language spoken in "Angle-land" was Anglo-Saxon. The epic poem *Beowulf* was probably written in 700 C.E. and is considered a classic in Anglo-Saxon literature. The influence of the Germanic (Teutonic) languages emerged in Old English nomenclature. In Old English it was common to use name words consisting of two parts, as in *Aelfraed* (*aelf,* "elf" and *raed,* "counsel"). This system of naming can be traced back as far as 3000 B.C.E. to the prehistoric Indo-Europeans. Most Old English names did not survive past the thirteenth century and were forgotten, thanks to the strong arm of the church. The only names that were allowed to emerge out of the distant antiquity of Paganism were those attached to Christians.

Elements Found in Old English Names

Aelf/Alf/Elf: elf.

Beald/Bald: bold.

Aethel/Ethel: noble.

Beorht/Bert: bright.

Beorn/Born: bear; warrior.

Afterwards a son was born to him, a young boy in his house, whom God sent to comfort the people: he had seen the sore need they had suffered during the long time they lacked a King. Therefore the Lord of Life, the Ruler of Heaven, gave him honor in the world: Beowulf was famous, the glory of the son of Scyld spread . . . in the Northlands.

—BEOWULF

Ead/Ed: happiness, prosperity.

Frith/Fred: peace.

Helm: helmet, protection.

Herd/Heard/Hurd: strong, hard.

Her/Here: army, soldier.

Mund/Mond: protection.

Os: deity.

Raed/Rede/Red: counsel, wisdom.

Ric/Rick: rich; rule.

Vin/Win/Wine: friend.

Weald/Wald: power; rule.

Weard/Ward: guard, protection.

Wil/Will: resolve.

Old English or Anglo-Saxon Names

Aethelweard

Aethelwine

Aethelwulf

Alfeah

Aelfric

Aylwyn

Cada

Cuthwulf

Dene

Edmund

Edward

Ethelbert

Hereward

Hereweard

Hilda

Kragg

Mildburh

Mildgyth

Mildred

Mildthryth

Regenbeald (later Reynebaud, then Rainbow)

Regenweald

Thurbeorht

In Old English, although they did not use last names, family ties were created by choosing names that all began with the same letter, or all used the same prefix or suffix. Thus daughters of the same family might be called Mildthryth, Mildburh, and Mildgyth.

750 C.E.: THE VIKING INVASION

Powerful Viking sea raiders from Denmark, Sweden, and Norway ravaged the coastal settlements of Scotland and England around 750 C.E. The raids often involved the abduction of local women, who then became the property of the victors. The Danes finally conquered England in 1017 C.E., when King Canute of Denmark and Norway ruled England and made serfs of the Anglo-Saxons. The Scandanavians who settled in Britain made their mark on the culture and their history speaks to us through the fossils of current names. Names like Osborne, Booth, Svegn, Thorkill, Woolf, Seagram, and Osmond may come from ancient Viking raider ancestors.

Current Names and Their Ancient Viking Roots

Osborne (Asbiorn, God-Bear)

Booth (Bothe, herdsman)

Secker (Sekkr, sackmaker)

Woolf (Uhlfr, wolf-cunning)

Seagram (Saegrmr, sea-guardian)

Knowles (Knol, turnip-head)

Knott (Knutr, square-body)

Osmond (Asmindr, protector)

1066 C.E.: THE NORMAN INVASION

William the Conqueror and his army of Norman warriors were of Scandanavian descent, which is to say they were of Indo-European origin. The Normans came to England after having conquered parts of France. Although the Normans and Anglo-Saxons both originally used a dithemic system (a stock of name words), Norman customs changed slightly after their invasion of France. In France, the language was of Latin descent and people did not use the dithemic system. When the Normans stormed England they brought a very limited stock

of name words with them, fewer name words than there had been for 400 years previously. This accounts for the overuse of a few men's names, such as Richard and Robert. Using the few names they had, they dramatically altered the face of English nomenclature. The Normans brought with them biblical names, saint's names, and Old German names. Almost all the Old English names disappeared within three generations. By 1313, a list of 800 jurors in the Eyre of Kent showed only five Old English names; the rest were Norman.

The Normans instituted the first survey of England. Twenty-one years after their arrival in Britain, an army of clerks armed with quills and thin sheets of vellum invaded every home and interviewed the lord of every manorhouse. Production of crops, numbers of workers, sizes of homes, and heads of livestock were noted. From this information the Norman rulers were able to assess and charge taxes. The information, now only barely readable, was assembled into a two-volume set of books known as the *Domesday Book* (1087). In terms of nomenclature, it is an invaluable resource for historians. The *Domesday Book* indicated that, a mere twenty-one years after the Normans came to England (a very short period of time in terms of nomenclature), Norman names were most prevalent. In fact, virtually every name in the Domesday survey book was Norman.

Norman Names

Emma

Helewis (Heloise)

Henry

Hugh

Matilda

Maud

Ralph

Richard

Robert

Roger

Walter

William

What eclecticism there was decreased by the middle of the thirteenth century. Unless an ancient name was associated with an early Christian saint, it probably dropped out of use. This was because the early church made repeated attempts to obliterate all memory of Pagan classical history, the source of such names. Old Germanic and English names were almost entirely replaced by the names of saints, although some Old English, Norman, Breton, and Latin names were occasionally used.

THE PROLOGUE OF THE CANTERBURY TALES

By the 1300s, Old English (Anglish) was replaced by a new form of English that was a mixture of Anglo-Saxon and French words, with a Norman influence. In 1380, this "new" English became the official language for Oxford and Cambridge Universities in England. Twenty years later, Geoffrey Chaucer wrote *The Canterbury Tales*. The "English" he used in this work is known as Middle English.

Original Middle English

Whan that Aprille with his shoures soote
The droghte of Marche hath perced to the
  roote,
And bathed every veyne in swich licour
Of which vertu engendred is the flour . . .

Modern Translation

When April with his sweet showers has
Pierced the drought of March to the root,
And bathed every vein in such moisture
As has power to bring forth the flower . . .

—GEOFFREY CHAUCER

1300 C.E.: THE NICKNAMES ERA

By 1300, one-third of the males in England were called either William or John. It was therefore necessary, to avoid confusion, to be called by a nickname. For example, Roger could be known as Hodge, and Robert as Hob. In fact, the late Middle Ages became the great era of nicknames. A man born Richard might never be called Richard, but Dick, Rich, Hitch, Hick, Dickon, or Ricket. Robin Hood, Will Scarlet, and Little John are good examples of nicknames in the Middle Ages. The name John today is frequently altered to Johnny or Jack. In the age of nicknames, however, shortened forms were used much more often and more creatively than they are today. In the Middle Ages, John was transformed into Jack, Johnny, Jenning, Jenkin, Jackcock, Jacox, Brown John, Mickle John, Little John, or Proper John. In addition to distinguishing a specific person from others of the same name, nicknames were also often a way to advertise one's trade or profession, such as Arthur the Smithy. The advent of the Puritan movement saw the end of the age of nicknames, as the pious Puritans saw diminutive forms of biblical names as irreverent. The Puritan era was when manners became very important and titles of "Miss," "Sir," and "Ma'am" came into common usage.

Some Nickname Forms in the Fourteenth and Fifteenth Centuries

Adecock (cock is a reference to one who is "cocky," or masculine)

Adkin

Alison

Annot/Annora/Alianora

Batcock

Colin

Dawkin

Diccon

Dickin

Diot

Dobbin

Drewet

Eliot

Emmott

Gibbon

Gilpin

Hallet

Hancock

Hankin

Hitchcock

Hopkin

Huggin

Hutchin

Ibbett

Jeffcock

Jeffkin

Lampkin

Larkin

Lesot

Marion

Maycock

Peacock

Perrin

Pipkin

Gillot

Robin

Simcock

Tibot

Tillot

Tonkin

Warinot (later Warren)

At present our only true names are nicknames.

—HENRY DAVID THOREAU

In the olde dayes of the Kyng Arthour,
Of which that Britons speken greet honour,
Al was this land fulfild of fayerye.
The elf-queene, with hir joly compaignye,
Daunced ful ofte in many a grene mede.
This was the olde opinion, as I rede;
I speke of manye hundred yeres ago.
But now kan no man se none elves mo . . .

—GEOFFREY CHAUCER

SURNAMES

At the beginning of the Middle Ages (1050 C.E.), the people of England, Scotland, and Wales had no surnames. As time went on, the name pools these cultures drew upon became too limited; as the population grew, it became confusing because so many people bore the same name. Surnames were once called sir names, because the nobility were the first to adopt this second name. The method by which the gentry chose a surname was usually by association with their property. Thus, Robert, Lord of Blackstone Castle or Edward, Earl of Thornfield Hall were titles that the gentry passed down to successive generations. By the year 1250 C.E., these titles were passed on whether the child was residing in the manor or not. Many of the people in England had adopted a second name by the thirteenth or fourteenth centuries, but even by 1465 C.E. the use of last names was not yet universal.

Before hereditary surnames evolved, the first surnames were often patronymic (named for the father by adding "son" to a father's name: "Fitz" in Teutonic or "Mac" [Mc] in Gaelic); some were place names (indicating residence or origin); others were names of trade or nicknames that described a characteristic of the person. Thus William Jackson, Robin of Loxley, Alywin the Smythe, or Bodrick the Forgetful were representative thirteenth-century names.

Many societies clung to the patronymic system, even though naming through the mother's line is much more accurate, as maternity, unlike paternity, is never questionable. There is evidence that some cultures were matriarchal, but with the advent of the patriarchal warrior tribes, customs changed. With patriarchy came the notion of female virginity at marriage and strict monogamy as means of assuring paternity. It was under this patronymic system that a woman first began to take the name of her husband. This was one of the profound changes in cultural history that is well illustrated by the history of nomenclature. Within these subtle changes of nomenclature, history bears witness to the subjugation of women in Western culture.

Patronymic Names

Fitzgerald

Jackson

Johnson

MacGregor

Wilson

Place Name Elements

Ay/Ey: island, marshy meadow.

By: farm, hamlet, town.

Cott: cottage.

Croft: fenced-in field.

Den/Dene: valley, pasture.

Don/Dun: hill, slope.

Garth: homestead, enclosure.

Gea: castle.

Hale/Hall: corner; house.

Ham: farm, homestead.

Holt: wood.

Holm: island.

Law/Low: small hill.

Lay/Lee/Ley: clearing, meadow.

Mor/More/Moor: marshy or barren land.

Shaw: small wood.

Stan/Staun: stone.

Stow: place.

Thorpe: settlement.

Ton: village, town.

Wal: foreigner; wall.

Wald/Weald: forestland.

Wick/Wich/Wyck: farm (esp. dairy farm).

Worth: enclosure, homestead.

NAMES FROM LOCATIONS

Atwood: forest dwellers.

Bradford: the broad ford.

Cheney: from the oak-wood.

Dean: valley dweller.

Endicott: from the end cottage.

Ford: place to cross a stream.

Shaw: shady glen.

Standish: a stony place.

Winthorp: from a friendly village.

They shall take unto them a surname either of some towne, or some colour as blacke or brown, or some art or science, as smythe or carpenter, or some office, as cooke or butler.

—THE LAW PASSED BY KING EDWARD IV

NAMES FROM TRADES

Baxter (baker)

Brewster (brewer)

Butler

Carpenter

Carter

Clark (scholar)

Cook

Currier (tanner)

Fowler

Gardener

Harper

Mason

Taylor

Tyler

Wainright (wagon builder)

Ward

Webster (weaver)

In the days of Edward IV (1465 C.E.), a law was passed to compel Irish outlaws to take a surname (conceivably, it was easier to identify and keep track of such people with a surname). It wasn't until King Henry VIII (early 1500s) that people in England began keeping a single hereditary surname. Henry VIII drafted edicts to the people of Wales trying to force them to adopt the custom of surnames, which had been popular in England for some time. King Henry VIII's full hereditary name was "Henry VIII,

By the Grace of God, King of England, France, and Ireland; Defender of the Faith, the Supreme Head and Sovereign of the Most Noble Order of the Garter." In Wales and remote Ireland, however, the people rejected surnames so strongly that there are people in the recent past who still bore a single name.

1500 C.E.: THE INCREASED INFLUENCE OF THE CHURCH

On Halloween night in 1517, beneath the light of the full moon, a German monk named Martin Luther nailed a proclamation to the door of a church and changed history. Luther, a Dominican monk in a small backwater village in Germany, did not like what he saw of Catholicism. His views presented a gentler, more forgiving god than the punitive one of the Catholics. He might have become one of hundreds of disgruntled monks the Vatican frowned upon and muzzled into silence but for the availability of technology.

While the ecclesiastical hierarchy in Rome was deciding the best way to silence this troublemaker, Luther had his ideas printed and distributed all over Germany. The social and religious rebellion that Luther inspired led to division and uproar. As the pendulum swung toward a gentler religion with Luther, it swung back to a stricter one with another leader. This time it was a Frenchman named Calvin, whose tenets were grim and filled with sin, describ-

ing the basic depravity of humanity and its inevitable end in fire and brimstone. This added to the reformation already in progress, and change swept across Europe. The Protestant Reformation shaped the lives of people at a deep level by making them submit to an intense scrutiny of their private lives and personal conscience, paving the way for the atrocities that were to come later in the Burning Times.

The Protestant Reformation also caused an upheaval in the customs of naming babies in England and the New World. Until then, people used only a few biblical names, but mostly non-biblical saint's names. These were not mentioned in the Bible but were names of supposed local saints, some of whom doubtless were whitewashed versions of local goddesses and gods.

The church preached the virtues of naming children after biblical saints, but the advice was not taken enthusiastically until after the Council of Trent (1545–63), when the Roman Catholic church required a baby to bear the name of a canonized saint or angel in order for the child to be baptized. The variety of saint's and biblical names was much greater than the old stock of name words and thus increased the number of names available for name making.

Even so, there was still not a very wide assortment of names from which to choose. Only 3,037 male names and 181 female names are given in the Bible. This new, albeit limited, supply of names, combined with the very strong pressure from the church, contributed to a complete switch in nomenclature customs. All the names of nonscriptural saints fell into disgrace and were no longer used. Austin, Bride, Blase, Hilary, Quenton, and Valentine all but disappeared in the sixteenth century. These changes did not happen overnight, however. Most of the name changes didn't happen until the Reformation took stronger hold and as the attitudes of a movement known as Puritanism developed.

1580 C.E.: THE PURITAN ERA

The Puritan era was my favorite period of time only in terms of its curiosities of nomenclature. It is good to find something of interest and amusement in these times; the Puritan era lies within those horrible years we have come to call "the Burning Times," and there was little to laugh about during this reign of terror.

Reformation abolished the old system of nomenclature, while Puritanism supplied a new one. The Puritans turned the Reformation into a crusade against all Catholic dogma and ceremonies. With obsessive zeal overpowering their good taste and common sense, the Puritans changed the customs of nomenclature in Britain and in recently settled (1620) Massachusetts. Puritans were fundamentalists in the extreme. The custom of picking names from the Bible was

taken beyond any other custom to date. Some very unlikely names were pressed into service. Old Testament names, incidental biblical references, biblical place names, and ordinary words and phrases were used as first names. Names were sometimes assigned without regard to the sex of the bearer. An example is a custom of using Maria as a man's name, while Dennis and Matthew were used as women's names. The extent of the Puritan influence on nomenclature decreased to the north in the British Isles, with Scotland scarcely having any Puritan names at all. The Puritans were in the minority in England, but in America they flourished. In the New World, this religious fundamentalism launched a revolution in nomenclature that saw the almost complete abandonment of all Norman names in the New World.

Some Actual Puritan Names (1500–1640 C.E.) Found in English Birth Records

Abstinence

Abuse Not

Acceptance

Accepted

Acts-Apostles

Adulterina

Aholiab

Anger

Arise

Asa

Ashes

Assurance

Barnabus

Be Steadfast

Be Thankful

Be Strong Philpott

Be Courteous Cole

Beloved

Bezaleel

Caleb

Changed

Charity

Chastity

Clemency

Consider

Continent

Deliverence

Delivery

Depend

Desiderius

Desire

Discipline

Do Good

Dust

Earth

Ebenezer

Elihu

Elilama

Eliphalet

Erastus

Experience

Ezekiel

Faint Not

Faith

Farewell

Fear God

Fear-Not

Fight the Good Fight of Faith (a first name)

Flea-Fornication (or Flee-Fornication)

Fly Fornication Richardson

Forsaken

Free-Gift

From-Above

Gamaliel ("camel of God")

Give Thanks

God Reward

Godly

Habakkuk ("the wrestler")

Hariph ("the flower of life")

Hate Evil

Help on High

Helpless

Hephzibah ("my pleasure or delight in her")

Hezekiah ("strong in the Lord")

Honor

'Tis good to impose such names as expresse our baptismal promise. A good name is as a thread tyed about the finger, to make us mindful of the errand we came into this world to do for our master.

—WILLIAM JENKIN
PRESBYTERIAN MINISTER
CHRIST CHURCH, LONDON (1652)

Puritanism: The haunting fear that someone, somewhere, may be happy.

—H. L. MENCKEN

Hope

Hopestill

Humble

Humiliation

Ichabod ("the glory has departed")

Increased

Isaiah ("salvation of the Lord")

Jaell ("ibex")

Jedidiah ("praise of the Lord")

Jehostiaphat Star ("the Lord judges")

Joab ("the Lord")

Joy

Joy In Sorrow

Joy-Again

Judas-Not Iscariot

Justice

Kerenhappuch ("splendor of color")

Kill Sin Pimple

Lament

Lamentation

Learn Wisdom

Live Well

Lively

Love

Love God

Magnify

Mahershalalhashbaz Christmas
(Mahershalalhashbaz means "haste to the spoil, quick to the prey")

Make Peace

Malachi ("angel of the Lord")

Merciful

Mercy

Meshach ("agile or expeditious")

Misericordia-Adulterina

More Fruit

More-Triall

Muche-Merceye

No-Merit

Obedience

Obey

Onesiphorus ("profit bearing")

Patience

Persist

Phineas ("mouth of brass")

Pleasant

Pontius Pilot Pegden

Postumus

Preserved

Prudence

Reformation

Refrain

Rejoyce Lord

Remember

Renewed

Repent

Repentance

Revolt Morecock

Riches

Sabbath Clark

Safe-on-High

Savage

Search the Scriptures

Shadrach ("rejoicing in the way")

Shelah

Silence

Sin Deny

Sin-No-More

Sirs ("Sirs, what must I do . . . ")

Solomon

Sorry for Sin

Stand Fast on High

Steadfast

Supply

Temperance

Thank

Thankful

The Peace of God

The-Lord-is-Near

Tremble

Tribulation Wholesome

Truth

Unfeigned

Virtue

Weakly

Wealthy

Welcome

Zachariah ("remembrance of the Lord")

Zaphnathpaaneah ("sorrow of the age")

Zeal of the Land

Of particular interest is the seventeenth-century Barebone family. One or two members of this family may be referred to by the name of "Barebones," but that is not accurate. The Barebone family consisted of at least four brothers who were named:

Praise-God

Fear-God

Jesus Christ Came Into the World to Save

If Christ Had Not Died for Thee Thou Hads't Been Damned

Due to his bad reputation, the Puritan taboo against shortening given names was waived by the public when referring to Dr. "Damned" Barebone. Praise-God Barebone was imprisoned after the Reformation, was released shortly afterward, and died an old man in obscurity in London.

My own family were farmers, and (ack!) one married the sister of the sinister clergyman Nicholas Noyes of Salem. The names I found in my genealogical research were representative of the Puritan influence of the day. At the three hundredth commemoration of the Salem Witch Trials at Dragonfest Pagan gathering in Colorado, I met another Pagan whose ancestor married another one of Noyes' sisters. At the same festival was also a descendant of one of the victims of the Salem witch hunt. Now we're all on the same side, witches all. It added an eerie and uplifting element to the ritual to know this history.

Puritan Influence in My Own Family

Abel

Abiel

Asa

Asahel

Azariah

Calvin Ely

Cyrus

Ebenezer

Elias

Eldad

Eliakim

Eliphalet

Elisha

Enoch

Ephraim

Hannah

Hezakiah

Hiram

Huldah

Isaac

Israel Ela

Jemima

Luther

Moses

Nathan

1600 C.E.: POST-REFORMATION

Following the piety of the Reformation came a period in which change crept quietly over society, especially in terms of nomenclature. One of the ways in which our naming practices changed was by using surnames as first names, even for girls. Names such as Gilford, Ashford, Rutherford, Ashley, Hill, Dudley, Stanley, Keith, Douglas, and Graham began to appear as early as the early 1600s during the reign of Elizabeth I. The church and pious community leaders condemned the use of these names, but to no avail. Usually the names were maternal family names used as first names to keep the names from dying out. The fashion is still popular today. Despite the desire of the church to retain control over nomenclature, the pendulum had begun to swing in the opposite direction and there was nothing that could be done to stop it.

The seventeenth century saw few other changes in naming practices, except for the adoption of multiple names. The giving of at least one additional name remains popular to the present time. As with most trends in nomenclature in England, new names were adopted by royalty, then became pop-

ular among the gentry, then the lower classes. It was the aristocracy who initially embraced this trend so enthusiastically that it appeared to be a contest to see how many ostentatious names could be hung on a child. The double names Mary Anne and Anna Maria appeared after the revolution of 1688, named for queens Mary and Anne. Double names lasted to the nineteenth century, and gradually became confined to the lower classes and eventually relegated to the southern United States.

THE EIGHTEENTH CENTURY

The eighteenth century saw classical or Latinized names for women take hold in fashionable society. Names such as Anna from Anne and Maria from Mary came into vogue.

Latinized Women's Names

Anna

Sophia

Olivia

Evelina

Cecilia

Juliana

Maria

In addition to this Latin influence in the eighteenth century, there was also a revival of the medieval names of Old English. Names that had been put aside for hundreds of years suddenly enjoyed a burst of popular appeal. Names such as Edgar, Edwin, Alfred, Galfrid, Emma, and Matilda flourished.

THE NINETEENTH CENTURY: THE ROMANTIC MOVEMENT

Many old names were taken out of the history books and dusted off for use in the nineteenth century, thanks to a social and a religious movement. First, the Romantic movement (1798–1832) introduced escapism, mysticism, and a new surge of imagination in literature. Poetry of the time revived old legends of ancient gods and goddesses, fairies, elves, and the tales of Robin Hood and King Arthur. Gothicism, a return to Celtic and Scandinavian mythology, and a sentimental interest in the relics of an idealized past, was also characteristic of Romanticism. As an enthusiastic response to this new age, thought-provoking authors such as Scott brought us names like Wilfrid, Guy, Roland, Nigel, Quentin, and Amy. The romantic, idealized medievalism of Tennyson and the pre-Raphaelites popularized names such as Lancelot, Walter, Hugh, Aylmer, Roger, Ralph, Ella, Alice, Mabel, and Edith.

Religiously, the Tractarian movement was responsible for the acceptance of several antiquated saint's names, such as Aidan, Augustine, Alban, Theodore, Benedict, and Bernard.

ROMANTIC ERA NAMES

Aidan

Alban

Augustine

Benedict

Bernard

Clarissa

Cristabel

Guinevere

Gwendolyn

Lancelot

Marmaduke

Theodore

The Victorian era (1837–1901) saw the addition of names taken from everyday words, including names for gemstones, flowers, plants, and birds.

NAMES FROM NATURE

Cherry

Daisy

Fern

Ivy

Lilly

Opal

Orchid

Robin

Rose

Ruby

Violet

THE TWENTIETH CENTURY: NAMES FROM POPULAR CULTURE

The twentieth century has seen the fashions of nomenclature grow increasingly eclectic in the United States as well as England. There is a practice of using names from all over the world and from a variety of new sources. Novels, television, and the cinema have influenced our names and methods of name-making. It became popular in the early twentieth century to simply "make up" a name, or to combine two existing names to form a new one. It seems that about every ten years a new group of names becomes popular and the names that reigned the decade before are ousted. The names Doris, Peggy-Sue, Sunshine, Denny, Tiffany, and Morgan can be associated with the 1940s, 1950s, 1960's, 1970s, 1980s, and 1990s respectively.

Frank Zappa, a rock musician, has also etched a place in popular nomenclature by virtue of his choice of names for his children. They are named Moon Unit, Dweezil, Diva, and Ahmet. Moon Unit (a girl) was first-born; if she had been born male, her name was to be Motorhead. When the Zappas went to the hospital to have their son Dweezil, the admitting nurse became annoyed when Frank answered "Musician" to the question "What is your religion?" When she found out the parents intended to name the baby Dweezil, she pleaded with them to name him something else. Despite the fact that Ms. Zappa was in labor, the nurse was determined to let her stand at the admitting desk until they thought of a "proper" name for the baby. The angry parents rattled off an assortment of names of people they knew, and as a result the baby was legally called "Ian Donald Calvin Euclid Zappa." Of this name, the nurse approved. The child, nevertheless, was called Dweezil. He was five years old before he discovered his legal names on his birth certificate. Dweezil was upset and pleaded with his parents to legally change his name to Dweezil, which they did. Diva (a girl) and Ahmet (a boy) came along later, and presumably no one tried to enforce traditional names on these members of the Zappa family. Traditional, especially religious, input is not worthless to Frank Zappa, however. He found it useful in disciplining his children. When his children misbehaved, he would make them watch a televangelist. Eleven-year-olds do not find this to be fun and it was successful as a form of discipline.

Musical history played an important part of the naming process for actress Valerie Bertinelli and her rock-star husband Eddie Van Halen when they chose a name for their son. In honor of the two hundredth anniversary of Wolfgang Amadeus Mozart's death and out of respect for his genius, the couple named their son Wolfgang Van Halen. I applaud their creativity and individuality in choosing Wolfgang. A grand old name!

People make a lot of fuss about my kids having such supposedly "strange names," but the fact is that no matter what first names I might have given them, it's the last name that is going to get them in trouble.

—FRANK ZAPPA

It's good to take magical names that express our relationship with the Goddess. It will act as a string around the finger, to remind us of our place in the Universe, our roles as priest or priestess, our personal goals, and our responsibility to the earth.

—PHOENIX MCFARLAND

NAMES FROM BOOKS

The ever-increasing popularity of science-fiction, fantasy, and the swords-and-sorcery genres of literature and cinema has contributed to popularizing creative new names and opening our imaginations to accepting new and interesting names. Especially popular have been the Harry Potter books. I have devoted an entire chapter to names from literature in the latter half of the book.

AMERICAN NAMES

Creating names by flights of imagination is a long-standing American tradition. This method began in the southern United States, but soon grew in popularity in the north as well. This method involves new ways of spelling old names, such as Kathryn or Madalynne, or combining syllables from existing names in new combinations, such as Lauretta and Luvenia. This method is very popular in African-American names. Another American fashion, especially in the South, is to use pet name forms as formal names. Former President "Jimmy" Carter, for example, is legally named James, but insists on being called by his pet name.

Historical nomenclature is useful to us to examine the culture and influences of the day and learn something of the people who bear the names. At first glance, one would assume that this modern practice of making up new names is obscuring the clarity of historical nomenclature and confusing its social significance. Some Western countries have agreed with this notion and have created legislation to combat these trends. In France, for example, the Revolutionary Law of Germinal XI (1803) decreed names were to be chosen only from persons known in ancient history, or in use in the various calendars. Germany's laws state that a name must be one that can be proved to have been used before. While such laws keep the waves of modern popular names at a minimum, they simultaneously restrict the natural evolution of nomenclature. On one hand we are creating generations of meaningless, artificial names (which does say something about the culture in which we live); on the other hand, others are simply spinning out new generations of older name clones (which also says something about that culture). So by the very nature of our superficiality or resistance to change, historical nomenclature is as socially significant as ever.

chapter two

Naming
Children

I n naming a child, you must first decide just how conventional or unconventional you want to be. There are arguments on either side of this issue. The drawbacks of giving a child a unique name are that people do have a tendency to strive toward commonality and conformity and may pressure the child or discriminate against her or him. Unusual names may interfere with social interaction and make the child a bit of an outcast. But these days the norm is moving toward the unusual. Many parents are seeking the truly unique name for their child, so in order to be considered really unusually named, you have to go pretty far out there. You may not want to name your son something as unorthodox as Ichabod, Dweezil, or Sherlock, or your daughter

25

You don't just pick a name,
you name the child.

—PHOENIX MCFARLAND

MAUDE: *No beautiful names, okay? Not Nicholas or Christopher or Adam or Jonathan.*

ROB: *Or Jennifer or Gwyneth or Cherish or Innocence.*

MAUDE: *And no politics, right? Not America or Peace and Freedom . . . just short and to the point . . . Joe, Gus, Eddie. Not Edward, Eddie.*

ROB: *Sue, Pat—American Bandstand names, right? So, it's settled. If it's a girl, it's Tallulah No-Nukes Salinger.*

MAUDE: *And if it's a boy, it's Bartholomew Zachary Save-the-Whales Chastity-Belt Salinger.*

—*MICKI AND MAUDE,* 1984

Cinderella, Tallulah, or Tinkerbell. Those who bear very odd names may suffer from less attention given in classrooms and the prejudice of potential employers. They may encounter a certain lack of respect in general. Bear in mind that you do not know what sort of person this baby will grow up to be. They might well want to be a corporate lawyer or stock broker. It would be very difficult as Cinderella Leilani or Kennocha Tofu.

Despite the trouble the mundane world may give to a child with an unusual name, I feel that there are compelling arguments in favor of, at least, a moderately unusual name. On the plus side to giving the child an unusual name is that by setting the child apart from the "norm" of society, he or she may see life differently than the average "Joe." This may be a good thing. In my view, most of the truly brilliant, sensitive, creative, and ethical people are in some way outcasts. Most geniuses, artists, poets, and Pagans were outcasts, and they are better people for the experience. You might want to look at the society from which your child may be shunned. Do you really want your child to fit in with those people? If you are Pagan, your child being from a family of Neopagans, Wiccans, or New Agers will set the child apart in the first place, so sticking the child with a name like "Mary" or "Joseph" won't make the child fit in any better. If you look at the members of any metaphysical or spiritual community, you will see that we are all different from the "norm." We are set apart and we have come to see a great advantage in this. Why would we want less for our children? In addition, the traditional name stocks from which we choose names are often Christian in origin, and many people are reconsidering using such names for non-Christian people.

If enough people begin naming their children unconventional names, soon it will become the accepted practice. In fact, this trend is on the rise; fewer people want to name their children conventional names. There is growing acceptance for the unique rather than the traditional name-words. If you choose to take the road less traveled in picking a name for your child, tread thoughtfully. Finally, if little Kennocha Tofu does grow up to be a lawyer who longs to be called Lloyd, he can always change his name.

When choosing a name, the question of the sexual orientation of the parents (they are not always heterosexual) and the idea of gender identification comes up. As time goes by, names that had traditionally belonged to one sex are sometimes claimed by the other. For example, at one time, it was common to find boys named Maria, Marion, Leslie, Clare, Lucy, Ann, Patsy, Caroline, Vivian (Vyvyan), Carol, Dorris, Evelyn, Jean, and Shirley. As interesting as that fact might be, to choose a name that is sexually confusing takes its toll on the

Parents in Sweden were disappointed when the court refused to allow them to name their child an unusually spelled name. The proposed name was to be pronounced "Albin." It was to be spelled "Brfxxccxxmnpcccc111mmprxvc1m nckssq1bb11116."

To be normal is the ideal aim of the unsuccessful.
—CARL JUNG

child. The unhappy truth is that most North Americans are homophobic and frightened by anything that rocks the boat in terms of sexual identity. This fear usually takes the form of aggression against the dissident. Androgynous names can also become an object of ridicule and result in battery in the schoolyard. The *Saturday Night Live* sketch featuring "Pat" whose gender you cannot discover, is a good example of such gender questionable names taken to an extreme. But the lines are blurring between what are boy's and girl's names. There are actresses with "male" names such as Sean Young and Michael Learned. Sean's real name was Mary Sean Young. Sean apparently liked her gender-bending name for she named her two sons Rio and Quinn, both sexually neutral names and very good choices.

There is also the question of extremes in sexuality in choosing a name. If you are all frilly and perfumed and love ultrafeminine names, please be aware that your daughter may end up a rough-and-tumble tomboy or athlete. Picking a very masculine or feminine name could be embarrassing or overwhelming to your child.

As unfair as it is, names for boys have a more devastating impact on the youngster than girl's names. It's not easy being a young boy growing up in the school yard, especially if your name is "Rambo." Other boys will expect a certain level of testosterone to accompany a name like that. If you don't want your son to be a punching bag, or a defensive pugilist, stay away from the very "guy" names. In the same way, however, you can take it too far the other way. A boy named "Mortimer" or "Francis" will not have it any easier. It might be said that boys are under more pressure to conform than girls, and so the degree to which a boy's name may be unusual is more confining than it is for a girl. You might venture further out for a daughter's name, but come in closer to the norm for a son's. Researchers have found that boys who had peculiar first names had a higher incidence of mental problems than boys with common ones; no similar correlation was found for girls. Keep in mind that your "clever" choice of a name could end up causing your baby black eyes and split lips.

I was named Laurel at birth. It was an unusual name that, as I was often told, meant "honor." It set me apart from the many girls named more conventional names. So, from the time I was little, I learned to see beyond the norm of society. People frequently commented on the beauty of my name, which made me feel somehow special and magically empowered. I took the meaning of my name seriously and I tried to choose the honorable path. I think that my name helped me to develop magically. Try to imagine what effect the name you are considering might have on the child. Some of the impact of the name comes from what you tell the child about the name you chose. My parents often told me that my name was about beauty, honor, and triumph (resting upon one's laurels). Remember that your child is his or her own person, a separate soul who may have other plans than adopting your politics or religion. Perhaps the kindest thing to do would be to give the child a name that would reflect your Pagan beliefs but work equally well in other worlds. Laurel was such a name for me. The only difficulty in being a Pagan who bore the name Laurel was when it came time to pick a magical name—I already had a beautiful one.

Often, even after the most thoughtful and well-intentioned parents choose what they consider to be the "perfect" name for their baby, the baby may grow up loathing their "perfect" name. A beautiful name to one person may be hideous to someone else. You do the best you can with what you have, and little Kennocha Tofu—I mean young Lloyd—will just have to deal with it as he sees fit. Names are not forever, even legal ones. Many people have legally changed their names for the sake of their careers, or just for their own pleasure. My cousin and her fiancée didn't like either of their last names, so when they married they chose a new last name and both had their names legally changed. If your parents did not discover your true name, take up the quest and discover it for yourself. Take control of the name by which the world knows you; own it or disown it.

chapter three

THE POWER OF THE
MAGICAL NAME

As we set foot on a spiritual path, we begin to change. Life, well lived, is change. To walk the spiritual ways, especially the path of the Goddess-based religions, involves an enormous amount of personal transformation. We change. We grow. We evolve into new people many times over as we progress through life. We are no longer static and unchanging; we no longer "fit" the names given to us by someone else, which we have carried all our lives. After having met the challenges the Goddess gives us, after having studied and developed our power and wisdom; having learned to work magic, the healing of the sick, the divination of the future, we just simply are no longer a "Kathy" or a "Dan."

We all wear many names through life's changes. We wear baby names, little child names, adolescent names, nicknames our friends give us, adult nicknames our colleagues give us, pet names our lovers give us. Women often take different names each time they marry or divorce. We take initiation names and often rename ourselves at each degree along the magical path. We name our tools, our homes, our pets, our children, our covens, and some have been known to name certain body parts as well. The reason we have so many names is that we are constantly evolving, and for each new stage in our development we choose a new name. If chosen thoughtfully, each name can be used as a tool to hasten our spiritual evolution and our understanding of ourselves.

Of all the times in our lives when we take on a new name, one of the most meaningful is the initiation rite. The ritual of initiation is one of the most significant religious experiences in human spirituality. This is an act that invokes great change, not only in the religious arena of a person's life but over his or her entire life. The ceremonial renaming of initiates is an archaic and powerful tradition still practiced today by Neopagans, Wiccans, and even Christians. Catholic nuns may, and often do, choose a new name upon becoming nuns. Roman Catholic popes traditionally choose a new name upon election by the College of Cardinals. This custom

began in 844 C.E. when a priest named Boca de Porco was elected pope. (*Boca de Porco* means "pig's mouth.") Pope Pig Mouth was perhaps not in keeping with the image the church wished to have.

Baptismal names are customarily chosen for the Christian initiation ritual. The rebirthing experience that occurs in many other initiations includes the taking up of a new appellation to represent the newly "born" initiate. The new name is also used to introduce the new person to the deities within them, as well as to the companions witnessing the ritual. Most of all, however, the new name is intended for the benefit of the initiate. If the name is the initiate's true name, the act of discovering it will have been a meaningful exercise in self-discovery. A person's true name is believed to resonate to the sound of his or her soul. A magical name can represent the initiate's newly discovered spiritual persona. Naming it validates that facet of the person's personality but validates the person's spiritual quest as well.

Another powerful renaming rite is the manhood/womanhood ritual. There is a trend in North America to reinstate rituals of adolescent initiation. The coming of age rituals are transformative ceremonies that span nearly every society, past and present. As with religious initiations, a coming of age initiation may involve a renaming of the initiate to reflect the mature personality as contrasted with the youthful personality.

The rituals involve a clear understanding of the qualities of that which is sought (manhood or womanhood). It involves the initiate's understanding of his or her strengths and weaknesses. Having undergone a trial of some kind to prove his or her worth to the community, and most of all, to themselves, the individual is given their first adult name. This concept appears in many novels of the science-fiction/fantasy genre.

There are many tools and traditions available to us as we walk the path of the Goddess. People involved in the New Age disciplines use many of these. Many tools are used to help us understand our power, and some tools work better for us than others. Some use tarot cards, some candle magic; both are effective and both have merit. One of the tools often overlooked by Pagans is the power in the name we bear.

Witches don't twitch a nose and wild things just happen. The source of our power is in our own minds. Our power comes in the form of psychology, self-awareness, strength, vision, bravery, self-transformation, discretion, curiosity, and comfort with change. To understand ourselves is to gain control over that which creates our reality. Most people haven't a clue as to who they are. Perhaps such understanding begins with the name by which we call ourselves. This may be a key to spiritual transmutation.

The names we choose for ourselves can serve as magical tools as we travel on our

Verily, she is a magician, and of divine might, which hath power to bring down the sky, to bear up the earth, to turn the waters into hills and the hills into running waters, to call up the terrestrial spirits into the air, and to pull the Gods out of the heavens, to extinguish the planets, and to lighten the very darkness of Hell.

—APULEIUS
THE GOLDEN ASS

Magical names can help our minds manifest the magic.

—PHOENIX MCFARLAND

*First, the initiate is given a Witch name, which
she or he has chosen beforehand. The choice is
entirely personal. It may be a God-name or
Goddess-name expressing a quality to which
the initiate aspires, such as Vulcan, Thetis,
Thoth, Poseidon or Ma'at. . . . Or it may be the
name of a legendary or even historical figure,
again implying a particular aspect, such as
Amergin the Bard, Morgana the Sorceress,
Orpheus the Musician, or Pythia the Oracle. It
may even be a synthetic name made up of the
initial letters of aspects which create a balance
desirable to the initiate (a process drawn from a
certain kind of ritual magic). But whatever the
choice, it should not be a casual or hurried one;
thoughtful consideration before the choice is in
itself a magical act.*

—JANET AND STEWART FARRAR
THE WITCHES' BIBLE

individual paths. A name can be an inspiration; it can label us by our attributes or our failures, and can inspire us to change. Our names can associate us with elemental powers and bring that energy into our lives. A name can help to improve how we feel about ourselves. It can emphasize where we are now or where we hope to go. It can make us feel more powerful, wiser, more beautiful, more commanding, gentler, stronger, more female/male, more exotic, more innocent, more sexual, more enthusiastic, more fertile, etc. There is no limit to what a name can bring into our lives, except for those limits we put on it ourselves.

For example, if you are skinny, shy, and awkward and long to be confident, powerful, commanding, and assured, a name change may be a positive and helpful tool for transformation. Take some time and think about yourself the way you are and the way you'd like to be. Let your inner voice guide you in choosing a new name. To become empowered, fire names or powerful God or Goddess names or simply a name of someone you see as having these attributes is an appropriate choice. Conversely, if you are learning to control an angry temper, then a change to a cooler water name might help put out the excess fire. There are endless images that can help to change your life.

Energy in this world tends to flow like water down an established path ever deepening the channel through which it flows.

Habits create ruts. If you begin to channel energy in a small way via a name change, pretty soon people will begin to associate you with that energy. Perhaps you will begin to collect imagery of that energy such as a water-named person beginning to collect seascapes or shells. You may incorporate some water imagery into your meditations and magical practices. You may connect more with sea deities. You may be drawn to blues and greens in clothing and room decore. As you envelop yourself with the water imagery, it invades your dreams, it works on the subconscious, and soon the water washes over, through, and into your life. With each etch in the pattern, the energy flows more readily until drop by drop, you are transformed by the shift in energies flowing into your life. Soon the old angry fire energy just feels out of place in your new world. You drop those associations with anger as a focus and attract new, more intuitive, emotionally calm people. Energy flows this way. It works this way with water as it turns mountains into plains. It works this way with habits and change. This is also how practitioners of feng shui manipulate the energy flows in one's home.

There is no reason for limiting yourself by having only one name. A name is a tool. You don't own just one tool and refuse to get others because of the one at home. "I can't get a wrench; my parents gave me a perfectly good screwdriver already! It's a family screwdriver, we all share the same one, generations

On the day the boy was thirteen years old, a day in the early splendour of autumn while still the bright leaves are on the trees, Ogion returned to the village from his rovings over Gont Mountain, and the ceremony of passage was held. The Witch took from the boy his name Duny, the name his mother had given him as a baby. Nameless and naked he walked into the cold springs where it rises among rocks under the high cliffs. As he entered the water, clouds crossed the sun's face and great shadows slid and mingled over the water of the pool about him. He crossed to the far bank, shuddering with cold but walking slow and erect as he should through that icy, living water. As he came to the bank, Ogion, waiting, reached out his hand and clasping the boy's arm, whispered to him his true name.

—URSULA LEGUIN
A WIZARD OF EARTHSEA

It is through our names that we first place ourselves in the world.

—RALPH WALDO ELLISON

of us. I plan to give it to my son." You have as many tools as you need and sometimes you use a tool for only a brief period of time. If it does the job, what difference does it make how long you used that tool? It is the same with magical names. Use as many as you need. The witches I've known who used the power of names well, have had dozens of names. These names needn't be public. I've used many names only in my journals or within my family, keeping my public name unchanged.

I find that everyone has a season in which he or she feels best and seasons which are harder to bear. For example, some people are summer people. I am not. While others bask in the sun, I sit in the basement, swatting at bugs, covered with calamine lotion for prickly heat, waiting impatiently for autumn. An ancient custom of British Columbian Indian tribes is to take a seasonal name. I could choose Sunstroke or Calamine to describe myself in the summer, or Summerwind or Phoenix to help me deal better with the fire energy. Taking seasonal names is another way in which we can become more connected to the chang-

ing seasons and the turning of the wheel of the year. Again, the most important connection made by taking up a name is the connection to yourself and who you are; in this case, who you are during each season.

Children grow rapidly and seem to be different people each time you look. They go through so many changes in their personalities that you, as well as they, can lose track of who they are. Magical names are wonderful tools children can use to illustrate the characteristics they see growing in themselves. These can be public names by which everyone in the metaphysical community calls the child, nicknames just the child's friends use, or they can be names that are used in the family setting only. Making an effort to call the child by his or her new name (even if she is going through dozens of them) tells the child that you accept and respect those changes and that you approve of who she is and who she is becoming. It also shows the child, in a clear way, how he has changed over a period of time. Magical names for children, as well as for adults, can help our minds manifest the magic.

chapter four

THE FOLKLORE
OF NAMES

The custom of naming ourselves and the
things around us is common to every culture in the world. Many cultures possess a
rich stock of folklore about the mysterious powers
of names. Nearly every aspect of naming has
information that dictates how and why cultures
choose the names they do. Some wonderful superstitions and native folklore from around the world
are listed here—some amusing, some profound.

NAMES TO BRING LUCK

Theater people are, by nature, creative, sensitive,
emotional, and superstitious. There are many
superstitions having to do with luck and the theater. One play in particular seems to attract a lot

He who is called a bear is apt to act like a bear.
—FINNISH PROVERB

Sticks and stones may break my bones but names can never hurt me.
—ENGLISH PROVERB

of "bad luck." It is considered unlucky to speak the name of the play *Macbeth* aloud, the only known exception being when a religious leader (more recently, witch) has blessed the theater first. It is believed by many actors that if an actor unwittingly says *"Macbeth,"* she or he must immediately step outside the theater and recite lines from anything else written by Shakespeare to remove the "curse."

Some bizarre customs exist even though there is ample evidence to show that the superstition isn't true. For example, in England it is believed that any boy named George will never be hanged, despite the fact that several Georges have been hanged.

It is considered lucky to have initials that spell a word. My late mother-in-law was born Beatrice Agnes Brownie Young (B.A.B.Y.). Her father, the artist Charles Warburton Young, wanted to make the initials spell *baby* but couldn't think of anything else starting with "b," so he chose "Brownie." Many of the quaint practices found in folklore harken back to legitimate ideas and habits which have passed out of memory. The curiosities of letters and words perhaps were once the domain of a few learned people, and so to the ignorant peasantry this might seem like magic, and thus lucky.

NAMES TO AVOID ILLNESS

There are many names given to children in hopes of avoiding illness or misfortune. In the Midlands of England, there is a curious belief that any person named Agnes will invariably go mad. Sometimes a sickly English child was given many names of saints and dead relatives in an attempt to elicit supernatural aid on the child's behalf. Yet there is also a widely held superstition that if a child is named for another child who died in infancy, the same fate awaits the child who bears its name.

The name is seen as the link, in many cases, between illness and good health. Thus, by changing the name you could also change the physical condition of the name bearer. In several groups of North American Indians, when a person became ill, it was thought that his name was disagreeing with him and the name was "washed off" and a new one chosen. This is a primal, symbolic ritual that is shared by many cultures.

NAMES TO HONOR OTHERS

We all are aware of the practice of naming a child after someone to honor that person. This is a common occurrence today. When Alexander the Great entered Palestine in 333 B.C.E., legend has it that all Jewish boys born that year were named Alexander. Whether this was done out of respect or by force is not known.

On a deeper level, the giving of a name of a great warrior, healer, or thinker has the resonance of sympathetic magic to it. (Sympathetic magic is the invocation or evocation of a desired trait by mimicry.) Ancient Norsemen honored their dead in hopes that the good characteristics would be reborn in their children.

HOW NAMES ARE CHOSEN

This area of folklore yields the greatest diversity in naming customs. The naming of a child is an important event. We have always named our children and always will, but the ways in which these names are chosen is evolving. The ancient Jews had a custom of naming the baby after the first thing the mother saw after the birth of her child, so a woman in labor was surrounded by pleasant things. Priests interpret dreams for the natives of Brazil before choosing a name for a child. In Derbyshire, England, it was common to select a baby's name from the first name the eye fell upon when opening the Bible, regardless of the sexual orientation of the name. In Burma, a child is named according to the day of the week on which she or he is born. Each day has letters associated with it, and the child's name begins with one of those letters. Native Hawaiian children are usually named with words describing nature. Some examples of Hawaiian name words are Lani (sky), Lei (child), Kapu (sacred), Kala (sun), and Nana (beautiful). Many people choose a name based upon the number of letters in the name.

Many tribal peoples recognize a link between people, especially people of a common tribe. Tribal kinship is described as a "seamless web of humanity" by villagers in Ghana in western Africa. Kinship ties are strong and extend to the whole tribe. In Ghana, a child is given two names: one a soul's name (from a deity associated with its birthday), and the second given by the father. In New Guinea and western Africa, a name is chosen by divination. The behavior of the child is observed in response to certain objects belonging to dead ancestors, or its reaction while a list of ancestors is recited. The baby is used as a divining tool to find its own name.

A people's relationship with deity may have a hand in the naming process. Hindus believe God is manifested in everything. They may name a child after common household objects, because every time they say the name they are pronouncing the name of God and reminding themselves that deity is all around them. Other sources of Hindu names are nature, made-up names, rivers, and Hindu gods.

Names in Uganda indicate birth order, describe family circumstances, or express hopes for the future. A child's name may be amended up to ten years later. A child's name often reflects the tribe's totem (a plant, animal, or object that serves as an identifying emblem for the clan).

NAMES AND SECRECY

Having a secret name is a powerful idea that children like to use in their play, along with secret passwords and secret codes. Every wizard had secret names, as did secret agents, cowboys, and most superheroes. When a Wiccan is asked to choose a "secret" name, it touches on the inner child excitement. Although it was expedient during the Inquisition, the need to keep names (especially inner-self and magical names) secret went further back than the dangers of the Burning Times. In many North American Indian cultures, it was believed that everyone and everything had a name that may remain hidden, perfectly describing one's innermost nature. The name might be revealed confidentially at some point, but the word had such sacredness to it that it was considered an extreme discourtesy to utter it aloud.

Secret names known only to the owner have to do with a belief in name-soul connection. In myths and folklore, the discovery of the secret name gives the discoverer power over the owner of the name. In many religions, the names of the gods are the secret property of the priests, and thus the power of the gods was held by the clergy. Many cultures thought it was unlucky to reveal the name of a newborn to anyone outside the family before the child was christened.

When it is necessary that a person's name be kept secret to protect that person from ill will from his or her enemies, many cultures name people after their children, reasoning that children have no enemies. So people are named "Mother of so-and-so," or "Father of that child." As any parent can tell you, when one is a parent she or he is often called "Cheryl's father" or "Trey's mother," by other parents who you think of as "Little Erica's mom."

NAMES AND DEITY

Along with the idea of secrecy goes the notion of compromised security if the name is revealed. As the Romans approached a city, they would have their priests lure the city's guardian deity to their side, promising many sacrifices and better offerings. Thus the name of the protective deity of Rome was kept a secret lest some foe lure their own gods away.

In many Pagan traditions, it is common to choose a secret "inner court" name to be known only by one's covenmates and never revealed to outsiders. This is done not so much for security anymore but for the name's magical properties and the transformative idea of taking a name. In the past, however, the taking of a secret name was a great defense against discovery.

In some Pagan traditions, it is considered inappropriate to name yourself after a goddess or god. Similarly, in the ancient Egyptian, Babylonian, and Hindu religions, just naming the gods compelled them to answer, so these names were not used for fear of their gods. Today, most Pagans are encouraged to have at least one Goddess or God name to instill the idea that we are all deity, that we are Goddess and God. This way, names act as a transformational tool to help us accentuate our God or Goddess-like traits.

This idea is also used in reverse to try to convince the powers of death that a child is unattractive. Often a child in India is given an unpleasant name to trick the gods into not taking the child away. The Nigerian Ibo tribe treasures children, and often gives them an unpleasant name such as Chotsani (take-it-away) in an affectionate attempt to hide their joy so ancestors or deity won't take back the infant.

CHANGING NAMES

There are endless opportunities for new names. I have heard of Pagans who take a new magical name each year to reflect personal growth. Names can be used to mark the seasons or the turning of the years. The Kwakiutl Indians of British Columbia had both winter and summer names.

Among some African cultures, a child is given a name at birth (a childhood name) that describes the birth or the baby's appearance. Seven to forty days later, the child is given an adult name by the parents or paternal grandparents. Adults often change their names when the person has reached some sort of crossroads in life, or has achieved a personal milestone. A name is descriptive of the person who bears it and since we are always evolving and changing, it seems logical that our names evolve with us.

NAMES TO INVOKE CHARACTERISTICS

To shout at a baseball game calling the batter a less than flattering name is a form of magic. You are labeling the batter in a derogatory fashion in hopes that the person will take on the traits of the name and perform badly. This common kind of curse is not very powerful against the batter, but it is an old sort of curse. Some societies call their enemies by names suggesting clumsiness, because they believe that such attributes will attach themselves to their enemies, rendering them harmless. They are careful not to use the real names of these enemies lest their foes regain power and attack and slay the careless name-droppers. Similarly, some cultures will call a dangerous foe by a mild-mannered name to encourage it to become less of a threat. Tribes in India and Africa will call a snake by names meaning a stick or a strap to convince the snake to lie still and act like a harmless stick.

NAME TABOOS

The fear of and reverence for totem animals lends us many interesting naming customs and taboos. North American Kiowa Indians say that unless you are named for the bear, you must not say "bear." They believed that a bear could render one insane just by saying its name.

The ancient Finns believed that if you knew the secret name for something, then you could control the thing. The ancient Finns used the phrase "words of power" frequently. Finns believed in a pantheon of spirits and deities that could be controlled by magic; the magic was in knowing its name. The Finns also believed in the taboo against uttering the name of a totem animal aloud for fear of needlessly invoking it. So, speaking of a bear, a Finn says "The little brother in the warm coat," Baltic peoples say "Beautiful honey-paw," "Broadfoot," or "Grandfather." Ural-Altaic peoples of Siberia call him "Little old man," "Grandfather," "Dear uncle," or "Wise one." The Tete de Boule Indians in Quebec also call the bear "Grandfather." In Sumatra, the tiger is called "He with the striped coat." In Java, the crocodile is called "Old One." To the Bechuanas, the lion is called "Boy with a beard." To the Kols, the elephant is known as "You, with the teeth."

To the ancient Greeks, the names of the priests who performed the Eleusinian mysteries might never be uttered during their priesthood. After a rite of consecration into the mysteries, the names of these priests were written down and thrown into the sea to hide them from the eyes of humans. They then were given new and sacred titles. They did not wish the powerful priests to be lessened by someone calling them by their old mundane name.

The misogynistic attitude of the Christian church and the societies it has influenced has lead to many naming customs that were used to subjugate and belittle women. The taking of the husband's last name while the woman loses her own is a good example of this. The Christian idea of women being the root of all sin and menstruation being a "curse" is shamefully used in some naming customs. Most restrictive customs are especially confining when a woman is menstruating. In several cultures there is a taboo against women speaking the name of their husbands, their husband's male relatives, or their own son's name. To do so results in death to the person whose name the woman uttered. Many tribes also will not allow women to speak the name of valued livestock, but refer to animals with descriptive terms, such as "the woolly ones" for sheep.

"Luck is my middle name," said Rincewind, indistinctly. "Mind you, my first name is Bad."

—TERRY PRATCHETT
INTERESTING TIMES

Naming Rituals

The naming ritual is a profound one. Most religions have a ritual for the giving of a name. Christians have christening and Wiccans have Wiccaning. Choosing the time when children are to be named is a source of many interesting customs. The Yoruba tribe in Nigeria names their boys on their ninth day, girls on their seventh day, and twins on their eighth day. Until the naming day, a child is called *Ikoko Omon* (newborn child). In the naming ritual, the baby's mouth is touched with substances to signify hopes for the future: water for purity of body and spirit, red pepper for resolute character, salt for power, honey and oil for happiness and prosperity, and kola nut for good fortune. After the child's name is pronounced, the feasting and dancing continues until the next day. The naming of a child and the first cutting of his hair was cause for an important ritual and celebration among the Incas. The custom became so popular that it spread to several forest tribes of the upper Amazon.

A name ritual can help transform negative traits of the person to whom the name belongs. In Finland, it is believed that if you shout the name of a young thief over a cauldron of medicated boiling water, then clap the lip on tight, leaving the name to steep in the medicated water for several days, then the thief will be reformed.

Names and Misfortune

The connection between the name and the soul was recognized by the early Egyptians. They believed that cursing a man by name may destroy his soul and when the name of a dead man was ritually placed on his statue, that statue became the residence of his soul. In Ireland, it is believed that to strike a line through a person's name would end that person's life.

We learn from folklore how names were once considered to be powerful, magical tools that helped shape the destiny of those who wore them. Let's look now at how we can shape the destiny of our children by the names we give them today.

chapter five

Naming Rituals, Spells, Exercises, and Meditations

A ritual has the ability to solidify ideas, to amplify intentions, to legitimize fantasies, and to influence the subconscious in a profound way. Some psychologists think that the loss of ritual has led to many of the ills of today's society. Ritual is more than pomp-and-circumstance and outmoded tradition. Effective ritual speaks to the subconscious and can bring about powerful change in the individual.

Using rituals for naming is a necessary step toward effectively using names as the powerful tools they are. Whether the name involved is a new magical name for an initiate, a baby's name, or a name chosen for a transition into another phase of life (such as adolescence or cronehood), the use of ritual is an integral part of the naming process. Here are some spells, meditations, and exercises to help you find and empower your name. At the end of the chapter is a full naming ritual.

TO FIND NAMES

Quickie Names
Exercise to help find and
name aspects in ourselves

We all have different aspects to our personalities. To find a name for some of these parts requires much thought. Other aspects come to mind immediately. One exercise with a group is to give the group members ten seconds to think of new names for themselves, then take turns telling their new names and why the name appealed to them. This off-the-top-of-your-head method is effective for naming certain aspects of oneself. It is also a good way in which to grow closer to coven mates or friends by seeing, naming, and discussing their various "selves."

Name Quest
A meditation to help find
a name for anything

A meditation for finding your magical name, a name for your baby, a pet's name, a house name, or the name of anything you care to name is what I call a Name Quest. In a Name Quest, go into a safe, meditative space (whether this means lighting candles and incense, putting up a circle, creating sacred space, closing the bathroom door, or merely closing your eyes), and mentally state your purpose before you begin by thinking "I am seeking the name for my new house" (or baby, cat, myself, etc.). Go into a meditative state in your favorite way. Visualize going deep within the thing in question (to the heart of the child, or of the home, etc.). Feel the essence of the thing. Notice any visual characteristics. Be open to any other incarnation (or former owner's) experiences imprinted on the thing. Sense its strengths and weaknesses, note how it makes you feel—do you sense a smell associated with the object (no, don't name your baby Mr. Poopy Pants)? Do you hear anything? When you feel you have a handle on the essence of the object, tell it your most secret name and ask to know the name of the object. If a name does not make itself immediately known to you, do not despair. It may occur to you over the next few days spontaneously or appear in a dream one night.

Names from Descriptive Words
A way to make a new name

This is the most common method of name-finding among Neopagans and Wiccans. As people did in ancient times, one can use name elements to create a new name. The ancient Anglo-Saxons put elements like "Aelf" and "Weard" together to make the name Aelfweard, which means "Elf-Guard" or "protected by the elves."

We can create new and totally unique names for ourselves from descriptive word elements. This exercise is also a good way to get to know oneself. Make a list of several positive traits of the person to be named (like brave, strong, noble, handsome, wise), and a list of objects that appeal to that person (such as elf, silver, singer, moon, music). Make these lists as long and as descriptive as you can. This is also a good exercise for building self-esteem or awareness of what we feel about the person being named. Simply combine as many elements as you like from the two lists until you find a combination that suits you, such as Silver Ragingwaters, Golden Music-woman, or Wise Mountain.

For baby names you can use name-words that are imbued with the characteristics you hope the child will have. Such as adding Joy, Blythe, Beau, Belle, etc. as a name for a child you hope will be happy or attractive.

Search the World over
for Your Name
Other places to look
for magical names

Reference books are good places to look for magical names. The technique of bibliomancy, or using books as one might use a crystal ball or tarot deck to scry the needed information, is a wonderfully fun way of looking for your name. If, for example, your magical totem animal is a cat and you wish your magical name to reflect this

energy, you could turn to these books for help. Under the listing of "cat" in *Webster's New World Thesaurus,* for example, you find: "House cats include the following: Maltese, Persian, Siamese, Manx, Burmese, Angora, Tortoise-shell, Alley, Tiger, Calico. . . . [Other cats are:] Lion, Tiger, Leopard, Puma, Wildcat, Cheetah, Lynx, Bobcat, Mountain Lion, Ocelot, Cougar, Jaguar." Any of these would make a wonderful feline-oriented name. A search through the foreign language section of the library gives us the names Paka (Swahili, "cat"), Sanura (Swahili, "kitten"), and Nyan Nyan (Japanese, "kitten"). So just from this short excursion into the reference section of the local library we can come up with names like Sanura Manx, Alley Paka, or Angora Wildcat.

TO EMPOWER YOUR NAMES
Coven Name Bonding
A ritual to bond a coven
to a new coven name

This ritual is about timing and flow. It works best with groups who are good at working together. This being said, doing this sort of ritual repeatedly makes groups good at working together. It could become something you do before or after every gathering of the group. This ritual should raise energy. If done right, it should raise the hair on the back of your necks and make you shiver with the "after-tingle." If it doesn't, you aren't getting the energy flowing well enough. Don't be afraid of energy, it's what fuels magic, heals the body, soothes the mind, and cleanses the spirit.

It's very simple to do. Form a circle. Begin a quick, repetitive, single drumbeat, very rhythmic without any deviation except to keep up at the climax. Begin with the priestess. She says her magical name or inner court name or whatever name she uses in circle. The person next to her says his name and around the circle you go. Try to add it on a beat. It needn't start fast, you can jump in every other beat at the beginning. Get into it (Phoenix . . . Kerr . . . Robin . . . Morning . . . Hill . . . Arthur . . . Mead). Put your energy into the flowing chant. Go faster and faster. As the names slide into the chant one after the other, feel the energy flowing around the circle from person to person. (Phoenix! . . . Kerr! . . . Robin! . . . Morning! . . . Hill! . . . Arthur! . . . Mead!). The priestess on her next turn (and at her discretion) inserts the coven name instead of her name. With practice the coven will get good at moving from one chant to the other. The priestess can signal that she is going to change it ahead of time, so be prepared. One by one the individual's name drops away and is replaced by the coven name. Soon all will be repeating the coven's name. Don't use the full name of a long-winded coven. If your group is the Temple of the Dancing Lady of the Lunar Light, I'd shorten it to shouting out "Dancing Lady!" or "Lunar Light!" Start clapping in the

Practice makes powerful.

—PHOENIX MCFARLAND

rhythm of the people saying the words. Go faster. Feel the heat being generated, feel your hairs begin to react to the movement of energy. Imagine it flowing increasingly rapidly around and around the circle of people. Repeat the coven name in sequence until they slide out smoothly with very few gaps between words. As it intensifies, clasp hands. This signals all to begin to chant the name simultaneously, faster and louder. You might shorten the name even further to "Lady" or "Light" in the example used above. Raise the energy to a crescendo and let the priestess signal when to release it. Let it flow back into the members' joined hands to seal and bind the group to this new name. The more you do it, the better it will be. Remember . . . practice makes powerful.

The Name Chant
To empower and enhance your chosen name

To empower yourself, try chanting your name (mundane, magical, or private or "inner circle" name, whichever aspect of you it is that requires empowerment). If you are a member of a coven or other spiritual group, you might try empowering one member of the group by surrounding that person and chanting his or her name. Adding the person's positive traits to the mantra not only helps create a positive self-image for the person, but also helps to share the group's impressions of him or her. This technique would also work in achieving a desired result that is not yet manifested. For example, if a covenmate is ill, the group could chant his or her name and add short comments like "Healthy body!" or "Clean lungs!" (or whatever is affected), "Radiant health!" etc. Be sure to include only comments from a positive perspective, because the subconscious doesn't readily process negatives. To prove this point, try telling yourself not to think of elephants. The mind must think of an elephant in order to know what not to think of. Comments, then, that communicate "Healthy body" are a better choice than "No more illness." If you walk a solitary spiritual path, get into a meditative space and chant or sing your names as above.

This technique is useful for groups or individuals and can be used to bring any number of attributes or changes into one's life. Chant the name in association with health, prosperity, happiness, a new home, a job, more fire, water, earth, or air energy (look in the Names by Their Characteristics for things you want to invoke into your life), or anything that you desire for yourself. Always remember to think about the ramifications of all magic! Ask yourself if this will harm anyone (including yourself) before you do any magic. Be careful about the wording of your spells; this exercise is a spell. Remember that words are magic, so choose them with due consideration.

By ancient custom, for the next seven days, there was but a single task with which [the father] would seriously occupy himself: the selection of a name for his firstborn son. It would have to be a name rich with history and with promise, for the people of his tribe—the Mandinkas—believed that a child would develop seven of the characteristics of whomever or whatever he was named for . . . Out under the moon and the stars, alone with his son that eighth night, [the father] completed the naming ritual. Carrying little Kunta in his strong arms, he walked to the edge of the village, lifted his baby up with his face to the heavens, and said softly, "Ffend kiling dorong leh warrata ka itea tee." (behold—the only thing greater than yourself.)

—ALEX HALEY
ROOTS

Look in yourself. Not at yourself.

—PHOENIX MCFARLAND

Mirror Image
To bind you and your name and to delve within yourself

This is an exercise to do alone. This exercise should take ten to fifteen minutes. Sit or stand before a mirror. Light a candle nearby. Spend a few minutes staring into your eyes while calming and centering your mind. Begin the name chant as in the exercise above. Gaze into your eyes and picture you in the desired situation. Picture someone calling you by your new name within that image. Softly chant your name to yourself. Imagine the name words encircling you and wrapping you snugly, protectively. Let yourself be soothed by this exercise. Spend the last few minutes silently staring into your own eyes. Look at what flickers below the surface. Read your thoughts. Get in touch with yourself. Repetitions of the name, and visually seeing yourself as you do it, will bind the name to you as well as any of the attributes you seek along with the name. Be careful to avoid looking at your appearance. Do not allow yourself to be critical or adjust your appearance in any way. This is a spell, not a make-over. Restrict your gazing to your eyes. It may take a bit of practice before you can do this undistracted. Look in yourself, not at yourself.

Name Amulet
A spell to empower names

Using magic to empower a name before taking it on will help to boost the power of the name. Try making a name amulet filled with your new name, appropriate spices, stones, oils, and imagery representative of the changes you are seeking. Everytime you smell the oils and spices, everytime you feel it around your neck, the magic will be helped along. If you are working with elemental energy, it is also helpful to bring the energy of the element into your environment. For example, if you are seeking to have calm water energy in your life, burn blue candles, hang photos of ocean scenes on your walls, put sea shells in blue bowls on tables, and make an effort to wear sea colors. All these things will work with your new magical name to trigger your subconscious and help manifest change. (Remember: As above, so below!) Magical names react with the inner child, the younger self within all of us. This is the part of you that likes dramatic robes, magical jewelry, elaborate rituals, candlelight, and incense. The more magical trappings you attach to your new name, the greater the effect on the subconscious. The subconscious mind will then work the magic and the growth will occur.

Tool Names
To ritually name magical tools
as part of a consecration ritual

Each magical tool has its own individual feel. Many Pagans name their swords, athames, drums, wands, staffs, and chalices. Incorporating a naming ceremony into the consecration ritual for your tools is a wonderful idea. Try meditating on the tool in question to seek its name. Remember the ancient notion that to know the name of something is to be able to control it. You can name your athame, for example, and ritually link the blade to you by linking the name of your athame to your inner circle magical name. By writing both your magical names on the blade (in water, if you want to keep them secret), you further emphasize the bond. You may also use the name of your blade in a dedication ritual by pledging your heart and your blade to the Goddess.

OTHER USES FOR MAGICAL NAMES

Sexual Orientation Switch
An exercise to get in touch with
the other in ourselves

Many people have expressed a desire to become more comfortable with the opposite sex, especially when it comes to the little boy or girl who lives inside all of us. It is a valid technique for a man who seeks to be at ease with his feminine self to take a woman's name as part of this process. It needn't be a public name, if he is shy about it. Women would also do well to name the little boy within. I have been to an inner child party given by some Pagan friends. We all came in our inner personas, played with crayons and toys, ate peanut butter, and drank Kool-Aid. We all also were called by our inner child names. It was a fun and powerful experience. Naming our opposite sex selves helps to accept these parts of ourselves and also draws us closer to the Goddess and God aspects that we all reflect. This is a healthy exercise for all of us who have clawed our way out of a misogynistic, homophobic society. We all have some aspects of that attitude lurking within our psyches. To openly name and covet the opposite aspect of ourselves will help us understand our motivations, and may lead us to discover and abolish some of our hidden prejudices.

Name, Name, Go Away!
A spell to rid ourselves
of unwanted habits

That addiction to cigarettes! That uncontrollable eating problem! That nasty temper! We all have traits we wish we didn't have. They shade our dark sides like trees along a country road. To help rid yourself of these unwanted tendencies, try giving them a name. Remember the wisdom of the ancients—to know a thing's name is to

control that thing. For example, give your temper a name. When you are choosing its name, think about it and what motivates it to explode. You will come to have a better understanding of it, and even an acceptance of it as part of yourself. Your temper becomes more personal when you know it well enough to name it. Then, when your temper erupts, you won't add guilt on top of it by feeling bad about your temper. You'll simply acknowledge it as "Old Hothead" or "Firebreather." You can work on overcoming your temper's negative aspects by giving it a watery name to reduce its fire power. You can do spells and meditations to break it into its parts (a temper is anger, insecurity, frustration, fear, desire to be noticed, and many other things specific to the individual). Keep and rename the valuable aspects, such as deeply felt emotion and your need for attention. Banish the unwanted parts, like unwarranted anger and fear. Your temper serves a purpose or you wouldn't have developed one. Find a way to express what needs expressing and toss out the rest. Name the parts you want to banish and do a ritual in which you burn the unwanted aspect's name or erase it, transform it into something useful, or flush it down the toilet. Use your imagination.

The same idea works for ridding yourself of addictive habits, such as an eating disorder, or a drug, or an alcohol addiction. Try naming that from which you wish to be free, and then ritually destroy that name. You could write the name for your problem on a piece of paper and tear it into many pieces, saying encouraging and forceful commands with each tear. Or you may choose to name the part of you that desires to be sober, clean, or in control of your addictions and empower that aspect. Give that aspect a power name filled with strength and wisdom and do exercises such as the Name Chant (discussed earlier) to help yourself become stronger and fight against the addiction. But, as with all magic, remember the old saying, "As above, so below." In addition to the magical working, you also need to work on a mundane level to fix the problem. Find a support group or go see a therapist.

A Name for Any Season
To use names as a yardstick
for personal growth

You can incorporate the idea of name magic in any seasonal ritual to create growth. For example, if at Beltane you felt ready for a spiritual growth period, you could choose a growth-oriented name like Sapling and ritually rename yourself. Pagans of my acquaintance commonly set seasonal goals for themselves at Beltane to be achieved by Samhain, and again at Samhain to be accomplished by Beltane. These goals would be more easily achieved by adding name magic to the ritual already taking place. Be sure to reward yourself if

you meet your goals and give yourself a new name. Try using your name as a sign-post along the path, marking your progress as each goal is achieved. Go from Acorn to Sapling to Oak to Mighty Oak to Oak Forest. Goals at Beltane should be growth oriented and at Samhain they should be things you want to release. It's better to go with the flow.

Bless This House
Use names in a house-blessing ritual

When Pagans move into a new home, one of the first things they do is a House Blessing ritual. This ritual is basically blessing the house with the four elements of air, fire, water, and earth; the easiest method is by using incense (air and fire) and salt water (earth and water). If there is some lingering negativity from the previous owners, a banishing is done before the blessing. A good way to ritually banish an area is to use a ritual broom to symbolically "sweep" away all that isn't welcome. When you are blessing the house, begin by formally naming the house and use the new name in your ritual. In essence, you are consecrating the house as you would a magical tool. You can add desired aspects (such as protection, safety, sanctuary, love, coziness, happiness, and comfort) to the ritual to further enhance the home magically. As a symbol of the protection I seek, I paint tiny pentagrams in clear nail polish on all the windows in my house as part of the ritual. This is symbolic of the invisible barrier to any unwanted negativity or trouble. The nail polish becomes mostly invisible, unless you see it from a certain angle when the light is right, then suddenly what looks like a crystal pentagram seems to appear in the window. You might want to carve or paint a sign with the house's name to hang by the front door. Working on the house's name sign while in circle will add to its effectiveness and magical potency. We once did that in a little cottage by the sea that we lived in just after we were married. We named it Gull Cottage. Years later they tore it down and put up a big three-story contemporary house on the site, but our old house name sign still hung near the front door as a rustic reminder of what once was. The name had bonded with the house and the new owners felt that it belonged there, although perhaps they didn't know why.

Handfastings and Names
Using names to bond
in handfasting rituals

Handfastings (Pagan wedding ceremonies) are highly personal rituals that cannot be generically produced for use by the masses. They are written from the heart and tailored to reflect the tastes and feelings of the happy couple (or threesome, etc.).

In Pagan traditions, handfastings do not require the woman to give up her name. Some women take their new husbands' names, some do not, and some couples change both their last names to new ones of their own invention. Some choose new magical names to reflect the union. One advantage to changing magical names rather than mundane names is that you reflect the changes that come from being "married" without having to change your driver's license.

Handfastings are more than just a way to acknowledge the love and/or commitment people feel for each other. The Handfasting ritual can help deepen the bond between people. Many feel that Handfasting will help those so bound to recognize the other in the next lifetime.

Many people exchange some kind of vow or promise during the ritual; this section inevitably includes using your names. ("I, Phoenix, do promise . . . ") Some people choose to use their mundane names in the ceremony and some use their magical names. Because we name different aspects of ourselves when we take a name, it might be a good idea to use all our names in this ritual. The mundane names, circle names, magical names, inner court names, outer court names, and even pet names should be included in the Handfasting ritual. This way it is a bonding of two (or more) complete people. All aspects are merged and shared equally with the other. This deepens the effects of the ritual on many levels. I was at such a handfasting years ago when two people spoke their vows with six different names.

Names of the Past
A meditation on names

We all have carried many names. Think about all the different things people have called you, some more affectionate than others. Everything from "Billy-Willie" your mother called you when you were a baby, "Big Geek!" in the schoolyard once, "Mr. Jenkins" at work, to the "Honey" your wife calls you. Spend some time thinking about all of your life's names. Settle yourself into a quite place and center your thoughts. Softly chant, repeating first one name then another as they occur to you. As you are softly chanting "Billy-Willie," try to feel what the sound of hearing your mother's voice calling that name meant to you at the time. Was it a joyful sound? Was it a comforting sound? Feel the joy and comfort. When chanting an unflattering name such as "Big Geek," send energy back to the person who said that to you full of forgiveness. Try to imagine reasons why someone would call someone else by a name like that. Try to understand and forgive. Use these names as tools of forgiveness, do not label yourself negatively. Look at your own past in that way. As you are chanting, try to remember if you called others by bad names. If so, try to remember what prompted you to do it. Try to understand and forgive yourself. Deal with each name before moving on. Get in touch with each name's intent, affection, love, humor, and how they made you feel. Send energy to those people who named

you, grateful of their bond with you. These names are part of who you are. The people who called you by them, have had a hand in forming the you that you are today. For that you can be thankful. Celebrate yourself by acknowledging your past and current names and those who felt you were sacred enough to name. End by chanting your latest name and recalling how far you've come from wee Billy-Willie.

The Naming
A naming ritual
for any new name

Set up an altar and quarter altars (if desired). If the name you have chosen has a visual symbol, use it in decorating your altar (with the name Owl, for example, use an owl feather or owl statue to accent the altar). Include a piece of paper, a pen, and a mirror on the altar. Make sure candles, incense, water, and salt are available, as well as any musical instruments you have. Call the quarters, cast the circle, and invite the deities.

> I, [old name], stand before you for the last time as [old name]. I have grown. I have changed. [Feel free to illustrate ways in which you have changed into this new person.]

> I have evolved to be the person here today. I am no longer described by [old name]; I no longer can be contained within that name.

Go to the altar and write your new name on the piece of paper. Then wave the paper through the smoke of incense, saying:

[New name], be consecrated and empowered by the powers of air to lend me strength of intellect, clarity of vision, and purity in the dawn of the life of this new name.

Hold the paper between you and the candle, seeing the light illuminate the name (but do not let it catch on fire), saying:

[New name], be consecrated and empowered by the powers of fire to give me determination, strength, drive, and energy, the fiery spark of enthusiasm during the noontime of the life of this new name.

Sprinkle the paper with water from the altar, saying:

[New name], be consecrated and empowered by the powers of water to lend me gentle intuition, deep understanding, and a deeper awareness of the mysteries of myself during the twilight of the life of this name.

Bury the name in the salt dish on the altar, saying,

[New name], be consecrated and empowered by the powers of earth to give me strength and solidity, deeper connection to my own earthiness, and a fearless awareness of the dark sides within

myself during the nighttime of the life of this name.

Take the name from the salt. Light it on fire and drop it into the censer, saying:

I am now [new name]. By air, fire, water, and earth I bear this name proudly. I am [new name]! I am [new name]! I am [new name]!

Go to the four quarters and say the following at each direction:

Hail, east [south, west, north]! It is I, [new name]. Know me when I call to you by this name. Help me by sharing with me your [intellect, strength, intuition, groundedness, etc.].

Go to the altar and call the deities.

Hail [deity names and specific greetings to them]! I am your child. I am your priest/ess. My names change to reflect my movement upon your path, but my heart remains true and steadfast. Know me, Mother/Father, I am [new name], your child. Bless me, Mother/Father, for I am your child. Know me by my heart that is true, my mind which strives for knowledge, my hands which shape your images, my eyes which behold your magnificence, my lips which speak your name which is all names, for you are All. Bless me, Mother/ Father, for I now am [new name].

Spend some time in contemplation, if desired. You might drum and chant your new name, weave it into your favorite chants, or drone it out in a meditative way. You can illustrate how your new name makes you feel in dance or song. The Name Chant (above) is good to do here to help reinforce the name in your mind and in the minds of your coveners. When you are finished reveling, dismiss the quarters using your new name, bid farewell to the deities, and take down the circle. Stay aware of the impact of the new name upon your life. (It will have an impact!)

Like all rituals, this is to be adapted to your personal needs. Change the traits the elements lend to the new name; change what you seek to become. Put in your deities and their qualities. Add, subtract, and tailor it to fit your life. Add music. Breathe your life into this ritual and into your new name!

chapter six

PAGANS AND
CHRISTIAN NAMES

Since the Norman Conquest of England, the church has influenced or dictated to the English-speaking world the names by which our children would be known. Of course, many people did not choose biblical names simply because the church encouraged it, but be-cause they were motivated by sincere religious reverence or in loving memory of someone who once bore that name. Later, after the Protestant Reformation, names were chosen out of the Bible in a new manner to illustrate the tenets of the religious reorganization of the day. The church was still dictating, even more loudly than ever, by what names our children were to be called, and more people complied out of fear. In these dark days, deviating from the Christian norm was severely punished and very soon no one walked

Religion is doing; a man does not merely think his religion or feel it, he "lives" his religion as much as he is able, otherwise it is not religion but fantasy or philosophy.

—GEORGE GURDJIEFF,
GREEK-ARMENIAN
RELIGIOUS TEACHER, MYSTIC

Names, once they are in common use, quickly become mere sounds, their etymology being buried, like so many of the earth's marvels, beneath the dust of habit.

—SALMAN RUSHDIE
THE SATANIC VERSES

alone. People may have been marching to a different drummer internally, but to the world they marched as Christian soldiers, all named the same. From 1750 C.E. to the present, the most commonly given names are drawn from a store of only 179 names. A dreary sea of Johns, Pauls, Josephs, and Marys washed over history for hundreds of years.

Today, many of us are not even aware of which names are biblical, or to what they refer in the Bible. We simply have a stock of "normal" names from which we choose. We have chosen the same names for centuries. What the church once had to force upon us, we now accept as rote. We have blurred the boundaries between church and society in so many areas that we have come to find that certain ideas are frowned upon by the culture, but actually stem from the disapproval of the church.

I think it is time for a change, for many reasons. Names have power, as many ancient cultures used to know. To choose a child's name from a religious tradition to which you do not subscribe is a meaningless, hollow concession to societal (and implied religious) pressure. How can this name ever have power and meaning to the child to whom it is so thoughtlessly given? How can a name so commonplace vibrate in harmony to the essence of so many people who carry that name? A name, ideally, is a reflection of the person who bears it. We have lost a sense of our own individuality and we perpetuate this trend by choosing names that do not represent the individual.

Another good reason to vary the program with regard to choosing traditional Christian names is boredom. We have used Joseph, Peter, Mary, John and the derivations of biblical names for centuries. Aren't we bored yet? When someone tells you they have just named their new baby John, do you ever comment, "Zonkers! What a rollickingly fascinating name! Wherever did you get a name like that? How on Earth did you come up with it? How original! How creative! Good name! How do you pronounce it again? By Jove, there's a keeper! You know, I have a bathroom named that?" Probably not.

Most of us were given our "given" names, and many of them are Christian names. Our parents may have been Christians, and had no inkling they were naming someone who would grow up to be a Pagan. The Christian name may have been given in a sentimental gesture, out of religious zeal, or just because the parents thought it was pretty and hadn't a clue that it was a Christian name. The names in the Bible were around a long time before Christianity came to be, so it may be argued that they are merely pre-Christian Hebrew names that happened to be used in the Bible. As such, don't they have as much power as any other non-Christian name? To a Pagan, I don't think so. For centuries, millions of people have put lifetimes worth of energy into the Bible. They prayed to many

of the names in the Bible; they read it aloud as they set fire to innocent people—it is the basis of many wars and much bloodshed. In terms of the collective unconscious, biblical names have "copped an attitude." If you disagree with me, try thinking about naming your son Judas, a popular name once upon a time, and see if the name isn't tainted by all that has gone before. There was certainly good and sincere energy attached to biblical names, but to our subconscious, which is the level in which names hold power, the names still say "Christian." It could be argued that Peter, for example, means "rock," so why not use it for stability and grounding work? Because to our subconscious, Peter carries the biblical images, not those of rocks. Why try to reshape and redefine all that energy when by choosing a name free from Christian imagery, you can also make a statement about nonconformity and help to free society from the clutches of any one religion?

So what's so bad about a little Christian energy in a name? Nothing, if you're a little Christian. But if you bought this book, odds are you aren't. Or if so, you aren't so Christian that you aren't open to other ideas. Don't get me wrong, there's a lot of good stuff in any religion and I encourage Christians to draw from that name-pool when naming their own children. But in the case of Pagans, particularly because the Christian church spent so much time taking over our names, it feels right for us to reclaim some of what was lost to zealotry. People assume that a Jewish baby will bear a Jewish name, and that a Muslim family will choose a name from within its own tradition. Because Neopaganism is so neo, we don't yet have established names that can be labeled as "Pagan names." But we can choose names that aren't Christian, Jewish, Muslim, etc. We can create some Pagan naming traditions of our own.

So, here we are, all fired up with an anarchistic, innovative, revolutionary fire in our collective belly. We are ready to chuck all the Johns, Marys, Josephs, Pauls, and Matthews right out the window and begin fresh with different, non-biblical names. We can now choose Pagan-friendly names or make up new names. The trouble is, in regard to Pagan-friendly names, what are they? The second half of this book lists over 7,000 non-Christian names suitable to Pagans. How do you go about making up a new name? It would be helpful to review how the ancients chose their names. Below is a listing of methods used prior to the Christian influence, as well as some modern techniques. All these techniques lend themselves well to selecting a baby name as well as a magical name.

METHODS OF NAME MAKING

Ancient

Metronymic: named for the mother. This makes great sense, because maternity is irrefutable. Merlin Stone speculated in *When God Was a Woman* that cultures as far back as the Upper Paleolithic period were matrilineal (based upon mother kinship). In Denmark, it is law that a person can choose to adopt the name of the father or the mother. Many people today use the mother's maiden name as a child's middle name.

Patronymic: named for the father. This system superseded the metronymic system.

Habitational: where you live. Robin Red Bluff, Laurel of White Rock, and Kerr of Gull Cottage are examples of habitation names.

Occupational: Baker, Weaver, Wainright, and Smyth are such names.

Nicknames: David the Forgetful, Atilla the Hun, and Becka the Buxom are names derived from affectionate or descriptive nicknames.

Anecdotal: based upon a significant experience in the person's life." An example is the name Dances with Wolves from the motion picture by the same name. I call my husband's renovation persona Dances with Ladders and he calls mine Fusses with Blueprints.

Seasonal: based upon a time of year particularly important to its bearer (May, June, Mabon).

Interests: based on what the person does, perhaps as a hobby (Mason, Gardener, Healer, Harper).

Appearance: based upon the person's physical characteristics, such as Aelfrick the Red.

Ambitions: hopes for what the bearer will achieve.

Mythological: named after famous mythical gods, goddesses, or heroes.

Birth: names chosen based upon birth order, birth process, or significant family feelings.

Totem animals: named for the spirit animal that makes itself known to be the person's totem animal through dreams or visions.

Special objects: names can come from many common sources (rocks, plants, flowers, herbs, spices, celestial objects, trees, animals, etc.).

Geographic: using the names of mountains, towns, or land forms as a source of names.

Modern

Nature: picking names from nature (trees, birds, plants, clouds, etc.).

Foreign names: picking names from other countries that mean something of significance to the bearer or their ancestry.

Psychology: names based on archetypes.

Elemental: names from the four natural elements (air, fire, water, and earth).

Mythical: names from mythology.

Cultural: TV, movies, and popular books as a source of names.

Name switch: choosing surnames as first names.

Seasonal: names associated with seasons or time.

Universe: names from distant galaxies, names of spaceships or satellites.

Light: names associated with light, dark, or colors of the spectrum.

Culinary: names from the foods we eat, spices, favorite dishes.

Names from both the ancient and modern methods above are included in the latter half of this book. Go through the next part of this book with a pen and paper and make notes of any names or ideas that appeal to you, go back when you've finished reading all of the book, and review your notes to narrow down the search. I wish you well on your name quest.

chapter seven

MAGICAL NAMES FROM
INNER SANCTUMS

ARCHETYPAL NAMES

D eep inside our beings lies our nature, often hidden from the world and even from ourselves. In the shadowy realm of id, ego, and superego is spoken the magical language of dreams. Symbols and archetypes exist within these inner sanctums. They speak to us in this dream language, guiding us along the magical journey to enlightenment. Archetypes are universally understood images, such as a baby representing beginning and an old man representing ending. They are the symbols of our deepest unconscious. Perhaps it is the language of our souls.

Archetypal realities hidden in the dreaming night of the collective unconscious are the building

*Gone, glimmering through the dream of
things that were.*

—LORD BYRON

We are such stuff as dreams are made on . . .
—WILLIAM SHAKESPEARE
THE TEMPEST

*A human being's name is a principal compo-
nent in his person, perhaps a piece of his soul.*
—SIGMUND FREUD

blocks of our psyche. It is by accessing these realities that we can learn about who we are, and find ways to become what we intend. These are powerful realities. A fully integrated psyche has elements of all the archetypes in balance. The warrior for self-discipline and a willingness to face one's fears. The rebel to discard tired ideas and embrace new philosophies. The lover to connect with others and nurture the self. The leader to make sound decisions and set goals for the future. The wizard to observe life and self and learn from them.

Some people choose such names on a cyclical basis. Every so many years, they cycle through the archetypes with new magical names, seeing what else they can learn when they become once again the rebel/warrior/lover/magician/leader. It can be a lifelong quest. Certain times in life are more disposed to relate to certain archetypes as well: Teen years and the rebel is an obvious choice; military service and the warrior is another; old age and the magician seems a good fit. The years in which the career is a main focus may fall into the realm of the leader.

These are just a few archetypes. There are many others. If you did not find yourself among these archetypes, find ones that resonate with your inner self and look for a name there. Those of you who are familiar with tarot will recognize that archetypes are like the major arcana to our life's reading.

They are the most powerful images, which signify the most profound changes. Archetypes are the stuff of dreams and it is in our dreams that we begin to be.

Names for the Warrior

The warrior is an instinctual energy form that cannot be repressed. In our culture's politically correct quest for sensitive, gentle, New Age, nonpatriarchal archetypes we sometimes overlook the warrior. But the warrior is not just about aggression, in fact in most cases, it's the opposite. The best warrior would never have to fight. It's more about an approach to life and to self. The Japanese warrior philosophy claims that there is only one position in which to face the battle of life and that is head-on. By learning to "attack" life from a fully frontal attitude, we can take from the warrior self-discipline, an awareness of our own mortality, and the consequent zest for living. The warrior is alert, in control, disciplined, with a clarity of thinking, and a relationship with their destroyer side. There are many things in life that need destroying—corruption, tyranny, hierarchies that do not work, oppression. On the personal front we can destroy our bad habits, character flaws, weaknesses, and fears in order to become a better person.

Choosing a warrior name is not the same thing as following the warrior path with all its benefits. But it can be a beginning.

And when they name you, great warrior,
then will my eyes be wet with remembering.
And how shall we name you, little warrior?
See, let us play at naming.

—DIDINGA OF SUDAN
FROM A SONG ON CHILD NAMING

All good fortune is a gift of the gods, and . . .
you don't win the favor of the ancient gods by
being good, but by being bold.

—ANITA BROOKNER, BRITISH NOVELIST

A warrior knows what he wants, and he
knows how to get it.

—CARLOS CASTANEDA
JOURNEY TO IXTLAN

First comes the name and with part of you aware and advertising that you are open to this energy, vehicles of change may present themselves. Of all the steps to a worthy goal, the first is the most important.

Adventure
Aim
America
Ask
Auspicious
Awake
Aware
Balance
Believe
Brandish
Care
Challenger
Chance
Constance
Criterion
Dare
Deeds
Deem
Destiny
Dignity
Diligence
Discipline
Duty
Emancipation
Encounter
Endeavor
Energy
Enterprise
Escapade
Everything
Exalt
Expect
Experience
Far-Wander
Fate
Flex
Fling
Flow
Fortune
Freedom
Genuine
Glory
Goodness
Guidance
Habit
Hallow
Happenstance
Harmony
Hasten
Hero
Honor
Hope

Idea

Illusion

Imagine

Independence

Insight

Intensity

Journey

Justice

Keep

Kindness

Knowing

Liberty

Luck

Luster

Manifest

Memory

Merit

Myriad

Outrider

Paradise

Paradox

Patience

Pluck

Possibility

Prize

Promise

Quest

Quirk

Quiver

Random

Respect

Revere

Risk

Sage

Scout

Scruple

Seek

Seeker

Serendipity

Silence

Simplicity

Skill

Spar

Stance

Steady

Stint

Stout-Heart

Strive

Thrive

Time

Train

Tranquil

Truth

Try

Valiant

Vanguard

We know not where our dreams will take us, but we can probably see quite clearly where we'll go without them.

—MARILYN GREY

Don't be afraid of the space between your dreams and reality. If you can dream it, you can make it so.

—BELVA DAVIS

Dreams are the touchstones of our characters.

—HENRY DAVID THOREAU

Tread softly because you tread on my dreams.

—WILLIAM BUTLER YEATS

Vantage

Venture

Vigil

Vision

Voyager

Wander

Wanderer

Wanderlust

Way

Whirl

Will

Word

Zen

NAMES FOR THE REBEL

Another archetype is the rebel, especially popular in a culture that has its roots in defying established religious traditions. The popularity of the Wiccan movement with the "hippies" of the 60s also makes the rebel a familiar archetype in much of Wiccandom. The rebel is the person who defies establishment and hierarchy. They overthrow tired establishments and fight for change, sometimes admittedly just for the sheer fun of doing so. Like Marlon Brando said in his archetypal role of a biker in *The Wild One,* when asked what he was rebelling against, he replied, "What have you got?"

The rebel is the youthful expression of the leader and the warrior. Teenage rebellion serves the purpose of emotionally separating the child from the parent and making way for the independent adult to emerge. It is a valuable stepping stone to fully adult archetypes. In order for the Holly King to emerge, the Oak King must die. The rebel in us causes us to shake up our world, the established traditions and dogma, to brave new paths, try new things, question authority, in fact, to question everything. In balance with other archetypes, it is a valuable and necessary facet to a complete personality. Like with all other archetypes, it is when one facet overwhelms all the others that we become out of balance. We all know extremists of one archetype or other and see how dysfunctional they are. The solution to such an imbalance is not to toss the archetype away, but to put it in balance with the others. The opposite of extremism is not another form of extremism. The opposite of extremism is balance. So cultivate the rebel as well as the others, but try to avoid being too much of any one archetypal projection. Balance is harmony.

Become

Blaze

Change

Curious

Defy

Defiant

Dreamer

Enlighten

Enthusiasm

Fantastic

Flux

Freethinker

Grandstander

Infidel

Joker

Liberal

Maverick

Misfit

New

Oddball

Outlandish

Outlaw

Outrageous

Quaint

Question

Quixote

Radical

Rebel

Reformer

Renegade

Shifter

Strange

Surprise

Trailblazer

Transfigure

Transformer

Trickster

Twister

Utopia

Veer

Weirdling

Why

NAMES FOR THE MAGICIAN

The archetype of the magician is keenly felt in the Wiccan world. The magician is the wise one, who knows "why" but also the master of technology who knows "how." She is an initiate and she initiates. It is in the realm of the occult, or hidden knowledge, that the role of magician takes on its full flower. Whether we see this archetype as Merlin making an utopian Camelot or Obi Wan with his knowledge of the occult science known as "the Force," the magician is a creator, a transformer, one who alters reality. This is the realm of the student, the apprentice, the holy man, the trainee, and the initiate—those who seek to learn that which is hidden or unknown. This archetype is full of power. The power comes from the ability to see the unseen, to navigate the occult, to heal with herbs, to foresee the future, to manipulate people and reality for good or ill. Historically it was the magicians who invented language, mathematics, engineering, astronomy, psychology, medicine, and law. The magician has a discerning eye to avoid being taken in by people's masks and see beyond to their inner self. It is through knowledge that

What is a rebel? A man who says no.

—ALBERT CAMUS
THE REBEL

this power comes. Knowledge from self-understanding, study of people, psychology, technology, spiritual study, energy work, self-discipline, and practice with the tools of the seer. This is an archetype of the thinking person. One of the closest professions today to this archetype is the psychologist. There are a large number of Wiccan/Pagan therapists and psychologists, and perhaps this is why.

Brujo

Canny

Challenger

Clever

Curious

Dark

Delve

Discover

Discovery

Diviner

Eerie

Elder

Enchanter

Enchantress

Envision

Ethereal

Exploration

Explorer

Farsighted

Fathom

Gandalf

Genius

Hex

Hocus

Imagine

Insight

Intuit

Keen

Know

Macabre

Merlin

Mystery

Mystic

Necromancer

Observer

Occult

Oddly

Phantom

Pocus

Ponder

Quest

Questor

Quietude

Ranger

Sage

Savant

Scout

Seek

Seeker

Sense

Singular

Sojourner

Soothsayer

Sorcerer

Sorceress

Spooky

Strange

Supernatural

Think

Thinker

Vision

Voyager

Wisdom

Wit

Witch Doctor

Wizard

Wonder

Sorcerers make their own destiny. They touch the earth lightly.

—TERRY PRATCHETT
SOURCERY

There's a kind of magic in masks. Masks conceal one face, but reveal another. The one that only comes out in darkness.

—TERRY PRATCHETT
MASKERADE

NAMES FOR THE LOVER

The lover is not the same thing as the stud muffin. This is not about the equipment, frequency, ability, or skill at sexual matters. The stud muffin, of either sex, who sleeps with everyone they can is not a great lover, no matter how skilled such repetition makes them. That is actually a lack of the lover in a personality. It is a fear of that intimate, sensual, fully open archetype that creates that sort of loveless lover. The lover is "tuned in" rather than "turned on," to speak in the 60s vernacular. Tuned into the world about them, the harmonics of the ripples on the sea of the unconscious; tuned in to others, to the world around them, and the one beyond them. It is not through lust that the lover relates to others, but through feeling. Being closer to the unconscious means being closer to the fires of our drive to sexuality, so that is why the lover has taken on a kind of tawdry Lothario patina. But that is only one facet of the total crystal.

The lover is connected sensually to the world around her. She doesn't just look at the forest, she wants to touch the bark, finger the leaves, wash her face in the morning's dew on its blossoms and breath in their perfume. The lover sees and experiences life as a kind of art form. They are so aesthetically aware of their environment that they see hundreds of colors and nuances that to us would just look beige. The dwellers of the arctic regions who have hundreds of words for snow seem to be connected in this way to their environment.

At different times in life we all have such moments of connectedness. When I was sixteen, I was in a car accident in which I broke my back. My VW Bug blew a tire, spun around, and overturned, tumbling down a hillside. I saw it all in precise slow-motion. I saw hundreds of scenarios of grass, dirt, weeds, and bits of sparkling broken glass followed by sky as we tumbled. I could see every blade, every cloud, hear every utterance and breath of my companions. I became enraptured by the color of blood on a bit of broken glass lying in the sunlight. It was more profoundly sacred than any stained glass window I'd ever seen in church. It came to me, very calmly and peacefully, "So this is dying." I wasn't afraid. I was filled with love and connectedness and was dazzled by everything I saw and felt, smelled and heard. I was, for that brief few endless moments, fully integrated in the lover.

Many people have had near-death experiences. While the forms these experiences take seem to alter with whatever the individual believed would happen (a lesson for us all to be careful what we allow ourselves to believe in), the one universal impression they all bring back is an overwhelming feeling of love for themselves and all of life. Some say that is God. Some say it's the collective unconscious. Some say it's neurons hiccuping in the brain. But whatever the explanation, it seems clear to me having experienced it, it is also being the archetype they call the lover.

So why would anyone be fearful of such a feeling? Because to feel love, one must be totally open to feeling pain—great emotional pain. Most people are closed off to that—as am I—in most circumstances.

The lover is at odds with restrictions to experiencing life totally. Religions typically persecute the lover, equating such earthly connections to Satan. When the church first took power it first closed the theaters, then the brothels. Soon to follow was the persecution of psychics and mediums. The Burning Times were to a large extent about the church's stance against the lover. Christian, Jewish, and Muslim faiths all tried to demean and banish the lover. But archetypes cannot be driven away. This may well explain why the sexual revolution of the middle last century occurred, and the rise in popularity of nature religions, nature being more closely akin to the lover energy.

Who are lovers then? Connoisseurs of life. Those who experience and are passionate about aspects of life. It is she who is inundated by the scent of roses. The gourmet who savors each taste like a symphony on his tongue. The actor who is pierced to the quick when she sees a brilliant performance and cries with abandon at what she experiences. People who become emotionally touched by a sunset. Lovers cry at movies. Lovers love food. Lovers love life. Lovers love love. Accessing the lover brings us connectedness, enthusiasm, compassion, romance, and, yes, sexuality. It tempers the other archetypes with a humanity that is necessary for a completely integrated being. The lover needs them as well, because the lover without boundaries, insights, and control is chaos or addiction.

Many people were so repressed in childhood that they have trouble experiencing the lover and so often side-step into the easy role of promiscuity. Some may find it difficult to

The lover of life makes the whole world into his family . . .

—CHARLES BEAUDELAIRE
L'ART ROMANIQUE

The lover of nature is he whose inward and outward senses are still truly adjusted to each other, who has retained the spirit of infancy even into the era of manhood.

—RALPH WALDO EMERSON
NATURE

actually feel joy or passion. We live our lives routinely and can't remember the last time we shouted with joy, enthralled in the total abandon of fun. Try to slow down, even for brief periods of time, and look at life through the lover's eyes. See the beauty of the simple things, the sacredness of life, taste, touch, feel, and smell things, and feel for the connectedness of the lover and be open to its embrace. And then . . . love responsibly.

Admire

Adore

Agape

Alive

Ardor

Aroma

Bask

Beau

Beloved

Bliss

Caress

Cherish

Darling

Delight

Ebullience

Ecstasy

Enjoy

Eros

Esteem

Euphoria

Exuberance

Fancy

Felicity

Fervor

Flame

Flavor

Fond

Fondle

Gusto

Honey

Joy

Kindness

Libido

Lust

Lusty

Nirvana

Paradise

Passion

Rapture

Relish

Revel

Revere

Savor

Sensua

Spice

Spirit

Tang

Thrill

Treasure

Verve

Vigor

Vivid

Wallow

Zeal

Zest

Zip

NAMES FOR THE LEADER

A good leader is also a good warrior, a talented wizard and a sincere lover, tempered with the fire of the rebel. The leader comes along last, formed from the wisdom and experience gained sojourning through the other archetypes.

People who worked in the White House tell of a newly elected president's coming into office. Each man came into the oval office and a magical thing happened. He automatically "drew down" the presidency like a psychic mantle worn by each person holding that office, the archetype of the leader. The energy is the same, only its bearers vary. It is the old cry upon a death of a king: "The king is dead. Long live the king." The leader archetype is timeless; only those who bear its mantle come and then go.

When we don't have that leader energy incorporated into our own personality, the result is a life spent at the whim of others. Giving over the leader role to others may lead us to places we don't want to go, such as into an abusive relationship. How do you assume the leader archetype role in your own life? The leader is achieved not by identifying and mimicking being a leader. It isn't about being bossy, critical, or even decisive. The first step is to realize, as each president had to, that they were merely a temporary piece on the chessboard, playing the king for a time. He was, in fact, a servant to that energy. It is the selflessness of the leader that makes her able to lead. A person who takes the leader role without this inner shift becomes a tyrant. When manifested properly, the leader lends our lives fullness, anxiety levels drop, feelings of calm and centeredness abound, and we speak with an inner authority, a genuine authority to which people cannot help but listen. The leader will see others as complete beings and have compassion for them, not lord power over them. Power with, not power over.

These names, like all magical names, need not be public. You can use these names to speak to that part of yourself in the privacy of your own head and still they will be effective. If you feel you are ready, take up the mantle and rule, even just over yourself. Hone the skills of leadership. Care about others, rule over yourself, learn from life and speak with confidence, and people will pay heed to what you say.

Arthur

Auspice

Axiom

Blandish

Caesar

Calm

Captain

Cap'n

Chief

Coax

Commander

Control

Counselor

Credo

Czar

Czarina

Deem

Empress

Emperor

Entice

Guard

Guide

Kaiser

King

Lady

Leader

Liege

Managers are people who do things right, while leaders are people who do the right thing.
—WARREN BENNIS, PH.D.
ON BECOMING A LEADER

The leader leads, the boss drives.
—THEODORE ROOSEVELT

To lead people, walk beside them.
—LAO-TSU

Lord

Marshall

Mighty

Mogul

Monarch

Overlord

Pacesetter

Paladin

Patrician

Pilot

Potentate

Prestige

Prevail

Queen

Regime

Reign

Reserve

Sovereign

Sway

Trailblazer

Triumph

Tycoon

Tzar

Tzarina

Vassal

Warlord

Win

chapter eight

MAGICAL NAMES FROM
OUT OF THE BLUE

BIRD NAMES

Magical names taken from bird names are usually chosen because the bird has special meaning to the individual. Perhaps a bluebird has a nest in the tree near where you do your magical work or a crow reminds you of how you act at times. Bird names are highly individualized and they mean what you think they mean. I have listed some of the more interesting or beautiful-sounding bird names. If any of the names interest you, watch that bird in nature (or on bird documentaries) to get a feel for it. Often it is helpful when contemplating a name to meditate on the names that you are considering. Your subconscious will guide you.

Blackbird

Bluebird

Brant

Bunting

Buzzard

Canary

Cockatiel

Cockatoo

*I'll bet your father spent the first year of your
life throwing rocks at the stork.*

Condor

—IRVING BRECHER AND
EDWARD BUZZEL J.
CHEEVER LOOPHOLE
(GROUCHO MARX)
AT THE CIRCUS

Conure

Coot

Cormorant

Crane

Crow

Dove

*Wake from thy rest, robin redbreast!
Sing, birds, in every furrow,
and from each bill let music shrill
Give my fair love good morrow!*

Dunlin

Eagle

Eider

—THOMAS HEYWOOD

Falcon

Finch

Flicker

*In a herber green, asleep where I lay,
The birds sang sweet in the midst of the day;
I dreamed fast of mirth and play.
In youth is pleasure. In youth is pleasure.*

Gannet

Gladwall

Godwit

—ROBERT WEAVER
LUSTY JUVENTUS

Goldeneye

Gull

Hawk

Ibis

Jackdaw

Jaeger

Jay

Kestrel

Kittiwake

Lark

Laughing Gull

Laughing Dove

Linnet

Lovebird

Macaw

Magpie

Mallard

Manx

Merganser

Merlin

Oriole

Owl

Parakeet

Partridge

Pelican

Petrel

Pigeon

Pipit

Platypus

Plover

Ptarmigan

Puffin

Quail

Raven

Robin

Rook

Sanderling

Sandpiper

Shearwater

Skua

Sparrow

Sparrowhawk

Starling

Stonechat

Stork

Swan

Swift

Tern

Turnstone

Wagtail

Waxwing

Whimbrel

Wigeon

Woodpecker

Wren

BIRD MEDITATION

Get yourself into a quiet, meditative space. Visualize walking through the forest. It is a fine, sunny, spring day. There is new growth on all the trees and flowers are blooming on the forest floor. You hear the song of a bird ahead. Follow it. Come to a grove of apple trees that grow around a clearing, in the center of which is a well. There are flowers decorating the well, so you know that it is a sacred well. Drop the bucket into the well

If I had to choose, I would rather have birds than airplanes.

—CHARLES A. LINDBERGH

Fish got to swim
Birds got to fly.

—"CAN'T HELP LOVIN' DAT MAN"
OSCAR HAMMERSTEIN
SHOWBOAT

Every year, back comes Spring, with nasty little birds yapping their fool heads off and the ground all mucked up with plants.

—DOROTHY PARKER

and draw yourself a drink of cool, fresh water. In the grove, there appears a beautiful woman dressed in white. She wears white flowers in her hair and lovely songbirds fly about her, chirping greetings. She is Rhiannon, goddess of the underworld. Notice what kind of birds you see. What color are they? "Speak to me of what you seek, my child," commands the goddess in a soft voice. Do so. She will reply. After she has finished speaking to you, pick a bouquet of flowers from the forest to leave at the well in thanks. Rhiannon reaches out her hand to you and hands you an apple. Taste it; enjoy its sweetness and juiciness and the comforts of the grove. Sit in the dappled sunlight with Rhiannon and let yourself be lulled by the sound of her birds' singing. Allow complete abandonment to the sensations. Return back from whence you came when you are ready.

The thing to focus on in this meditation is relaxation, allowing yourself to rest in the company of the Lady and let her rejuvenate your tired spirit. Keep in mind the birds you saw; when you are under stress, recall the birds and the lovely flute-like song they sang and take with you some of that contentment to counterbalance the stress.

CLOUD NAMES

Names inspired by clouds are perfect for air or water signs. They are not quite the same as air names. Clouds and birds are things that are found in air, not the air itself. Clouds are airborne but are composed of water vapor so they could fit an air or a water person. They invoke lightness, and a kind of cleansing quality. The stormier ones may suit the more emotional person. Some of these are good names to help a person lighten up, be more optimistic and less intense.

Billow

Cirrus

Cloud

Cloudlet

Cumulus

Darkcloud

Dew

Downpour

Drift

Drizzle

Droplet

Filament

Fog

Foggy

Haze

Mist

Misty

Nimbus

Pinkcloud

Puff

Rain

Rainbow

Redcloud

A BUSINESS CARD I SAW ONCE:
George Moyer
Admirer of Clouds . . .
—PHOENIX MCFARLAND

I have a magpie mind. I like anything that
glitters.
—LORD THOMSON OF FLEET

I sing of brooks
of blossoms, birds and bowers,
of April, May of June and July flowers,
I sing of May-poles, hock-carts, wassails, wakes
of bridegrooms, brides and of their bridal cakes . . .
—ROBERT HERRICK

Every dark cloud has a silver lining.
—TRADITIONAL

Sky

Sky Kite

Sprinkle

Steamy

Stratus

Thundercloud

Torrent

Vapor

Whisp

Whitecloud

Zephyr

I want Carl Sagan to explain the sky to me.
—WHOOPI GOLDBERG

Oh 'darkly, deeply, beautifully blue!'
As someone, somewhere sings about the sky.
—LORD BYRON

On Thursday ticket counters and airplanes
will fly out of Reagan International Airport.
—GEORGE W. BUSH

SKY MEDITATION

While in a meditative state, picture a sky. It is the sky over your life. Let the imagery flow. What does your life's sky tell you? Are there rainbows, birds, fluffy white clouds, blue skies, dark clouds, tornados, hurricanes? Examine the sky for clues of your life's weather. If it is dark and brooding, take a look at how you are dark. Find things to be grateful for. Look for the light as well as the shadows. Take steps to clear away the bad weather haunting your skies even if that means self-examination or professional therapy. Check in from time to time to see how things are in your wild blue yonder.

chapter nine

MAGICAL NAMES FROM THE SPACE/TIME CONTINUUM

NAMES FROM TIME

Names from time are wonderful choices for magical names because they evoke a definite set of mental and emotional images in almost everyone who hears them. The names "April" or "Beltaine" remind most people of springtime and romance. To a Pagan, April may also generate thoughts of the maiden, a young girl approaching womanhood, innocence, sweetness, the budding earth, the promise of fertility, warmth, or blustery emotions. Beltaine conjures images of Eros or Cupid; the idea of romance, of course, but also passion, eroticism, flirtation, amorousness, and lust. The wheel turns and we turn with it, perhaps taking a name, or a series of names as your wheel turns

She made the best of time, and time returned
the compliment.

—LORD BYRON

Here's the day when it is May
And care as light as a feather,
When your little shoes and my big boots
Go tramping through the heather.

—A TOAST
BLISS CARMAN

Do not squander time, for that is the stuff
life is made of.

—BENJAMIN FRANKLIN

Time is the wisest of all counselors.

—PLUTARCH

throughout your life. If you are young, you could take a springtime name now and progress as you move through life from spring to summer, fall and winter— each name marking a piece of your life. Life is measured by time and the value of your time is measured by how you live your life. Tick-tock.

Afternoon

Age

April

August

Autumn

Begin

Beltaine

Bygone

Cadence

Chance

Dawn

Day

December

Dusk

Eon

Eostar

Epoch

Equinox

Era

Esbat

Evening

Eventide

Fall
February
Imbolc
Instant
January
July
June
Lammas
Lughnasadh
Mabon
March
May
Midsummer
Moment
Morning
Nightfall
November
October
Samhain ("SOW in")
Season
September
Solstice
Span
Spell
Spring
Sunrise
Sunset
Tempo
Time

*The butterfly counts not months but moments,
and has time enough.*

—RABINDRANATH TAGORE

*I'd always heard your entire life flashes in
front of your eyes the second before you die.
First of all, that one second isn't a second at
all. It stretches on forever like an ocean of time
. . . I guess I could be pretty pissed off about
what happened to me. But its hard to stay
mad when there's so much beauty in the
world. Sometimes I feel like I'm seeing it all
at once and it's too much. My heart fills up
like a balloon that's about to burst. And then
I remember to relax instead of trying to hold
on to it. And then it flows through me like
rain and I can't feel anything but gratitude
for every single moment of my stupid, little
life. You have no idea what I'm talking about,
I'm sure. But don't worry, you will someday.*

—ALAN BALL, SCREENWRITER
AMERICAN BEAUTY

Time and tide wait for no one.

—TRADITIONAL

The future will be better tomorrow.

—DAN QUAYLE

Today

Tomorrow

Twilight

Unfold

Valentine

While

Winter

Yesterday

Yesteryear

Yore

Yule

NAMES FROM SPACE

We have given some of the most beautiful names to the objects occupying the great silent mysterious enigma that surrounds us. The deep silence of space is filled with breathtaking beauty and, as yet, unknowable secrets. What better place to find mysterious and beautiful names?

Alcyone: In Greek mythology, a daughter of King Aeolus. She was changed into a kingfisher. One of the stars of the Pleiades. A seeker's name; one who seeks to soar despite the risks.

Aldebaran: a star of the first magnitude in the constellation Taurus, forming the eye of the bull. A good name for those who require a strong inner vision and true insights.

Algol: a fixed star in Medusa's head in the constellation Perseus. It is a binary star and loses most of its brightness when eclipsed by its dark companion. A fine name for someone who was (or is) overshadowed by others.

Alioth: a star in the tail of the Great Bear. A name for someone who requires the strength of the bear.

Altair: the bird; a star of the first magnitude in the constellation Aquila. Altair is a name for one who seeks a broader perspective in life (a bird's-eye view).

Andromeda: in Greek legend, Andromeda was the daughter of Cepheus. Perseus rescued her from a sea monster and married her. It is also a constellation in the Northern Hemisphere. A name for a person who needs to feel safe, rescued, and secure.

Antares: a star of the first magnitude in the constellation Scorpio. It is also called scorpion's heart. For those who require strength of heart.

Aquarius: Latin for "the water carrier." It is a large central constellation of a man pouring water from a pitcher. It is also the eleventh sign of the zodiac. A good water energy name.

Arcturus: from *arktos* (bear) and *ouros* (guard). It refers to a fixed star of the first magnitude in the constellation Boötes. A strong, courageous name.

Aries: a northern constellation between Pisces and Taurus that outlines a ram. It is the first sign of the zodiac. A name that, like people who are born under this sign, is strong, self-absorbed, and fearless.

Asteroid: any of the small planets (planetoids) found between the orbits of Mars and Jupiter. A name about movement, balance, and finding one's niche in life.

Astral: a word meaning starry or starlike, or referring to the field of energy that envelops the human form. This is a name for dreamers, poets, and others whose hearts soar upon the astral.

Aurora: in Greek mythology, Aurora was the goddess of the dawn. It also refers to the beginning or early period of anything. It is the name of the magnificent crackling, shimmering displays of light that occur in the far northern and far southern skies. Many native cultures have taboos about being outside when the lights are active. An air elemental name that invokes a bit of fire as well.

Canis: refers to the constellations Canis Major and Canis Minor, the greater and lesser dog. A name for a dog lover or someone who has a hound as a totem animal.

Capricorn: a southern constellation of the goat. Also the tenth sign of the zodiac, which the sun enters at the winter solstice (December 22, Yule). This is a name that brings images of the goat climbing easily to high, rocky crags, leaving everyone else below. This is a good name for an achiever, a social climber, one who cares about succeeding.

Cassiopeia: in Greek legend, Cassiopeia is the mother of Andromeda and the wife of Cepheus. It is also a northern constellation between Andromeda and Cepheus. A proud mother's name, but beware the price of pride.

Centaurus: a constellation in the south between Hydra and the Southern Cross. The brightest star is Alpha Centauri, which is the closest star to Earth. From centaur, a cross between a horse and a human. For bringing fleetness, strength, and courage. A good name for a horse lover.

Cepheus: in Greek mythology, husband to Cassiopeia and father to Andromeda. He was placed among the stars after his death. Also a northern constellation surrounded by Cassiopeia, Ursa Major, Draco, and Cygnus. A proud father's name.

Chiron: a new planet discovered in 1977. It is located on an irregular orbit between Saturn and Uranus. In mythology, Chiron was a centaur who was unlike other centaurs. He was wise, kind, and skilled in music and medicine. He was a friend to Hercules, but was accidentally injured by him. Because centaurs are immortal, he would not die but suffer endless pain, so he asked Zeus to grant him death. Zeus placed him in the stars after allowing him to die. Chiron is a name to bring an end to suffering and provide wisdom, skill, and faithfulness. It is a name for one who walks to the beat of a different drummer, and does not live as others expect you to live.

*Houston, Tranquillity Base here. The Eagle
has landed.*

—NEIL ARMSTRONG, U.S. ASTRONAUT
FIRST MESSAGE TO THE EARTH FROM THE
APOLLO 11 LUNAR MODULE *EAGLE* AFTER
LANDING ON THE MOON JULY 20, 1969

*For a very few the sky's the limit.
And, sometimes, not even that.*

—TERRY PRATCHETT
SMALL GODS

*You're from outer space?
No, I'm from Iowa; I work in outer space.*

—STORY BY ALAN DEAN FOSTER,
SCREENPLAY BY HAROLD LIVINGSTON
STAR TREK IV: THE VOYAGE HOME

Space—the final frontier.

—GENE RODDENBERRY
STAR TREK, PREAMBLE

*Time, space and causality are only metaphors
of knowledge, with which we explain things
to ourselves.*

—FRIEDRICH NIETZSCHE

Comet: from *kome* (hair), because the tail of a comet is like long hair. A celestial body having a starlike nucleus with a luminous mass around and trailing after it. Comets follow an orbit around the sun. A name that brings fleetness, alertness, and fire energy; a quick, sparkling energy rather than a slow, steady flame. For those who seek fire elementals but who wish also for spontaneity and passion.

Draco: from the Latin *draco* and the Greek *drakon,* meaning "dragon." A constellation lying between the Big and Little Dippers. A subtle fire name for dragon lovers.

Earth: the fifth largest planet in the solar system and the third planet from the sun. Also referring to the soil covering the surface. One of the best names for becoming well grounded. A great name for promoting fertility. A good choice for gardeners or a would-be parent.

Ethereal: very light, airy, delicate, or referring to the upper regions of space. One of the more beautiful names for those who seek the power of air names.

Galaxy: a grouping of millions of stars that appears to be a luminous band across the sky, referred to as the Milky Way. A remote air name; although there is no "air" in space, such things are seen to live in the sky and thus are associated (distantly) as air names. Because stars are distant fires, starry names are also fire names. Galaxy has a marvelous lilt to the name with associated images encompassing many things within it.

Gemini: a northern constellation between Cancer and Pollux represented by twins sitting together. Also the third sign of the zodiac, entered by the sun about May 21. Gemini brings a duality to one's life, a recognition of one's other side.

Jupiter: in Roman mythology, the supreme god figure equated to the Greek Zeus. It is also the largest planet in the solar system and the fifth planet from the sun. A name for power, leadership, control, and omnipotence.

Leo: a constellation between Cancer and Virgo that outlines a lion. Its brightest star is Regulus. A cat name, one that brings feline power, sleekness, and strength.

Libra: a southern constellation between Virgo and Scorpio that resembles a pair of scales. Also the seventh sign of the zodiac, which the sun enters about September 23 (the autumn equinox). A name that lends its bearer balance and harmony.

Lumina: a measurement of the flow of light. A fire name that sheds light on the darkness, and also a name for personal enlightenment.

Luna: in Roman mythology, the goddess presiding over the moon and the months. In alchemy, luna refers to silver. A cool, calm, moon-driven name for those who wish to be in harmony with her cycles.

Lunar: moonlike. (See above.)

Lyra: a northern constellation containing the white star of the first magnitude called Alpha Lyra. A poetic name with a hint of music to it (lyre).

Mars: the god of war in Roman mythology, similar to the Greek god Ares. Also refers to the fourth planet from the sun, which appears red. In alchemy, Mars refers to iron. A name that brings strength, power, victory, and bravery.

Mercury: in Roman mythology, the messenger of the gods, god of commerce, manual skill, eloquence, cleverness, travel, and thievery; equated to the Greek Hermes. Also the smallest planet in the solar system and the nearest to the sun. A name that speaks of commerce, success, and movement along the economic scale. An ambitious person in business would do well using this name.

Mira: from Latin *mirus*, "wonderful." A star, Omicron Ceti, in the constellation Cetus, which is remarkable for its varying brightness increasing from the twelfth to the fourth magnitude in a period of six weeks. A flexible, variable, quixotic name for one who seeks to extend beyond limits.

Moon: the heavenly body that revolves around the earth once every twenty-eight days. A cool, tidal, changeable name.

Nebula: any of several misty, light, cloudlike patches that consist of interstellar clouds of dust or gas seen in the night sky. An airy, subtle, and sparkling name.

Neptune: in Roman mythology, the sea god equated with the Greek Poseidon. Also the third-largest planet in the solar system. A strong water name to induce the power to deal with the deepest emotions.

Nova: a star that suddenly increases in brilliance then gradually grows fainter. Nova is a name of brilliance and achievement.

Orion: in Greek and Roman mythology, a hunter whom a goddess loved but killed. Orion was also thought to have desired the Pleiades and so ran after them. Zeus saved them by turning them all into stars. Also an equatorial constellation near Taurus containing the first magnitude stars Rigel and Betelgeuse. A name that brings quick instincts and basic desires.

Perseus: in Greek mythology, the slayer of the gorgon Medusa. A northern constellation between Taurus and Cassiopeia. A youthful hero's name that brings bravery and accomplishment.

Pisces: a constellation south of Andromeda resembling two fish. Also the twelfth sign of the zodiac entered by the sun around February 21. A water name.

Pleiades: in Greek mythology, the seven daughters of Atlas and Pleione who were placed by Zeus among the stars. A large group of stars in the constellation Taurus. Six of them are visible, the seventh being the "lost" Pleiad. A good name for an all-female coven.

Polaris: the north star. A star of the second magnitude forming the end of the tail of Ursa Minor, it marks the position of the north pole. A name that involves polarity and alignment with the earth.

Rigel: the brightest star in the constellation of Orion. Rigel is a blue star of the first magnitude.

Sagittarius: from the Latin, meaning "archer." A southern constellation depicting a centaur shooting an arrow. Also the ninth sign of the zodiac, which the sun enters about November 23. A hunter's name, bringing attributes of a stealthy hunter.

Saturn: in Roman mythology, the god of agriculture and husband to Ops, the goddess of the harvest. He is equated with the Greek Cronos. Also the second largest planet in the solar system. A powerful fertility name for those who seek to make things grow.

Scorpio: a southern constellation resembling a scorpion located between Libra and Sagittarius. Also the eighth sign of the zodiac, which the sun enters about October 24. A fiery, passionate name.

Star: in Middle English *sterre*, Anglo-Saxon *steorra*, Icelandic *stjarna*, Gothic *stairno*, Dutch *ster*, Old Dutch *sterne*, German *stern*, Latin *stella*, Greek *aster*, Cornish *steren*, and Persian *satarah*. A star is a heavenly body seen to be fixed in the night sky. Each of these points of light are distant suns. A fire name, bringing sparkle and illumination.

Taurus: a northern constellation which includes the Pleiades. Taurus outlines the shape of a bull. Also the second sign of the zodiac, entered by the sun about April 20. A powerful earth name; the great bull who is strong, large, and prolific.

Terra: earth. A good name for grounding. Terra brings fertility and sensibility.

Vega: a blue-white star of the first magnitude in the northern constellation Lyra.

Venus: in Roman mythology, the goddess of love and beauty equated with the Greek Aphrodite. The most brilliant planet in the solar system. Ancients called it Lucifer as the morning star and Hesperus as the evening star. In alchemy, Venus is related to copper. A name that is a powerful expression of self-worth, appreciation of beauty and love, and strong sexuality.

Virgo: the sixth sign of the zodiac, which the sun enters about August 22. Its symbol is the virgin. An equatorial constellation between Leo and Libra outlining the shape of a woman or virgin. Virgo contains thirty-nine visible stars, of which Spica is the brightest. A maiden's name bringing youth and innocence.

Zodiac: an imaginary belt in the heavens extending for eight degrees on either side of the apparent path of the sun and including the paths of the moon and the other planets. It is divided into twelve equal parts, or signs, each named for a different constellation. A name that brings an awareness of the stars and astrology.

NAMES FROM SPACECRAFT

There are many satellites orbiting around the earth, more than most people think. They have some interesting names. Here are some high-flying spacecraft names for a high-flying witch.

Aeros

Agila: "eagle" French.

Ajisai: "hydrangea" Japanese.

Aldebaran

Alexis

Almas: "diamond" Russian.

Alouette: "lark" French.

America

Anik: "brother" Inuit.

Antares

Argon

Argos

Asterix

Astro

Aura

Aurora

Azur

Badr: "full moon" Pakistani.

Bion

Buran: "snowstorm" Russian.

Casper

Cerise: "cherry" French.

Clementine

Cobalt

Corona

Cosmos

Delta

Eagle

Echo

Echostar

Efir: "ether" Russian.

Ekran: "screen" Russian.

Endeavor

Etalon: "standard" Russian.

Ether

Explorer

Falcon

Firewheel

Fram: "forward" Norwegian.

Freedom

Fuyo: "rose mallow" Japanese.

Galaxy

Gamma

Geizer: "geyser" Russian.

Ginga: "galaxy" Japanese.

Gumdrop

Haruka: "far away" Japanese.

Jindai: "cherry tree" Japanese.

Kakehashi: "bridge" Japanese.

Kiku: "chrysanthenum" Japanese.

Koronas: "corona" Russian.

Kristall: "crystal" Russian.

Magion

Mariner

Midori: "green" Japanese.

Mir: "world peace" Russian.

Molniya: "lightning" Russian.

Momo: "peach blossom" Japanese.

Myojo: "venus" Japanese.

Nadezhda: "hope" Russian.

Nahuel: "tiger" Araucano.

Nauka: "science" Russian.

Nimbus

Nimiq: "unity" Inuit.

Nozomi: "hope" Japanese.

Oblik: "appearance" Russian.

Observer

Odyssey

Ohzora: "sky" Japanese.

Okean: "ocean" Russian.

Oko: "eye" Russian.

Omega

Orbus

Palapa: "unity" Indonesian.

Pegasus

Pioneer

Pollux

Priroda: "nature" Russian.

Prospero

Proton

Quantum

Raduga: "rainbow" Russian.

Ranger

Redstone

Rhombus

Rokot: "roar" Russian.

Rubis: "ruby" French.

Sakigake: "pioneer" Japanese.

Sakura: "cherry blossom" Japanese.

Salyut: "salute" Russian.

Scout

Sigma

Skipper

Skynet

Sojourner

Soyus: "union" Russian.

Spartan

Stardust

Starlette: "little star" French.

Strela: "arrow" Russian.

Suisei: "comet" Japanese.

Taiyo: "sun" Japanese.

Tansei: "light blue" Japanese.

Tempo

Tenma: "pegasus" Japanese.

Tselina: "untouched soil" Russian.

Tsikada: "cricket" Japanese.

Tsiklon: "cyclone" Russian.

Uhuru: "freedom" Swahili.

Ume: "apricot blossom" Japanese.

Uragan: "hurricane" Russian.

Uribyol: "our star" Korean.

Vanguard

Vector

Vega

Venera: "venus" Russian.

Viking

Voyager

Yantar: "amber" Russian.

Yohkoh: "sunlight" Japanese.

Yuri: "lily" Japanese.

Zarya: "dawn" Russian.

Zenit: "zenith" Russian.

Zeya: after the Zeya river.

Zond: "probe" Russian.

chapter ten

MAGICAL NAMES FROM
LIGHT, DARK, AND
IN-BETWEEN

Much of our celebrating takes place on solstices and equinoxes where light and dark are at extremes of balance with each other. So the coming and going of light and dark seasons is part of our yearly journey. Magical names from either extreme on this spectrum offer some illuminating choices. Glisten Lightlady, Darken Moonwood, and Gossamer Wink are fun names from the light and shadow sides of life.

LIGHT NAMES

Aglow

Alight

Ardent

Beacon

Rage, rage against the dying of the light.
—DYLAN THOMAS

When it is dark enough, you can see the stars.
—CHARLES A. BEARD

Enlightenment is not imagining figures of light but making the darkness conscious.
—CARL GUSTAV JUNG

Newman's Second Law: Just when things look darkest, they go black.
—PAUL NEWMAN

Beam
Blinker
Brand
Bright
Brilliance
Cheer
Cheery
Enkindle
Flambeau
Glimmer
Glisten
Glitter
Gossamer
Illumination
Iridian
Iridescent
Keen
Kindle
Light
Luminous
Merry
Neon
Niveous
Pale
Prism
Radiant
Ray
Shaft
Shimmer

Shimmery

Shine

Spark

Sparkle

Sunny

Twinkle

Vibrant

Vivid

Wink

DARK NAMES

Arcane

Ashen

Cloak

Cryptic

Dark

Darken

Darkness

Dusk

Dusky

Eclipse

Evening

Eventide

Gloom

Gray

Grim

Grizzled

Haunt

Hidden

Mirage

Misty

Murk

Murky

Mystery

Mystic

Nightfall

Nightshade

Penumbra

Phantom

Sequester

Shade

Shadow

Silhouette

Somber

Spector

Sylvan

Tenebrous

Twilight

Ulterior

COLOR NAMES

Choosing names from colors is not new. Look at Red Buttons, Deep Purple, Pink, or Indigo Girls for instance. Colorful names are great choices for anyone who is sensitive to the pallet of color that surrounds us. Artists, photographers, decorators, and anyone visually stimulated by hues of color might look here for a name. These are visual names with a

lot of punch such as Stonewash Moon-
flower, Cream Crone, Demeter Cornsilk,
Cornflower Blue, Sea Green Beeswax, Jet
Black.

Absinthe

Alabaster

Almond

Amber

Amethyst

Antique White

Apricot

Aqua

Argent

Aubergine

Auburn

Avocado

Azure

Beeswax

Beige

Black

Blue

Blue-violet

Brass

Bronze

Brown

Buckskin

Buff

Burgundy

Butterscotch

Canary

Caramel

Carmine

Carrot

Cerulean Blue

Chamois

Champagne

Chartreuse

Chestnut

Cinnabar

Citron

Claret

Copper

Coral

Cornflower Blue

Cornsilk

Cream

Crimson

Currant

Cyan

Ebon

Ebony

Ecru

Emerald

Evergreen

Fawn

Fiery

Firebrick

Flaxen

Fresco Cream

Fuchia

Garnet

Ginger

Gold

Goldenrod

Gunmetal

Heliotrope

Henna

Hot Pink

Hue

Indigo

Jade

Jet

Khaki

Lapis Lazuli

Lavender

Linen

Loden

Magenta

Mahogany

Malachite

Marine Green

Maroon

Mauve

Melon

Moonstone

Nile Blue

Ochre

Olive

Onyx

Orchid

Parchment

Pastel

Peach

Peacock

Pearl

Periwinkle

Pink

Pistachio

Platinum

Plum

Poppy

Primrose

Puce

Purple

Roan

Rosewood

Rufous

Russet

Sable

Sand

Sapphire

Sea Blue

Sea Green

*And there I saw myself as a man might expect,
except that my skin was very white, as the old
friend's had been white, and my eyes had been
transformed from their usual blue to a mingling of violet and cobalt that was softly iridescent. My hair had a high luminous sheen, and
when I ran my fingers back through it I felt a
new and strange vitality there.*

—ANNE RICE
THE VAMPIRE LESTAT

*With color one obtains an energy that seems to
stem from witchcraft.*

—HENRI MATISSE

Seashell

Sepia

Shadow Blue

Sienna

Silver Slate

Slate Blue

Smoke

Snowberry White

Stonewash

Straw

Tan

Tangerine

Taupe

Tawny

Teal

Tint

Turquoise

Ultramarine

Verdant

Verdigris

Vermilion

Wheat

Wicker

Wine

Yellow

chapter eleven

MAGICAL NAMES FROM
THE SILVER SCREEN

NAMES FROM HOLLYWOOD

Since I sometimes work in "the business," I thought I'd list some interesting names from Hollywood. I have worked as a background performer (extra) in the movies and TV for several years now and have worked with many stars. What I have noticed is that many stars have unusual names, and a great many favor them for their offspring. These are people who walk into a room and are instantly noticed. They are not hard to pick out of the crowd and not just because of their famous mugs, but because of their unique and vibrant energy. You can feel them coming. There is something special about many, many of the stars I've worked with, a unique vibration that sets them apart from the average "Joe." Sometimes they are different in a good way, and sometimes not. Perhaps this difference came as a result of having grown up with an unusual name in the first place. It set them on the path to being seen as special, out of the ordinary, and they learned that being different could be a good thing. So perhaps some of these stars first learned to twinkle when they were named and went on to dazzle us all. So if you, like me, have stardust in your eyes, finding a name from among these stars might help you or your baby sparkle a little brighter.

A note regarding celebrity: My philosophy of life is that I see us all as ambling along our individual paths at our different speeds and with our own sets of challenges and goals. When we see someone we admire, especially someone successful or famous, we stop and gaze in awe. They seem to have it so together. We tend to see the glamour of beauty, fame, and wealth, forgetting that our path is just as valid even though we aren't yet where they are in terms of fame, for instance. But remember that they may not yet be where you have already been.

You've gotta own your own days and name 'em! Each one of 'em, every one of 'em! Or else the years go right by, and none of them belong to you.

—JASON ROBARDS, JR.
HERB GARDNER, SCREENWRITER
A THOUSAND CLOWNS

It ain't what they call you, it's what you answer to.

—BILL CLINTON

HOLLYWOOD . . . THE NEXT GENERATION

Here are names of some of the children of celebrities.

Alec Baldwin: **Ireland**

Andre Agassi: **Jaden, Gil**

Angelina Jolie: **Maddox**

Anne Heche: **Homer**

Billy Ray Cyrus: **Blaison, Chance, Destiny, Hope**

Bob Geldof: **Fifi Trixibelle, Peaches, Pixie, Heavenly Hiraani Tiger Lily**

Brandy: **Sy'rai**

Calista Flockheart: **Liam**

Camryn Manheim: **Milo**

Cate Blanchett: **Dashiell**

Catherine Zeta Jones: **Dylan, Carys**

Christie Brinkley: **Alexa Ray, Jack Sailor, Lee**

Chris Rock: **Lola, Simone**

Cindy Crawford: **Presley, Kaya**

Cuba Gooding Jr.: **Spencer, Mason**

Cynthia Nixon: **Samantha**

Demi Moore: **Rumer Glenn, Scout LaRue, Tallulah Belle**

Diane Keaton: **Duke, Dexter**

Don Johnson: **Jasper, Atherton**

Eric McCormack: **Finnigan, Holden**

Forest Whitaker: **True**

Garrison Keillor: **Maya, Grace**

A self-made man may prefer a self-made name.

—GRANTING COURT PERMISSION FOR SAMUEL GOLDFISH TO CHANGE HIS NAME TO SAMUEL GOLDWYN, QUOTED BY BOSLEY CROWTHER

. . . we might as well face the truth that to researchers of the future, poking about among the ruins of time, we shall all be tiny glitters. But then, so are diamonds.

—JAMES THURBER

Twinkle, twinkle, little star How I wonder what you are.

—ANN AND JANE TAYLOR
RHYMES FOR THE NURSERY, 1806

Gary Oldman: **Gulliver, Flynn**

Geena Davis: **Alizeh, Keshvar**

George Stephanopoulos: **Elliott, Anastasia**

Gillian Anderson: **Piper**

Harry Hamlin: **Delilah, Amelia**

Hunter Tyler: **Izabella, Katya**

Jada Pinkett-Smith: **Jaden, Willow**

Jenny McCarthy: **Evan**

John Mellencamp: **Hud, Speck**

Johnny Depp: **Lily-Rose**

Jude Law: **Rafferty, Iris, Finley, Rudy**

Julianne Moore: **Liv**

Kate Winslet: **Mia**

Liam Gallagher: **Lennon**

Madonna: **Lourdes, Rocco**

Mariel Hemingway: **Langley Fox**

Melanie Brown: **Phoenix Chi**

Melissa Etheridge: **Beckett**

Nicole Kidman: **Connor, Isabella**

Noel Gallagher: **Anais**

Paula Yates: **Pixie**

Phoenix family: **Rainbow, Leaf, River, Liberty, Summer Joy**

Richard Gere: **Homer**

Rob Morrow: **Tu**

Robert Downey Jr.: **Indio**

Sean Young: **Rio, Quinn**

Shania Twain: **Eja (Asia)**

Sheena Easton: **Skylar**

Spike Lee: **Satchel, Lewis**

Steven Speilberg: **Destry, Allyn, Sasha, Sawyer, Theo**

Teri Hatcher: **Emerson, Rose**

Tom Robbins: **Fleetwood, Starr**

Toni Braxton: **Denim, Cole**

Victoria Adams: **Brooklyn, Romeo**

CELEBRITIES PAST AND PRESENT WITH UNUSUAL NAMES

Ace

Alistair

Anaïs

Arliss

Arsenio

Audie

Björk

Blythe

Bo

Bramwell

Buster

Cary

Charleton

Charlize

Cher

Colm

Courtland	Evel
Cox	Ewan
Crispin	Fabian
Cuba	Famke
Darling	Fancy
Delphine	Farrah
Demi	Gaby
Denholm	Garson
Denzel	Gates
Desmond	Geena
Dewey	Gemma
Dexter	Gig
Dixie	Goldie
Dodie	Gore
Dolph	Gray
Drue	Gretta
Dweezil	Haley
Elden	Honor
Elia	Iman
Elton	Ingmar
Elvis	Jada
Elya	Jersey
Enya	Joachim
Errol	Judge
Erskine	Keanu
Erykah	Kelsey
Esmé	Kermit
Ethan	Kia Joy

Kiefer	Orson
Kieran	Ossie
Kirk	Otto
Lafe	Ozzy
Lainie	Percy
Lana	Picabo
Leaf	Pierce
Liv	Piper
Lolita	Rain
Macaulay	Remy
Mamie	Rex
Markie	River
Marlo	Rock
Mata	Rockcliffe
Mathonwy	Roland
Mayim	Roma
Mena	Roscoe
Millard	Rudolph
Milos	Rufus
Mitzi	Sade
Moe	Salma
Montagu	Sandrine
Montel	Scatman
Nat King	Season
Neve	Sela
Night	Shae
Olympia	Shane
Oprah	Shania

Shaquille	Treat
Shevonne	Trini
Sig	Trinidad
Sigourney	Troy
Silken	Truman
Sinbad	Tuesday
Sinead	Twiggy
Skeet	Tyrone
Spencer	Uma
Sterling	Una
Stone	Ving
Stryker	Whoopi
Swoozie	Winona
Tabitha	Winston
Talia	Woody
Tallulah	Wyatt
Tamblyn	Wynne
Teal	Xander
Tempest	Yul
Thayer	Yves
Tipper	Zane
Titus	Zeta
Tobey	Zsa Zsa

chapter twelve

MAGICAL NAMES FROM
THE KITCHEN

The kitchen, more than any other room, represents hearth and home. For most of us these days, the kitchen doesn't find people gathered there to can fresh vegetables, make quilts, put up fruit preserves, or hang herbs to dry after the harvest. Today, it's mostly a friendly spot where people gather at parties. It is still the hub of family life. It is the place we store, cook, and eat our food, and so it holds an important place in the household. Food represents abundance, prosperity—a tangible kind of wealth.

Kitchen names are great choices for people who love to cook or who love to eat. Names taken from the kitchen can help us toward abundance. But more than that, kitchen names are homey, cozy, comforting names. These names are good to take if you are seeking a new home, if you want to make your existing home happier, or if you want to use your name to celebrate life's harvests.

FOOD NAMES

Ambrosia

Arrowroot

Barleycorn

Bayberry

Bearclaw

Belladonna

Berry

Bisque

Bittersweet

Bizzom

Bly

Brameberry

Bran

Brioche

Brochette

Brownie

Brulé

Bryony

Buckwheat

Burgoo

Buttermilk

Butternut

Butterscotch

Caffeine

Camomile

Cappuccino

Caraway

Carberry

Cardamon

Cassoulet

Caviar

Chantilly

Checkerberry

Cherry

Chicory

Chiffon

Chili

Chutney

Cockle

Cocoa

Coffee

Comfrey

Cookie

Couscous

Croquette

Crouton

Crumpet

Currant

Darjeeling

Dijon

Espresso

Fabiana

Farina

Filbert

Garbanzo

Gelato

Gingersnap

Granola

Griddle

Gumbo

Hazelnut

Hominy

Honey

Horehound

Hushpuppy

Jalapeño

Jambalaya

Java

Julienne

Kebab

Kipper

Kiwi

Kumquat

Latté

Licorice

Marmalade

Marzipan

Mead

Melba

Miso

Mocha

Muffin

Mustard Seed

Myrrh

Nectarine

Paella

Papaya

Parfait

Periwinkle

Persimmon

Pesto

Piccalilli

Pilaff

Pita

Polenta

Pomegranate

Poppy

Praline

Pretzel

Primavera

Pumpkin

Quiche

Quince

Rhubarb

Ricotta

Salsa

Sangria

Sauté

Sherry

Simmer

Succotash

Sugar

I know how hard it is to put food on your family.
—GEORGE W. BUSH

*In the childhood memories of every good cook,
there's a large kitchen, a warm stove,
a simmering pot, and a mom.*
—BARBARA COSTIKYAN

*And, indeed, is there not something holy about
a great kitchen? . . . The scoured gleam of
row upon row of metal vessels dangling from
hooks or reposing on their shelves till needed
with the air of so many chalices waiting for
the celebration of the sacrament of food. And
the range like an altar, yes, before which my
mother bowed in perpetual homage, a fringe of
sweat upon her upper lip and the fire glowing
in her cheeks.*
—ANGELA CARTER
"THE KITCHEN CHILD"
VOGUE (1979)

Sushi

Tabasco

Taffy

Tangerine

Tapioca

Tetrazini

Tidbit

Toddy

Toffee

Tortoni

Truffles

Vanilla

Wassail

KITCHEN MEDITATION

In a quiet moment, get into a meditative place and relax. Picture yourself inside a happy childhood kitchen. Feel the warmth from the oven, the smell of something good cooking (cookies work well).The familiar sounds of cooking—the kettle boiling, hood fan running, timer dinging, the sound of your caretaker's voice calling you to dinner. Collect all of these memories into one big emotion. Hold it in your hand like a ball of happiness. Put your hands around it and squeeze it until when you open your hands you find a name made from the happy energy. Bring your name up and smell it. What does it smell like? Cookies? Stew? Roasting meat? Fruit? Coffee brewing? Lick the corner of it. It tastes good. What does it taste like? Pop it in your mouth and eat it. Savor its warmth, flavor, texture, aroma, and feel satisfied as you consume your name. As you return to reality, remember the name that became part of you and how it made you feel.

SPICE NAMES

Spice names are splendid choices for magical names. There are gentle, sweet names and wild, lustful, and spicy names. If you find a spice name that brings out your natural flavor, then by all means, cook with it. Spice names correspond to images of coziness, hearth fires, warm and fragrant kitchens, and fresh-baked goods; in short, they invoke a feeling of home. They are marvelous plants that improve our lives and enhance the flavor of our food. In the early days of sailing ships, adventurers risked their lives to seek the treasures of the Spice Islands, bringing back the precious cargo of spice. Spices are used for healing and in magical spells. There is a vast amount of folklore about their uses.

Some spice names are better for certain physical attributes than others, such as for a redhead the names Allspice, Paprika, Cinnamon, and Cayenne work well. A blonde may prefer the name Vanilla or Lavender. A dark-eyed, black-haired person would do well with names like Star Anise, Licorice, or Pepper. Physical correspondences such as these are one way of connecting to a spice name, but there are many others. For example, the red spices are representative of fire energy and could be chosen based on elemental magic. Black spices are connected to earth energies. Sometimes there are interesting folk names for these spices; one of these may work for you.

Allspice: used for magical healing and is burned to attract prosperity. Oil of allspice is good for invigorating convalescing patients. This is a name that can be worn by any physical type of person, but one who is passionate and feisty, and comfortable with that. It is an invigorating and healing name.

Alum: when ancient Egyptians had been robbed, they would burn alum together with crocus to discover the identity of the thief. A good name for a quiet, mysterious, psychic person.

Angelica: angelica is used for its protective properties. It is a good name for a parent, teacher, healer, or for those who desire protection.

Anise: the essence of anise is said to be an aphrodisiac. Anise is very aromatic. It is thought to eliminate nightmares when you sleep on it. Many witches use it in their ritual baths together with bay laurel. It is supposed to promote clairvoyance. It is also known in Britain as sweet cicely or British myrrh. In the past, herbalists described the plant as "so harmless, you cannot use it amiss." Anise is a good name for a dark person. It brings deep passions.

Basil: promotes harmony and a sympathetic connection between two people. Perhaps this was why Spanish prostitutes used to wear the scent. It is also known as alabahaca and the witches' herb. Basil is used for purification, protection, exorcism, and to attract love. Basil is a name for one who is seeking a mate. It will emphasize their attractiveness to the right person.

Bay: also called baie, bay laurel, Grecian laurel, Roman laurel, or sweet bay. Bay is used for protection, improving clairvoyance, exorcism, and healing, and is believed to protect against lightning. Bay is a water sign name. Laurel is also a beautiful name that brings honor, truth, and intuition.

Bittersweet: used for protection and healing. It is good for curing vertigo. This is a good name for one who seeks to balance his or her light and dark sides, or for one getting over a relationship and going through the transition period.

Chamomile: also called maythen. Used for healing eye troubles, to increase prosperity, and to induce restful sleep. Chamomile is a woman's name. As a magical name, it is for bringing quietness to one's life. This is a peaceful, restful, healing sanctuary of a name.

Caraway: used for protection, to attract a lover, to strengthen memory, to protect against theft, and to ensure fidelity. Caraway is a good name for either sex, although it has a slightly more masculine feel to it.

Cayenne: a spicy red pepper. As a name, Cayenne brings out one's hidden passions and brings determination, righteous anger, and strong will.

Cinnamon: used for bringing success, spirituality, lust, increased psychic powers, protection, and love. In the past, cinnamon-leaf wreaths decorated Roman temples.

As with the other red spices, this would be a good redhead's name. It also represents passion, temper, hard-won loyalty, deep spirituality, fierce love, and the protective powers of a mother lion defending her young. Many of these fiery qualities are commonly associated with redheads.

Clove: used for protection, exorcism, attracting love and money, removing hostility, purification, stopping gossip, and attracting the opposite sex. As a magical name, Clove is a solid choice. This is a stable, respectable name for a person who has (or wants to have) a bounty of blessings, from a good job to a happy home life.

Comfrey: also called miracle herb or yalluc. Used for ensuring safe journeys and attracting money. Comfrey is a wonderful name for healers, herbalists, parents, teachers, or other people who are involved with making others feel better. This is a name for one who eases pain, one with great compassion and empathy for others. This is also a name to choose if you seek to be healed.

Coriander: amulets containing coriander are used to attract love, health, and lust. Coriander is also used to ease headaches. As a magical name, Coriander is likely to bring romantic qualities into your life. This is for a person who desires desire.

Cumin ("Q-min"): used for protection, fidelity, and lust. Cumin is worn by brides to insure happy weddings. Germans put cumin in bread to prevent the bread from being stolen. Cumin is a name good for either sex. It is a happy, rollicking, fun, friendly, protective, sexy name.

Curry: used for protection rituals. This is a spicy, exotic sort of name. Curry is an open person, sexual, attractive, and interesting. This name suggests fire.

Fennel: amulets made with fennel are used for protection and hung in doors and windows. Fennel is another name that is good for men or women. This name is for bringing wisdom, becoming well established in the mundane world, or becoming a powerful priest or priestess.

Ginger: used for attracting love, money, success, and power. As a magical name, Ginger is interesting. It's a good name for a lively blonde, and brings many good things with it.

Honeysuckle: also known as goat's leaf. Used to attract money and good luck. A sweet, feminine, charming name that can be used to attract success.

Laurel: a variety of the laurel tree was taken by priestess of the Delphic oracle prior to their oracular frenzies. It is a narcotic poison that contains levels of cyanide that can produce delirium. In the Vale of Tempe, the name Laurel (or Daphne) was given to the priestesses. (Also see Bay.) A good name for developing psychic talents. A good priestess' name.

Marjoram: also called joy of the mountain, mountain mint, and wintersweet. It is used in love spells, and is thought to brings happiness. Marjoram is a woman's magical name that hints at the great wealth of inner qualities that are hidden from casual view. This is a deep person, one who is romantic, steadfast, honorable, intelligent, and beautiful. The great strength of this person is not in what is obviously charming on the exterior, but what is inside. This name suggests becoming valued for your true gifts.

Mint: grown for its healing properties (it relieves headaches and stomachaches) and is used in cooking. Because of the rich green color of mint, it is used in incenses that attract prosperity. Spearmint is also called *mismin* (in Irish Gaelic) and Our Lady's mint. The mints are used for healing, attracting love, and increasing mental powers. Mint or its variations (Spearmint, Peppermint) are comfortable, feisty, funny, likeable names for witches.

Food is the most primitive form of comfort.

—SHEILA GRAHAM

"I wouldn't tell everyone, but I was only thinking the other day, about when I was younger and called myself Endemonidia . . ."

"You did? When?"

" . . . Oh, for about three, four hours," she said. "Some names don't have the stayin' power. Never pick yourself a name you can't scrub the floor in."

—TERRY PRATCHETT
MASKERADE

Nutmeg: used in luck charms, and strung on necklaces with star anise and tonka beans for a potent herbal necklace. It is used for prosperity spells. A wonderful name for a brown-haired person or one who desires riches.

Paprika: this is another great redhead name. A spicy, tumultuous, spirited name that brings fire energy.

Parsley: also called devil's oatmeal. It promotes lust. It is believed that parsley protects food from contamination, which is why it is traditional to place it on plates at restaurants. As a magical name, Parsley is a good choice. Parsley is a unique person with a strange sense of humor.

Pepper: used in protection spells. It is a great name for someone with black hair. This is a tempestuous, vivacious, sometimes depressed person. This name brings spirit.

Rosemary: also called dew of the sea, elf leaf, sea dew, and guardrobe. Used for protection, cleansing, and improving memory. Used in healing and as incense for thousands of years. It is used in the bath to ensure youth, hung in sick rooms to promote healing, and grown in the garden to attract elves. It is believed that rosemary makes one happy; this is a name that brings happiness.

Sage: used in promoting wisdom and in purification. Sage is a wonderful name for an older, wiser person. As the sage smudge purifies a temple, so can this name bring strong blessings to your life. A good crone's (or sage's) name to bring wisdom into your life.

Star anise: for developing psychic powers and bringing luck. It can be worn as beads to increase these attributes. Star anise is used to decorate altars because it empowers altars. Star Anise is a unique name for a powerful priest or priestess. This name brings power.

Thyme: used for promoting health, sleep, psychic powers, love, courage, and purification. A woman who wears thyme makes herself irresistible and able to see fairies, or so it is believed. Thyme is an interesting magical name for a person of either sex. It is for someone who is well rounded and interested in physical, metaphysical, and romantic matters.

Vanilla: a type of fermented orchid that inspires love, lust, and increased mental powers. Vanilla is a good name for a blonde. It is a name full of sweetness, warmth, coziness, home, and hearth. This is a bright person, a person to whom the home is important, a lover of people.

Spice Meditation

Relax. See yourself walking along a road, moving away from a city and into the countryside. You begin to notice fields of herbs and flowers. Walk into the fields. Notice that the fields all have Goddess statues in them. The plants aren't poisoned with chemicals and fertilizers, yet they grow green and lush.

As you walk through the fields, smell the tart mint smell of spearmint, the tang of dill; rosemary, thyme, and basils by the score are growing in abundance. Move toward the center of this magic garden, toward the Goddess statue upon an altar. On the altar are cords, cloth, and scissors for snipping herbs. Make yourself an amulet for whatever reason you choose. You may create one to attract a lover, to find a job, to be stronger or more sensitive. Roam through the field and let your intuition tell you which herb to take. Ask permission before you cut, and give thanks afterward. Take the cut herbs and bind them in the cloth. Tie it closed with the cord and allow for a length so you can wear it around your neck. Feel it hanging against your skin; smell the fresh-cut herbs mingling with your body's scents. Feel that which you seek. Associate this desire with the smell of these herbs. Whenever you have the need for bolstering this trait, remember the smell of these herbs. Leave the garden now and stroll along the dirt road. Notice the plants and flowers growing in lush display on either side of the trail. This road will lead you home in a very short walk. Notice the kinds of herbs you were attracted to and which flowers you saw on the way back. These may have meaning for you. Look them up in this section and find ways of using them in your life, such as amulets, incense, bath oil, perfume, or cooking with them.

chapter thirteen

MAGICAL NAMES FROM
SURNAMES

LAST NAMES AS FIRST NAMES

I think these are some of the most interesting ideas for baby names. They can be used as a formal name such as Jackson, or shortened informally to Jack or Jax. It is from this stock a lot of African-American names were drawn, at least partially. There is a trend currently to use last names as first names. Hollywood stars, particularly, have adopted it for use with their own children. Harrison Ford (a double last name) has done well with his. These names are a treasure of the unusual cloaked in a familiar-sounding name-word. Because we see these names frequently as last names they are not unusual, but using them as a first name makes them unique. They contain the best of both worlds, familiar yet unusual.

Ackerman	Benedict
Adamson	Bennett
Ainslie	Benning
Ainsworth	Benson
Ajax	Bligh
Alden	Bolton
Aldridge	Bourgeois
Anca	Bowen
Anderby	Bowie
Anderson	Boyd
Andrus	Bradbury
Arrowsmith	Bradford
Asher	Bradley
Atchison	Bradshaw
Avalon	Branson
Axelrod	Bray
Baird	Brennen
Balfour	Brett
Ballantyne	Brewster
Bannon	Brinkley
Barker	Bristol
Barnes	Brock
Bartlett	Browning
Barton	Bryce
Baxter	Buckberry
Beamish	Buckland
Beauregard	Buckley
Becket	Burnaby
Bellamy	Burroughs

Burton

Busby

Butler

Buzby

Byrne

Calder

Caldwell

Calladen

Callahan

Callaway

Calligan

Cameron

Campbell

Carmichael

Carnegie

Carrigan

Carruthers

Carter

Charleston

Chase

Chaundhry

Cohen

Colfax

Connolly

Conroy

Conway

Cooper

Corbett

Cox

Crawford

Danoa

Danson

Darby

Davidson

Davis

Davison

Derksen

Derrien

Dickenson

Drake

Dwyer

Eastwyke (-wick)

Elder

Eldridge

Elliot

Elton

Endicott

Ennis

Ericksson

Ethridge

Evans

Fabian

Fadden

Fahey

Fairbanks

Fairchild

Fairweather

Farkas

*Undine Celeste Mandala Palantine Thompson
and Myrddin Emrys Arthur Gunter Pinder
Thompson*
>—CHILDREN OF MICHAEL THOMPSON,
>BOOKSELLER, COLLECTOR OF
>RARE SCIENCE-FICTION BOOKS

*My father's family name being Pirrip, and my
Christian name Philip, my infant tongue could
make of both names nothing longer or more
explicit than Pip. So, I called myself Pip, and
came to be called Pip.*
>—CHARLES DICKENS
>*GREAT EXPECTATIONS*

INSTRUCTIONS ON A FORM I SAW ONCE:
*Last name first, first name last. If you were
previously married and had another last name
put your last last name first, first name last in
chronological order. Do this first . . . .*
>—PHOENIX MCFARLAND

Farrly

Farrow

Faulkner

Fawcett

Fawkes

Fenrick

Fenton

Fergusson

Ferris

Fielding

Findlay

Fisher

Flander

Flax

Fletcher

Flynn

Fogarty

Ford

Forrester

Forsythe

Fossett

Foster

Fowler

Foxworthy

Foyle

Franklin

Fraser

Frasier

Fuller

Fulton

Funk

Galbraith

Gallagher

Gallick

Galloway

Gardner

Garland

Garrett

Garrison

Gillanders

Grant

Griffith

Hadley

Hamilton

Handford

Hansen

Hanson

Harley

Harrison

Hartley

Hartwick

Hayden

Heath

Henderson

Hilton

Holden

Howell

Huntley

Ivanhoe

Iverson

Jacklain

Jackman

Jackson

Jamieson

Jansen

Jefferson

Jenkins

Jenson

Jervis

Kauffman

Kellerman

Kendall

Kennedy

Kenrick

Kent

Khan

Kirby

Kramer

Krieger

Lamont

Langley

Layton

Llewellyn

Lucas

Lyman

Maddock

Maggoo

Magowan

Malcolm

Malone

Mandrake

Manhattan

Markham

Markus

Marshall

Matheson

Mathison

Matlock

Maxam

Maxcy

Maxfield

Maxim

Maxima

Mayan

Mayberry

Mayer

Mayfield

Maynard

McAdam

McBeth

McCann

McCarthy

McCartney

McCleary

McCormack

McCullough

McDonald

McEvoy

McEwen

McFadden

McFarlane

McFee

McGarrity

McGarvey

McGavin

McGee

McGill

McGowan

McGreggor

McGuinness

McGuire

McHollister

McInnis

McIntosh

McIntyre

McKay

McKenna

McKenny

McKenzie

McLachlan

McLaine

McLaren

McLeod

McMillan

McMurray

McNabb

McNeill

McPherson

McQueen

McRae

McSweeney

McTaggart

McTavish

Melville

Mercedes

Meredith

Merrell

Merrick

Merrifield

Merryweather

Metcalf

Michner

Middleton

Milbern

Milburn

Millaney

Miller

Milligan

Milliken

Mingo

Moffat

Molloy

Mondo

Mongomery

Monroe

Montague

Mooney

Moorcroft

Moore

Moreland

Morgan

Morris

Morrison

Mortimer

Mosley

Mowbray

Moxey

Muir

Mulder

Mullins

Murphy

Naylor

Nelson

Nicholson

Nisbet

Niven

Noble

Nolan

Northwick (-wyke)

Nottingham

Novak

Otto

Owen

Oxford

Paige

Palmer

Parker

Patterson

Pearce

Peirce

Pendergast

Pennington

Percy

Perry

Peterson

Pettigrew

Pickford

Pickton

Piper

Porsche

Porter

Portnoy

Powell

Prentice

Presscott

Preston

Prichard

Pryor

Quinlan

Quinn

Quinnell

Rankin

Ratcliff

Ravencroft

Rawling

Redburn

Redfern

Redford

Reid

Reilly

Reily

Renton

Reynold

Richardson

Riley

Robertson

Robinson

Robson

Rochester

Rockford

Rockwell

Rooney

Roper

Ross

Roth

Rothman

Rothwell

Rourke

Rowland

Salisbury

Sandberg

Sanderson

Scanlan

Scarborough

Sebastian

Selby

Sexsmith

Shaw

Shepherd

Sheppard

Sherwin

Silverman

Simpson

Sinclair

Slater

Sloan

Snyder

Sorrenson

Southwick (-wyke)

Spangler

Spence

Spencer

Sprague

Stevenson

Stockdale

Stratton

Sullivan

Surrey

Sutherland

Sutton

Swanson

Sweeney

Sylvester

Taggart

Tandy

Tantra

Taylor

Thackary

Thacker

Thackery

Thompson

Thornhill

Thornton

Thorpe

Thunderbird

Thurber

Thurston

Tilden

Tilley

Tomlin

Tomlinson

Tonner

Treiger

Trent

Tucker

Turner

Ulrich

Underwood

Unger

Upton

Vargas

Wadsworth

Wagnall

Wagner

Wainwright

Walden

Walker

Warner

Warrick

Watson

Waxman

Waymouth

Webber

Webster

Weston

Westwick (-wyke)

Wheeler

Whitaker

Whitby

Wilcox

Wilkinson

Wilson

Windsor

Winkler

Winston

Woodcock

Woodward

Wyatt

Wyke

Yardley

PLURAL FIRST NAMES

It isn't a trend yet, to use plural names as first names, but I predict it will be. It's another way to find the interesting in the slightly unusual. They go particularly well with plural last names such as Evans Jones, Forbes Adams, Hans Briggs, etc.

Abrams

Adams

Adkins

Akins

Andrews

Baines

Banks

Bowers

Bridges

Briggs

Brooks

Burns

Burroughs

Byrnes

Cairns

Coles

Downs

Evans

Fields

Flanders

Forbes

Haines

Hans

Hayes

Hicks

Hopkins

Howes

Hughes

Ives

Jones

Lowes

Marks

Meadows

Menzies

Meyers

Miles

Mills

Monks

Parks

Perkins

Peters

Phillips

Powers

Rawlins

Reynolds

Richards

Robbins

Roberts

Rogers

Sanders

Saunders

Sears

Shields

Smithers

Tomkins

Watkins

Wells

Wiggins

Wilkins

Williams

Woods

Yates

Yves

chapter fourteen

MAGICAL NAMES FROM
MAGICAL PEOPLE

Sometimes when stumped for a name, it helps to hear what others call themselves. It might inspire a train of thought in you that will lead you to your name.

MY NAME

I'll begin this chapter by talking about my name. The one on the cover, Phoenix McFarland, is just my latest of a long line of my magical names. I chose Phoenix because I had lived in Phoenix, Arizona, once upon a time. Also I had been through some difficult relationship lessons that I was working toward understanding. Since the Phoenix of myth created its own death by flapping its wings to start its own funeral pyre, I thought it was a good name to take to learn to accept responsibility for my own part in choosing those relationships. And finally, I chose Phoenix because I came out of those hard lessons into such a great relationship with my darling husband, Kerr, I felt that the Phoenix rising from the ashes of its own making to begin life anew was as apt a name as I could hope for. McFarland came because my ancestry belongs to the McFarland clan in Scotland. Also I chose it because Kerr lived a couple of thousand miles away from my home and in another country, so to find my new life, Phoenix had to move to a "far land."

To give you some idea of where my names came from, here are some other names I have worn:

Bruce Gustov: this is what my parents were naming me when they thought I was going to be a boy. This is what they called me as a fetus.

Laurel Jean: what I was named when I turned out to be a girl.

Aurel Neen: the persona who lived in my mirror who lived everything the opposite of my life. She's struggling with trying to put on weight.

Squirrel Girl: I was five.

LaRue: teenage nickname, I lived on LaRue Street.

Nokomis: a dreamed name, it's Native American and also from Longfellow's "Hiawatha," "daughter of the moon, Nokomis."

Athena: a magical name.

Gaia: a magical name.

Mother of All Living Things: Kerr's nickname for my nurturing side.

Kermode: ("kerr-MOE-dee"). A rare albino black bear that came to me in dreams. Similar to the White Buffalo.

Lessa: a dieting name.

Tender Love: I pronounce Kerr, "Care" so it's Tender Love and Kerr. This name was bestowed upon me by Fritz Muntean in 1990, so it's clearly not my fault.

Fusses with Blueprints: Kerr's nickname for my renovation persona.

Lauriolis: Kerr's name for my energy force. It is she who steals all the covers, also clearly not my fault. Lauriolis made me do it.

Here are some great names of Pagans that have appeared in the public forum. Notice how the people who have chosen a last name are more distinctive from those who just have one name? Remember that. We are growing too numerous for there to be a Robin or Rowan who is known to everyone. Like the people in Henry's England, we now need last names to tell us apart.

Please don't just copy another's name, just use it for inspirational purposes as a tool to lead you to your own name. They worked hard to find interesting unique names, so don't steal that from them. Unlike other religions that forced people into a mold, especially in name-choosing, we don't copy each other's names in an attempt to be one of the many, we are proud to be one of one. Stand alone. Stand proud in your own name. Dare to be different.

Names of Individuals

Aeon

Ashleen O'Gaea

Bramble

Calliope Darkmuse

Canyon Dancer

Cinder

Coyote Joe

Cronebee

Daffin

Danaea

Dendera Wisepsychic

Deosil Dancer

Draconis

Draganna

Dreamweaver

Eleasaid

Farwalker

Galen Skyeagle

Garnet Redstone

Gaulic Shaman

Grian Redlion

Hensiarad

Inanna Blue

Indigorose

Kaliwillow

Kayleigh Summerfaery

Kerr Cuhulain

Kitty Willow

Kutulu Kelly

Kuu Noitah

Lady Aprille

Lady Drogheda

Lady Isabeaux

Lalani Moonshadow

Laurel Early

Lil' Wiccan Dude

Lord Silver Shadow Knight

Lord of the Grass

Lyral Patterndancer

Lysander Moonlight

Mairwen

Maisie Silver Panther

Medea Seventeen

Merlin Neo

Moonfeather

Moonmoma

Moonwater

Mountain Witch

Mysteries

Naryan Firedancer

Nichaolaa the Fiery Little Elf

Night Fire

Nightlad

Nowan Mandrake

Oberon

Phoenix Silvermoon

Prairie Witch

Puck

Quill Mastercraft

Rainbow Zend

Raven Fire

Ravenmocker

Rayne Raven

Red Dwarfer

Rhainy

Rosemayden

Roy-Ke Khan

Ruby Moonstone

Salem Alder

Selena Moonstorm

Sequoia Stormwind

Shadow Knight

Shun'kata

Silver Ragingwaters

Soltahr

Starhawk

Starwind Evensong

Stormy Windwalker

Strix

Swamp Witch

Sylver Myst

Sylver Nightshade

Tayzia

Teal

Techwolf

Teerose Thorn Warrior

Terra Autumnwynd

Theora Ronin

Traveller Farlander

Vinicius

Whispering Willow

White Wolf McRaven

Willow Moonsong

Winter Night Tiger

Wolfkin

Wyldefyre

Wynn D'Willows

Xanadu

Zanna

NAME JOURNAL:

For those of you who have the opportunity to attend a big Pagan festival, pay attention to things like the sign-up sheets for volunteers or anywhere where there are listings of people's names. Jot down any favorites and keep them in a name journal. Jot down favorite character's names from books or movies. When you read about celebrities having children, look to see if it's a name you like. One day you may be looking for a new name, or having a baby and turning to your name journal may inspire you toward your new name. I had a name journal once. It turned into this book.

MAGICAL NAMES FOR MAGICAL GROUPS

Coven-Naming Exercise

Coven names are hard to find. It's hard enough finding your own name but to find a name that everyone in the group likes? That's tough. Not every group is democratic with every member getting a vote. Some are set up with a couple to a few people running the group and the others are participants. Depending upon your group's hierarchical arrangements, those involved in naming the coven should get together to begin the name-finding quest. Even if your covenmates are not involved in this decision, you can still put out feelers to the coven for suggestions. You can also ask friends in other covens for their input. The first session should be a brainstorming session with someone writing down all the suggestions, just let it be an open forum. Nothing is accepted or rejected, no matter how far-fetched it sounds. Even terrible ideas could lead you down the path to a good name. This is a free-for-all of naming. Just shout out the ideas as they come to you. Names should fly through the air like witches at a quidditch match. Don't hold back. Then when the creativity has been spent, take a look through what you've got.

Sometimes when you hit on a name in a name-frenzy like that, everyone just knows instantly. It makes the hair stand up on your arms. A naming frenzy like that can be very freeing, helpful, and a lot of fun.

COVEN NAMES

Coven names often begin with a title such as Circle, Coven, Guild, Clan, Temple, Our Lady of, Our Lord of, Caer, Grove, Order, or Council followed by a descriptive and often poetic name, such as Circle of the Mystic Wood. Many devotees of J. K. Rowling's Harry Potter books have incorporated Hogwarts into their teaching coven names. Below are some real covens. I hope they inspire you and yours.

13th House Mystery School

Ancient Earth Study Circle

Blue Moon Circle

Butterfly Garden Coven

Caer Avalon

Celestial Circle

Changing Light Circle

Children of the Tropical Moon

Circle of the Starry Starry Night

Circle Sanctuary

Circle of the Silver Moon

Circle by the Sea

Clan of the Cauldron

Company of Wolves

The beginning of wisdom is to call things by their right names.

—CHINESE PROVERB

Pagans should be proud of being Pagan and learn to think outside the church.

—PHOENIX MCFARLAND

The power of grace, the magic of a name.

—THOMAS CAMPBELL

The most important question was: what should she call herself? Her name had many sterling qualities, no doubt, but it didn't exactly roll off the tongue. It snapped off the palate and clicked between the teeth, but it didn't roll off the tongue.

—TERRY PRATCHETT
MASKERADE

Coven of the Mystic Moon
Coven of Amorica
Coven Lothlorien
Coven of the Raven
Coven of the Whispering Wind
Coven of the Dolphins
Coven of the Obsidian Grove
Coven of the Cauldron
Dana's Circle
Daughters of the Meadow Coven
Daughters of the Muse
Desert Henge Coven
Dragon Palm Circle
Dragons of Avalon
Dreamdance Coven
Elvenhome
Full Moon Paradise
Gaia Consort
Gaia Community
Greenwood Grove
Invisible Evening Twilight Tribe
Mage Circle
Merlyn's Grove
Mississippi Moon
Moon Song of Central Texas
Moon Grove Coven
Mystery Cult of Bill the Cat
Oak Clan
Order of Osiris

Order of the White Star

Our Lady of the Earth and Sky

Pagan Knights

Rowan Grove

Sacred Oak Grove

Sacred Circles

Sanctuary of the Winds

Shared Vision

Silver Elves

Silver Midnight Coven

Sisterhood of Avalon

Standing Stone Coven

Starmist Coven

Stone Haven Circle

Sylvan Grove

Temple Stardust

Temple of Gaia

Temple of the Elder Gods

The Chalice of Our Lady

The Santum

The Mystica

Thorn & Oak

CHRISTIAN NAMES FOR PAGAN GROUPS

A few groups use religious terms borrowed from Christianity such as calling a Pagan organization a "church" or its leader a "bishop." Some do this because Christianity is the only other religion they know. They equate religion with these words. We needn't feel we have to be Christian-lite to be accepted in society, nor should we need to do so to be considered a "real" religion by ourselves. We don't need to remake Paganism in the mold of Christianity. This is something different. I think we should be proud of the differences, not cloak Paganism with Christian terms to make it prettier for others. Buddhism is a Pagan religion. They don't have Our Holy Lady of Shinto Tabernacle churches with bishops and congregations. They do their own thing. Pagans should be proud of being Pagan and learn to think outside the church.

Here are some definitions of such terms so you can decide whether to use them in your religious path. Some clearly are usable in the Pagan path, others don't fit. Make your own choices, but know what you are saying when you use these words.

Bible: a collection of sacred writings of the Christian and Jewish religions.

Bishop: a supervisor of other churches in the Greek, Roman Catholic, Anglican religions.

Cathedral: principal church of a diocese containing the bishop's throne.

Church: a building for public Christian worship. Christian believers. Christendom.

Congregation: a group of people who come together for regular religious worship.

Covenant: promises made to humanity by God in Christian scripture.

Minister: a person authorized to conduct religious worship, member of the clergy. A pastor.

Ministry: the service, functions, or profession of a minister of religion.

Missionary: a person sent by the Christian church to carry on religious work and convert followers.

Prayer: devout petition to God or an object or worship.

Priest: a minister of any religion.

Priestess: a woman who officiates in sacred rites.

Sacred: pertaining to or connected with religion.

Tabernacle: a house of worship, especially one intended for a large congregation.

Temple: a building used for the service or worship of a deity or deities.

Worship: to feel adoring reverence, honor, or regard for a sacred personage or object thought to be sacred.

chapter fifteen

MAGICAL NAMES FROM
MOTHER EARTH

F ind out if an elemental magical name is
right for you. Circle the letter of the description that best applies to you.

ELEMENTAL MAGICAL NAME QUIZ

1. Which way would you most like to be
   regarded by others?

   A. Being thought nice.

   B. Being thought of as a "together"
      person.

   C. Being considered desirable.

   D. Being thought of as a strong person.

2. Which mythical character most resembles
   where you are right now in your life?

   A. I'm a phoenix rising from the ashes.
      I'm starting over. I want a clean slate.

B. I'm the Salmon of Knowledge, learning lessons in life.

C. I'm the Trickster who races from one thing to another irreverently. Laughter is my thing.

D. I'm the Green Man/Woman who relates to nature.

3. Which goddess is most like you?

A. Diana, virgin huntress. Young, strong, independent, waiting for the right one.

B. Morgan, water goddess. Healer, magician, psychic abilities.

C. Aphrodite, goddess of love and beauty. Sexy, passionate, bold, outrageous.

D. Hestia, goddess of the hearth. My home is my hobbit hole. Cozy, warm, nourishing.

4. In which direction would you like to be moving?

A. Starting a new relationship, finding a new job, moving to a new town, finding a new coven.

B. Getting in touch with my emotions, going into therapy, getting an addiction under control.

C. Falling in love (or lust), getting into great physical shape, being successful at work.

D. Buying a house, renovating, having a baby, retiring, saving for the future.

5. Which film genre is your favorite?

A. Love stories. Happy endings, *Sleepless in Seattle*, *Beauty and the Beast*.

B. Heros overcoming obstacles. *Lord of the Rings*, *Apollo 13*.

C. Sexy. Steamy, R-rated or above, racy and hot. *Body Heat*, *The Big Easy*.

D. Dramas, people fighting for their land. *Gone with the Wind*, *Braveheart*.

6. Which book genre is your favorite?

A. Fantasy or romance.

B. Self-help, metaphysical, or feminist literature.

C. Erotica or adventure.

D. Science fiction or cookbooks.

7. Are you more excited by . . .

A. Storms with high winds, hurricanes, tornados, hailstorms?

B. Flooding, torrential rains, mud slides?

C. Volcanos erupting?

D. Earthquakes?

8. Your biggest social problem is

A. Shyness, not confident interacting with strangers.

B. Nobody understands you. You are a deep person with many facets but people just think you're weird.

C. You're too apt to sleep with the wrong person. You jump into bed too fast.

D. You want a serious relationship and a commitment, and that freaks possible partners out.

9. Which role do you play most often?

A. New Agey spiritualist, some would call you airy fairy but you forgive them.

B. An in-your-face feminist. You spell it womyn or wymoon.

C. Temptress, lover, femme fatale.

D. Healer, mother, crone.

10. Do you see yourself more as

A. Spiritual.

B. Witchy.

C. Hot.

D. Earthy.

11. What kind of person are you attracted to?

A. The hippie. Peace-loving, cool guy. Macrobiotic, 100-percent-cotton-stonewashed-tie-dyed guy.

B. The sensitive, New Age guy. Meditating, analyzing, getting-in-touch-with-his-issues guy.

C. The stud muffin. Tight jeans, tight everything else. Exudes a sexy, hot-root-chakra-vibe guy.

D. The elusive husband. Homebody who likes kids and wants to be married —sometimes thought to be on the endangered-species-list guy.

12. Which quality is lacking in you?

A. Groundedness. Stability. Real world concerns. Budget savvy.

B. Willingness to get your hands dirty in life. Just jumping in and doing it.

C. Think before you speak. Wait and see what happens. Patience.

D. Fun and frolic. A sense of whimsy. Lightheartedness.

13. Of the elemental energies, which one draws you the most?

A. Air.

B. Water.

C. Fire.

D. Earth.

14. If you won a gazillion dollars in the lottery tomorrow, what would be the first thing you'd do?

A. Take a friend and fly away on a whirlwind tour of romantic far-away places.

B. Bring your best friend on a cruise and float away, being pampered with massages and facials.

C. Throw a huge party somewhere fabulous and invite EVERYONE.

D. Buy your dream house, but saving some of your fortune for a rainy day.

Answers

If you answered mostly As

These are air issues. An air person tends to be on the shy side. Often young, or young at heart. She delights in intellectual ideas, spirituality, love and romance, and like the air quarter in circle, it is a place of new beginnings. This is the realm of the maiden. These are good names to pick when wanting to start over after a painful break-up, or when beginning a new job.

There are more than just air names (Aeolous, Whirlwind, Tempest) that would work for this kind of energy. You could also use names that evoke other characteristics too, but ones that are aligned with air energy. There are many air names in this section but you can also look for these names listed in the Names by Their Characteristics, beginning on page 351. Look under these characteristics:

Air names

Beauty names

Happiness names

Love names

Wisdom names

Youth names

Lunar names

If you answered mostly Bs

These are water people. Water people tend to be analytical, psychic, emotionally based people who benefit a lot from self-help books and introspection. These are people who take healing very seriously and do well overcoming obstacles such as addictions or personal problems. This is an ever-changing kind of person, as changeable as the tides. Moods flow in and out moment to moment. Intuition is a strong aspect of this person. This is the realm of the mother. These are good names to choose when wanting to get in touch with your inner world, when trying to overcome an addiction, or invoke serious change in your life.

There are more than just water names (Aquarius, Cascade, Quicksilver) that would work for this kind of energy. You could also use names that evoke other characteristics too, but ones that are aligned with water energy. This section has a lot of good water names, but if you still don't find the right one, look for these names listed in the Names by Their Characteristics, beginning on page 351. Look under these characteristics:

Water names

Protection names

Psychic names

If you answered mostly Cs

These are my fellow fire people. Phoenix, of course, is a fire name. Fire people are passionate, sexual beings who may be hot tempered or impatient at times. They are also fantastically loyal, impishly spontaneous, playful, and funny. This is the realm of the lover. These are good names for when you want to invoke a passionate love or get more ambitious in achieving your goals. This is a good name for a shy person who wants to kick start her search for love, or for a person who wants to drip with power. It's an assertive, bold kind of name.

There are more than just fire names (Ardan, Phoenix, Summer, Mare) that would work for this kind of energy. You could also use names that evoke other characteristics too, but ones that are aligned with fire energy. You can also find these sorts of names listed in the Names by Their Characteristics, beginning on page 351. Look under these characteristics:

Fire names

Success names

Love names

Passionate names

Strength names

Warrior names

If you answered mostly Ds

You are an earth child. Warm, welcoming, earthy, natural, and usually possessing excellent parenting and money management skills. This is someone who loves puttering around at home or in the garden. You would rather be home than anywhere. Successful people who handle their money well are said to have their "earth altars in order." But it can also be about people with a dark shadow side. I would guess that Anne Rice

would be an earth child. This is the realm of the crone. This is a good kind of name to choose when trying to start a family, retire from a job, buy, build, or renovate a home. This is a firm, secure, well-grounded kind of name.

There are more than just earth names (Amber, Clay, Demeter, Moss) that would work for this kind of energy. You could also use names that evoke other characteristics too, but ones that are aligned with earth energy. If you don't find what you are looking for here, look for these names listed in the index of Names by Their Characteristics, beginning on page 351. Look under these characteristics:

Earth names

Elder names

Success names

The object of this quiz was to help you pinpoint the general kinds of elemental names that might work for you at this stage of your life. These answers are either things that describe you, or things you *want* to describe you. Names can be labels or spells. As you change, your name should change. So hang on to your answers to this quiz and use it as a guidepost for choosing any new magical names in the future. This quiz was designed to help pinpoint the general name categories suited to your circumstances. The specific magical name is something only you can choose. Choosing your name can be a great tool for self-awareness, so don't ever let someone else pick your name. I can't tell you how many people write to me asking for a name, but I won't do it. I'd never take that journey away from you. Find a name that suits you and revel in it. Roll around in its energies and get it stuck between your teeth, squish it between your fingers, immerse yourself in it. Let it work its magic on your life. Wear your name like a precious spell and be glorious in it! Don't despair if yours isn't an elemental name. There are other categories and another quiz along the way to help you narrow down your search.

ELEMENTAL NAMES

Now that you have an idea of which element calls your name, you can look here for more ideas. Each of the four elemental earth-shaping forces has a "voice" of its own, its own energetic feel. These four very different elements make for very good name choices. The elements of air, earth, fire, and water are four powerful, natural forces for growth and change; they shape the very face of nature. Why not use them to change the nature of yourself?

Air

The process of weather gives us many of the air names. Air names bring airiness, lightness, and intellectual qualities. This is the quarter of the circle that faces east—dawn—when the clean and shining day begins. The power of air can be the gentle, refreshing breezes reflected in a pretty name like Ariel, or a maelstrom of wind-borne power in a name like Thunder. Air names are for heightening intellectual prowess, clear and orderly thinking, for soaring high above the ground on the wings of thought. Air moves us. Choose a name to help move you where you want to go.

Aeolus: Greek god of wind.

Aleyn: Phoenician god of wind and clouds.

Aria

Ariel

Aurora

Boreas: Greek god of the north wind.

Breeze

Celestial

Cirrus

Cloudy

Cumulus

Cyclone

Doldrum

Dustdevil

Eos: the dawn.

Ethereal

Eurus: Greek god of the east wind.

Gale

Gusty

Hathor: Egyptian goddess.

Hurricane

Jumala: Finnish sky god.

Maelstrom

Nimbus

Notus: Greek god of the south wind.

Puff

Skye

Storm

Stratus

Thor: Norse god of thunder.

Thunder

Tornado

Tradewind

Tsunami

Typhoon

Ukko: Finnish sky god.

Whirlwind

Wind

Zephyrus: Greek god of the west
    wind.

Fire

Fire names erupt like surging volcanos of change. Fire names are for bringing the passion and warmth of the south into your life. These names are for warmth, passion, determination, fiery conviction, increased sexuality, for becoming a "hot- blooded" person. As the volcanos erupt beneath the sea, so fire names ignite change and the reshaping energy fire can give. Fire transforms us. They bring determination, courage, unbending willpower, passion, enthusiasm, vivacity, sexual electricity, and drive. Read the following names and find one that reflects how high you want to turn up the heat.

Names can be labels or spells.
    —PHOENIX MCFARLAND

Wide open and unguarded stand our gates,
Named of the four winds, North, South,
East and West;
Portals that lead to an enchanted land . . .
    —THOMAS BAILEY ALDRICH

Agni: Hindu fire god.

Aton: Egyptian sun god.

Arani: Hindu goddess of sexual fire.

Ardor

Bask, Blaize, or Blaze

Blast

Brighid: Irish "fiery arrow."

Crackle

Dazzle

Electric

Fever

Fire

Firecracker

Firefly

Flame

Flash

Glow

Grainne

Li: Chinese sun god.

Lightning

MacGreine: Irish fire elemental.

Paiva: Finnish sun god.

Pyre

Ra: Egyptian sun god.

Salamander

Seb: Egyptian sun god.

Seker: Egyptian sun god.

Shamish: Babylonian sun god.

Solar

Spark

Sparkle

Sultry

Sundance

Sunny

Sunshine

Surya: Hindu sun goddess.

Wildfire

Water

Water names are a good way for a person to tone down an overabundance of fire energy in one's life. Water names are cool, tranquil, and soothing, and even the most serene ones are able to quench a raging fire. Water names bring about a coolness of mind, a quenching of tempers, a watery, emotional, moon-driven twilight merging with the Lady of the Lake. Water shapes us. Water names smooth over rough emotional terrains as water slowly smoothes the craggy face of the planet.

Archelous: Greek river god.

Atlantic

Bay

Brook

Cascade

Cove

Creek

Deep

Drizzle

Dylan: Welsh sea god.

Ebb

Egeria: Roman water goddess.

Flow

Geyser

Glacier

Hail

Harbor

Jet

Lagoon

Lake

MacCuill: Irish primordial water elemental.

Marsh

Monsoon

Nu: Egyptian water elemental.

Ocean

Pacific

Pond

Rain

Rana: Norse sea goddess.

Raindrop

Rainforest

Rapid

River

Sea

Sea Priestess

Shoney: Scottish sea god.

Snowflake

Splash

Spring

Stream

Tamesis: British river goddess.

Tefnut: Egyptian moisture goddess.

Vellamo: Finnish water goddess.

Waterfall

Wave

Whirlpool

Whitewater

Earth

Excuse the pun, but earth names ground. These names help one become more rooted in reality, more stable, quieter, and slower to speak, more thoughtful, fertile, and strong. Earth heals us. One can use earth names to heal old wounds and grow stronger as a result. Let your earth name absorb your pain and ground it harmlessy; grow straight and tall like a redwood. Earth energy is about endings and beginnings. In many ways earth names are the final stage of a personal development journey through the elemental names.

When people say someone has his "earth altar in order," they are saying that they have a handle on their responsibilities. That they are usually in a committed relationship, stable, employed, and well established, much like a well-rooted tree. It is a way of saying one has put down roots. Try digging in and try on an earthy name. Let it help you take root and grow.

Acre

Aker: Egyptian earth god.

Chalk

Chestnut

Coast

Desert

Eartha

Faunus: Roman god of forests.

Flidais: Irish woodland goddess.

Flora

Forest

Gaia: Greek earth goddess.

Glade

Glen

Gondwanaland: an ancient landmass.

Grove

Inland

Island

Laurasia: ancient continent.

Magma: molten rock.

Meadow

Mesa: plateau.

Mielikki: Finnish forest goddess.

Moraine: glacial debris.

Moss

Pangaea: ancient continent.

Planet

Rhea: "Earth" Greek.

Rock

Salt

Sandy

Savanna

Shore

Steppe

Stone

Talus

Tapio: Finnish forest god.

Terra: Roman earth goddess.

Terrain

Terrestrial

Tundra

Tuulikki: Finnish forest goddess.

DUAL ELEMENTAL NAMES

The planet is controlled by the interaction of elemental forces with each other. Many of us have elemental energies that form parts of our personalities. Taking a name that reflects the merging of two or more elements may speak to the energies that are exhibited in your nature and help them flourish. For example, the dual-elemental names Sea Fire, River Rock, Eagle Flame, and Whirlwind Raindrop all combine elements and may suit those who are working toward an inner balance of elemental forces.

ROCKS

Rocks and minerals are the gems of the earth. As a gift of the planet to its children, rocks are an excellent choice for a source of names. The study of the power of crystals is well-known, but all rocks give off a vibration and have unique qualities that can benefit the wearer. As with other magical names, rock names can be used to describe who you are, or can help you become what you want to be. In terms of the sympathetic magic aspect of names, rocks can lend one a wide variety of attributes, the most powerful of which is the groundedness that comes with these names.

Agate: magnificent stones with endless variations of brightly colored bands in swirling patterns. This is such a conspicuous and brightly colored stone that it was probably one of the earliest stones to be noticed and used, especially in the carving of ancient religious symbols. Agates were at first thought to have supernatural powers that gave them such intriguing beauty. The name agate was given because the stone was first discovered by the ancient Greeks beside the river Achates. Agates were popular stones for carving magnificent works of art in ancient Egypt, and later in Greece and Rome. In fact, agate was used by nearly every ancient culture due to its workability, strength, and beauty. Agates have a very calming effect and are frequently used as worry-stones

O, then I see Queen Mab hath been with you.
She is the fairies' midwife, and she comes
In shape no bigger than an agate-stone
on the fore-finger of an alderman.

—WILLIAM SHAKESPEARE
ROMEO AND JULIET

Listen where thou art sitting
Under the glassy, cool, translucent wave,
In twisted braids of lilies knitting
the loose train of thy amber dropping hair;
Listen for dear honour's sake,
Goddess of the silver lake . . .

—JOHN MILTON

Nature was in her beryl apron,
mixing fresher air.

—EMILY DICKINSON

Emerald as heavy
as a gold course,
Ruby as dark
as an afterbirth,
diamond as white as sun
on the sea . . .

—ANNE SEXTON
FURY OF JEWELS AND COAL

(polished versions kept in pockets and stroked when tension increases).

Agates are formed when lava from an erupting volcano flows and gasses escape from the lava to the air, leaving cavities that fill with concretions formed by the cooling rock solutions. Agates are hard and more durable than the rock around them. As the rock cools, the layers form in wild patterns that mimic the cavity in which they are formed. Sometimes the center of an agate is hollow space in which crystals form. Often crystals or fiery opals form some layers to create some of the most beautiful stones in the world.

As a magical name, Agate suggests a person of variety, unpredictability, fire, color, beauty, strength, durability, popularity, and age-old appeal. It is an especially fine name for a Pagan, as it is reflective of its birthplace in the earth and because of its cultural history as a medium for some of the greatest works of Pagan religious art ever created.

Amber: a fossilized rock formed from prehistoric tree sap. It is a pale-yellowish stone with a soft, waxy luster, usually cloudy (but more transparent when heated). It is always a lightweight stone, sometimes containing fossils of Tertiary period insects that had been caught in the tree sap as it flowed.

Amber was one of the most prized precious stones in primeval times. It was used for making simple ornaments and as a form of money during the Paleolithic period. Archaeologists have found ornaments made of amber dating from the second millennium B.C.E. Nearly every ancient society had its own name for amber, which reflects its popularity. To the Greeks, amber was *elektron,* meaning "lustrous metal"; in Rome, *succinum;* to the ancient Germans, amber was called *bernstein,* derived from the word meaning "to burn" (amber does burn).

During the geologic period known as the Tertiary (fifty million years ago), dense forests grew and thick sap flowed from wounds on the trees. The drops of sap would fall from the trees to the earth below, and were buried by the process of sedimentation until they were exposed once more to the atmosphere. The sap from the trees in the Tertiary period was thicker and richer in resin and sometimes dripped over insects that rested on the trunk of the tree, resulting in a thick, sticky death. These creatures were sometimes preserved inside fossilized pieces of amber, as in one famous example of the specimen that held a complete prehistoric wasp.

In terms of its significance as a magical name, Amber brings to mind one who is pale, thin, durable (yet soft), natural, tempered by life experiences; an ancient soul, one with a connection to trees and their well-being; a slow-moving, thoughtful person; a well-grounded person; a solid, well-rooted individual; a forest lover or an environmentalist. Amber is an excellent choice for a magical name because of its connection to ancient life and its gentle, glowing, golden appearance. Amber brings a slowness to judge, gentleness, and a deep sense of patience and tolerance. Amber beads together with jet are traditionally worn by a high priestess. Amber beads are the tears of ancient trees.

Amethyst: a purple variety of the mineral crystal quartz. To the Greeks, amethyst was *amethystos,* which means "unintoxicating," and was thought to be a cure for inebriation. The Greek word from which the word *crystal* was derived means "ice." Ancient wealthy Roman patricians used quartz crystal balls to cool their hands and face in hot weather. Quartz stays cool; it is a very poor conductor of heat. Amethyst is also believed to be a cure for insomnia.

Amethysts have always been very popular stones. All quartz crystals were used early in history due to their beauty, abundance, strength, and their resistance to erosion by all external influences. Early tools were made of another form of quartz (flint) from the Paleolithic period to the Neolithic period. The popularity of amethysts continues to the present day. In the Middle Ages, artists cut impressive goblets with magnificent carving out of amethysts and other varieties of quartz. Amethyst was used for jewelry and ornaments during the Renaissance. All manner of quartz crystals became popular during the Victorian era, decorating lamps and chandeliers. The awareness of crystals as amplifiers of energy was well documented from the writings of Pliny the Elder all the way up to the present day. A great surge of popular interest in the magical properties of amethysts (and all other stones) surfaced with the advent of the New Age movement.

Amethyst is thought to be a gentle stone, yet a powerful protector by those who use crystals in healing. Keeping a large cluster of amethyst in your home is thought to protect the space from negativity. It is used in meditation to help channel away any negative feelings from the bearer. It is suggested that amethyst should accompany any ritual of protection and purification.

Amethyst is a good magical name for someone who is (or who wants to be) sharp, clear thinking, regal, cool-headed, sober, resistant to societal pressure, naturally attractive; an honest person who is a transparent liar; a catalyst or a spokesperson for organizations; a sharp and battle-seasoned warrior; someone who needs protection from negativity; a trustworthy friend, but a poor enemy; and a person of strong psychic abilities.

Aquamarine: a clear, light bluish-green variety of beryl is called aquamarine. Aquamarines are formed in connection with coarse-grained granites, called pegmatite.

Aquamarine (blue-green), heliodor (golden), morganite (pink), and emerald are all forms of the crystal beryl.

Aquamarine is a fine name for one who is ruled by a water sign, who is beautiful, colorful, emotional, intuitive, cool headed, drawn to the ocean, tends toward depression and feelings of inadequacy yet comes to realize his or her true worth. This is a good name to take after an especially transformative experience.

Arkose: a sandstone composed mostly of quartz and feldspars, the most common and important rock-forming minerals. Arkose quite easily decomposes and is a vital source of nutrients for plant life.

This simple rock is not flashy, colorful, unique, or adorning the necklace of Cleopatra, but without it there might not have ever been any Cleopatra. This mineral-rich rock that easily erodes feeds the planet with its own quiet "death" and transformation.

This is a good name for one who is plain, hard working, modest, unadorned; one who does not hold a position of power in any organization, yet without whom the organization would collapse; a nurturer, parent, or teacher; a good cook; a purist; an animal and plant lover or gardener; an unemotional, basic, back-to-nature, natural-food-eating vegetarian, middle-of-the-road sort of person. It is also a good name for developing a more modest and helpful side to one's personality.

Basalt: during the Tertiary period (fifty million years ago), volcanos erupted and spewed glowing magma from the bowels of the planet. As the liquid rock flowed over the surface of the earth, it slowly cooled, creating a variety of rocks. Basalt is one of those rocks. Basalt is a rich, black rock that can sometimes be formed into interesting land forms such as Fionn Mac-Cumhail's Giant's Causeway in Ireland (and Scotland), and Devil's Tower in Wyoming.

A person bearing the name Basalt may be one who has a temper; one who accomplishes many things; a creator; a fiery, passionate person who comes from an overly emotional, even violent home; a fire sign; a successful person who is at his best when thinking cooly and rationally (but who doesn't always do so); a dark, brooding personality who will rise to great heights of accomplishment. Basalt is a good choice for bringing more fire energy into your life.

Beryl: a rock that commonly occurs within a coarse-grained granite called pegmatite. Varieties of beryl range in color from the deep green of emerald to the delicate blush pink of morganite. Plain beryl is not of gemstone quality. The crystals are sometimes very large and quite heavy. The largest crystal yet found weighs eighteen tons. Beryl crystals are milk-colored and opaque. They are valued for the manufacture of beryllium, one of the lightest metals.

Beryl is a pretty name. It is well suited to a salt-of-the-earth sort of person who is occupied in building and maintaining foundations of organizations, relationships, or families. This is a plain person who can be quite large in size; someone who is pale in appearance; a person who is often thrust into the role of outcast, yet who outperforms those around her; a private person whose inner thoughts are hard to read—you never quite know what this person really thinks; someone who often has very beautiful offspring and siblings. Beryl is a name for someone who gets things done. Beryl brings with it a sense of solidity and modesty.

Clay: a firm, fine-grained earth composed of aluminum silicate that is created by the erosion of fine rock particles mixed with water. It is used to make pottery, bricks, sculpture, and ceramics.

This is a nice magical name for one who is a sculptor, potter, or who works with ceramics. It is also a good name for becoming well grounded. This name evokes a feeling of earthiness, the fertile potential without which growth cannot occur; it is a creative and fertile person.

Copper: very likely the first metal used by humans because of its abundance and the fact that copper is easy to work. The Romans called copper *cuprum*. Copper is a reddish-brown metallic element that is most frequently found covered by blue azurite and green malachite. Copper is used for jewelry, ornaments, wall and building coverings, and

more recently in electronics, as copper is an excellent conductor of electricity.

Copper is an excellent name for a person with auburn or red hair, for one who is easy to get along with, who enjoys being "one of the guys (or gaias)," and for adept trance mediums and psychics. Copper suggests a charming and bubbly, sometimes highly sexual person. This is a name for working on a temper, becoming clean and tidy, and staying healthy; a good name for a hard-working and passionate activist. If you wish to play with fire names, then a name like Copper will bring fire energy to your life.

Crystals: crystals of all kinds have played a major part in the history of humanity. It is likely that one of the first rocks to become important to primitive people was rock salt. By watching the behavior of animals who came to lick the salty crystals for their important nutrients, early humans may have discovered this edible crystal. Later humans discovered and used many crystalline rocks, such as sharp-edged quartz, for tools and weapons, but ornamental crystals have always held a fascination for us. We fashioned jewelry out of them, sewed them on to our clothing, and imbedded them in the walls of our sacred temples.

The discovery of gold, copper, and bronze brought a way to fashion the beautiful crystals into ornaments to decorate the body. People have always liked the feel of crystals against the skin. Beautiful crystal jewelry has been found in tombs as ancient as the fourth century B.C.E. In the early days before we could explain the origins of these fascinating crystals, it was commonly believed that they were formed by (and in some cases possessed of) supernatural powers. Crystals were commonly worn as magical amulets.

The Greeks were adept at carving upon precious gems; the hard crystals of diamonds, rubies, emeralds, and others bore the work of accomplished artists. In Rome, the artisans acquired knowledge from a variety of sources and soon became superior to the Greeks. The Romans perfected the technique of carving the cameo.

In the Middle Ages, ownership of precious crystals was confined to rulers and the church. The natural joy of adorning the body with beautiful crystals and stones was frowned upon by the early Christian church.

The emphasis then was on the life to come and the pleasure of gems was forbidden to the masses as a temptation to be avoided, although high church officials and the churches were laden with magnificent jewels. The incredible developments in stone carving, especially the carving methods for the creation of the exquisite cameos, popular in the ancient world, withered into a faint memory until the art form finally faded into oblivion in Byzantine times.

In the eleventh century, Constantine Psellos wrote a book on the healing and magical powers of gemstones, which was based on the works of the ancient author Pliny the Elder, but with added ecclesiastical dogma. Even in this time, the popularity of crystals could not be denied. Moonstones became exceedingly popular and were worn as amulets to enhance beauty and health, and attract money, glory, and happiness through their strange, supernatural powers.

The expansion of the arts in the thirteenth and fourteenth centuries triggered a rebirth in the carving of precious gems. As the degree of interest and craftsmanship rose, so did the demand for the crystalline raw material. Trade routes from the sources of the gems into much of Europe developed. The prices for the gems were once again very high.

Crystals became extremely popular during the Renaissance in the later part of the seventeenth century. The demand for precious stones was so great that the supply of diamonds and rubies became strained and artisans used quartz and amethyst instead.

Crystals have remained popular and enjoyed a recent upsurge of popularity with the advent of the New Age. As the knowledge of the powers of crystals resurfaced, it once again became popular to wear crystals against the skin. As the influence of the Christian church has waned, the natural joy we have always felt in the wearing of crystals against the body has returned, stronger than ever.

As a magical name, Crystal is a clear favorite. It is for becoming someone who sparkles and shines; a pretty, vivacious, clear-headed, well spoken, honest, sincere person; one who communicates clearly and loudly when necessary; a concerned activist and boisterous opponent; one whose voice is clear and lilting, with a laugh as light as a bell. A truly likeable person. A great name for one who seeks to bring her light out from under the basket; this name will help shy people shine.

Diamonds: an almost pure form of carbon. Coal, many millions of years old, was exposed to massive forces of heat and pressure to create the diamond. It is a magical stone. To have come from such dark, earthy origins and be transformed into the clear brilliance and sparkling radiance of pure light has always been seen as extraordinary. These gems refract the light, splitting it into tiny sparkling rainbows of color, especially when cut to enhance this natural ability. Diamonds are also the hardest known natural substance.

The ancients used diamonds as jewelry. Pliny the Elder (79–23 B.C.E.) wrote about diamonds. Issac Newton, the physicist, assumed that the diamond was combustible, based upon its exceptional ability to bend light rays. It was believed that a diamond would help maintain unity and love, and so it became traditional for use in wedding and engagement rings. It was thought that this power only worked when the diamond was freely given. Diamond is a good name for one

What Youth deemed crystal,
Age finds out was dew.

—ROBERT BROWNING

Rich and rare were the gems she wore,
and a bright gold ring on her hand she bore.

—THOMAS MOORE

Let us not be too particular. It is better to have
second-hand diamonds than none at all.

—MARK TWAIN

Diamonds are forever.

—DE BEERS CONSOLIDATED MINES

who is bright, clear thinking, sharp, strong of will, stubborn, many faceted, and who shines in intellectual pursuits. This is the name for a highly intelligent person. A tough-minded MENSA member would be well suited to this name. Prepare to shine. This is a name to take to enhance your self-image in regards to your intelligence, to bring admiration of your speaking abilities, and to appear confident and sharp.

Emerald: the deep-green emerald is the most valuable variety of beryl. Emeralds have been mined and worn as far back as 1650 B.C.E. in ancient Egypt. Cleopatra had her image carved on an emerald. The ancient Romans (and later, the Arabs and Turks) came to Egypt and searched for the elusive and valuable emerald. The mines that lured these cultures are now deserted. Trade routes known as the "Emerald Road" led to the emerald mines.

It is said that the natives of Peru worshiped an emerald the size of an ostrich egg. Montezuma, the Aztec emperor from 1502–1520 C.E., is said to have owned at least one very large cluster of emerald crystals. Today, in a remote Buddhist temple in the jungles of Sri Lanka, is an ancient statue of Buddha carved from a huge single piece of emerald.

In terms of magical names, Emerald is a fine choice. It brings to mind a lucky individual, a beautiful person (perhaps with a green tint to his or her eyes), someone who seems to outshine those around him or her, a hard and enduring personality who overcomes all adversities and comes up shining, an attractive person to whom beauty is important, or one who may have come from humble beginnings but who is destined to attain a measure of greatness. This, then, would be a good name to attract employment or success of any kind.

Emery: a compact form of corundum, a variety of rock that includes rubies and sapphires. This crystal is found in deposits of metamorphic rocks (those rocks that have undergone metamorphosis by heat and pressure) and in alluvial deposits (deposits of the eroded debris of metamorphic rocks). It is mined for use as abrasives for polishing (emery boards).

This magical name is one suited to someone who has had a hard time, especially in the past. This difficult time has tempered the individual and also, perhaps, has interfered with the proper development of self-esteem, confidence, or trust. This is a wounded bird, but one who can soar. This may be a bitter and abrasive person on the surface, with a warm heart underneath. This is a name to take as a part of getting over a dysfunctional relationship or recovering from family disorders. Emery is a transitory name that may help lead one to a better place, for emery is abrasive, yet it helps to bring a glowing polish to dull, lifeless things.

Flint: during the Stone Age, flint was commonly used for tools and weapons.

Flint is the brownish-black mixture of chalcedony and quartz, which, because of how the stone broke when it was chipped, was easily formed into sharp-edged tools. This type of tool, made by prehistoric peoples, was common from the Paleolithic to the end of the Neolithic period. In addition to its exceptional ability to be shaped into useful tools, flint (and quartz in general) was widely available because it was sturdy and resistant to the forces of erosion. Most old arrowheads one still finds in the West were made of flint.

Flint is a strong magical name. It is suitable for one who is tough, useful, and helpful; one who is able to remain unswayed by pressure; a rugged survivor, there is little softness in this person. A sleek, athletic person; one who uses and understands the use of tools; or perhaps a woodworker or a sculptor might choose the name Flint. Flint is a strong name; if you are dealing with fear in your life, take a strong name like this one to help see you through.

Galena: a shiny gray stone made of lead sulphide, which cleaves into perfect cubes when struck. It is a very common mineral of ore veins and occurs in tandem with many other substances.

Galena was mined and processed to remove the lead from it as early as the time of the ancient Romans and Babylonians. The Romans used lead from galena to make water pipes for their famous sewer systems. The Babylonians used the lead to form lead vases. The process of extracting the lead from the galena was fairly simple, and known and used in early times.

In terms of Galena as a magical name, it is for one who works well with others; whose hidden, inner core is strength; a glowing individual with a shining intellect; a well-grounded person; one who may be prone to weight problems; a predictable, organized person; one who is neat and tidy; a person with an excellent memory; and one who might have a number of good partners. This is a good magical name for a student who seeks to share the shining intellect of galena.

Garnet: Pliny the Elder used the term *carbunculus,* meaning "small, red-hot coal" to describe the garnet. The garnet group includes minerals of similar composition that mix with one another. They include a greater variety of colors than any other mineral. They often form granular to large clusters in rocks. They vary in color from ruby red to green, yellow, or violet. Pyrope, a deep red variety of garnet, is named from the Greek *pyropos,* "fiery-eyed." Another kind of garnet is almandine, named for its discovery in the ancient Turkish city of Alabanda. Almandine garnets have a violet hue. The demantoid garnet is the most valuable. It shines with its dispersive power, or its ability to break up white light into the colors of the spectrum. Garnets are among the most widespread minerals.

Garnets occur under a variety of conditions, but always under high temperatures.

They are very resistant to weathering and so occur in alluvial deposits. Rocks that form on the boundary between igneous (volcanic) rocks and other rocks often consist of garnet rocks.

Garnet is an excellent name for a redhead or one with fire playing an important role in his or her life. Garnet is a fiery, in-the-fray kind of opponent; he or she is always on the edge of dissent. If there is a confrontation, you can bet this person will be close at hand. This is an opinionated, hard-headed, stubborn, smart, and vociferous individual. Someone who will not be swayed by public opinion, who will not shut up and hang back; this is a fiercely independent, feisty, likable person. This name brings great courage, determination, grit, staying power, and often a ruddy-cheeked beauty. These individuals are able to take a nasty thunderstorm of confrontation and turn it into rainbows of understanding. This is a person you need as a public spokesperson or organizer of events. The sparkle you always see in Garnet's eye will soon spread to those around him or her, like fairy dust.

Gold: gold has played a major role in the history of humanity. Archaeologists tell us that gold was probably the first metal worked by the ancients. The oldest gold decorative objects date back to the early Stone Age, and gold coins were used as early as the seventh century B.C.E. In the Dark and Middle Ages, gold was used to adorn churches and the clothing of priests. The allure and power of gold has touched practically every culture, from the Aztecs to the California gold prospectors. Gold is the metal that is symbolic of the God, where silver is the metal of the Goddess.

Gold does not oxidize and normally does not combine with other elements, so it is found in nature in a relatively pure state. It occurs in the original rock through deposition from hot water or through decomposition of gold-bearing sulphides, such as pyrite. Gold is very soft and is usually cast with harder metals to lend it strength and durability. Only platinum surpasses the density of gold.

Gold or Golden as a magical name conjures up images of the sun. This is generally a man's name, as it is a symbol of the sun and the God energy. Gold is a rarity; it is soft and pliant, bright and beautiful. The man who chooses this name is sentimental, flexible, soft; tender, yet sometimes easily manipulated; one who must rely upon his partner for strength; one whose early years may have been spent in mental abuse or emotional turmoil. He is a handsome man who doesn't indulge in harmful habits, such as smoking or drinking, and who is concerned about his health. This is an individual who is like no one else. His attitudes and preferences set him aside from the mainstream of society and he has learned to accept this ostracism. This is a man who prefers the company of men to that of women.

Granites: intrusive rocks (volcanic rocks that solidified before they reached the surface of the earth). They are used primarily in sculpture and for architectural uses. Granites are a combination of feldspar, orthoclase, quartz, mica, and sometimes larger crystals. Granite is the most abundant rock in the world and is commonly found beneath the earth's crust. Mountains are land forms largely made of granite, which have been thrust up into the atmosphere from below the surface. Granites appear white to pinkish with sparkling bits of mica or crystal.

Granite is a strong name that leaves a lasting impression on people. This name is for one who is strong, with a mixture of spirituality, self-knowledge, and well-grounded energy. This name brings earth energy, for having one's feet on the ground; practicality; reality; surviving a violent past, and yet crediting the violence of the past as a character-building experience.

Gypsum: formed from massive beds of decaying shells that were deposited on the ocean floor. Gypsum is easy to identify, as it can be scratched with the fingernail. Gypsum is quite soft and occurs in crystals. When these crystals are clear, white, or transparent, it is known as selenite; when granular, it is alabaster; and when it's fibrous, it's called satin spar. In the Sahara Desert, perfectly formed gypsum crystals are found lying loosely in the sands. (This variety contains a great deal of sand.) They appear as flat crystals, usually quite large, and grouped into clusters resembling rose petals or leaves. They are called "desert roses" and are formed by evaporation of water from salty lakes. It was

Gold cannot be pure,
and people cannot be perfect.
                    —CHINESE PROVERB

True gold fears no fire.
                    —CHINESE PROVERB

believed that gypsum was a lucky stone that would bring good fortune to its owner.

Gypsum is used to create plaster. When you heat gypsum it yields plaster of Paris, which sets hard after being mixed with water. Pliny the Elder, who wrote a great deal about rocks and minerals and how his culture used them, mentioned the use of gypsum by the sculptor Lysippus to make a mold of a human face. This was the first recorded time plaster was made from gypsum.

Gypsum is a name for water energy, especially ocean energy. It suggests sensitivity, being easily hurt, and showing this when injured. Gypsum is a carefree name of a plant lover, one who carries the whisper of the ocean in the eyes, an environmentalist, a highly emotional person, an intuitive being with great spiritual depth to their soul. For those who wish to be more water oriented, more emotional and intuitive, then bearing Gypsum as your name would help accomplish this.

Jade: one of the toughest known minerals and is widely used as an ornamental stone for carving, due to its strength. The Chinese have carved ornaments from jade for thousands of years. The cool, smooth, waxy feel to jade is characteristic of the stone.

The very mention of the name Jade conjures images of oriental beauty and mystery. There are stories regarding the mystic and magical properties of jade stones. It is said that jade transmits wisdom, clarity, justice, courage, and modesty. Jade is a fertile and lush name. Jade suggests cool, quiet mystery. It brings to mind lush, tropical plants and plenty of running water. Jade is a wise name, a name for one who understands life's mysteries, who has many gifts and much luxury (or the appreciation for it). This is a name for understanding one's gentle strength. This is one who works on instinct and emotion before calculated thought. This is a growth-oriented name. Jade is a name for bringing tranquil, watery energy to one's life.

Jaspers: brightly colored stones with wild patterns and designs similar to those of agates, but more beautiful. The colors vary greatly from piece to piece. The layers or bands create the wild designs, which may be cloud-shaped or rainbow patches where one color gradually blends into another. The designs are so intricate in jasper that it sometime appears to be a landscape scene drawn on to the stone rather than the natural, random layers of rock. The extreme beauty of a jasper may be why it is called "the mother of all stones." Crystals often form at the edges of jaspers. Jasper is formed by crystallization of hot solutions in cracks of igneous (volcanic) rocks. The minerals in this volcanic rock were decomposed by the hot solutions. This siliceous gel oozed into the cracks in the original rock, where it crystallized into an opaque quartz containing chalcedony.

The various colors come from minerals dissolved in the solution.

The ancient Egyptians, Romans, and Greeks used jasper for making ornaments and magical amulets. Magic signs and religious carvings were engraved on the surface of jasper in ancient days. Pliny the Elder wrote about the colorful splendor of jasper. This popularity lasted through the Middle Ages. The chapel of one Bohemian castle has walls decorated with blood-red jaspers that date from 1347. A table made of jasper was once considered one of the wonders of the world. A large tabletop from Emperor Rudolf II's collection, made of a great many colored jaspers that depicted the countryside, was one of the most famous examples of the incredible beauty of jasper. The Winter Palace of the Russian Tsars holds many ornamental works in jasper, including huge pillars carved from single pieces of jasper.

Jasper is a beautiful name for a Pagan. This is a name for developing inner beauty, the beauty that comes from the subtle intricacy of the mind and the beauty of the soul. Jasper suggests the hard-won ease and luxury that adorns one like a mantle. This is a name for a delicate and shining person; someone who may have been hurt in the past, but who has come out a lovely person much improved by the trial. Jasper is a name for a survivor.

Lapis: in Latin, *lapis* means "stone." The stone lazurite or lapis lazuli was always popular as a precious stone due to its beautiful blue hues. Marco Polo (1254–1324) first describes lazurite mined in what is today Afghanistan. The ancient Egyptians used the stones from these mines for amulets, especially for those representing the sacred scarabs. When lapis was ground it was used as paint, perhaps to adorn the eyes of Cleopatra. Oriental artisans also carved ornamental objects from lapis and prized its rich blue to mauve tones. It was believed that lapis lazuli would bring tranquillity and happiness.

Lapis is another cool water name, evoking the cool blues of a tranquil stream or lagoon, soothing the fires of temper or confusion. A name bringing a smile and a light and cheery disposition that is enjoyed by all.

Mica (pronounced "MY-cah"): a mineral that can be split into individual plates of transparent, elastic, thin material ideal for window panes prior to the use of glass. It is also prevalent in a large number of rocks, which fit into my very unscientific childhood category of "magic sparkle rocks." The sparkle you see when you look at some granites is mica.

Mica is a great magical name for a seeker, because it reflects the desire to see through the veils. Mica is not hard, tough, or resistant to change, quite the contrary; but Mica's very weaknesses make it special. This is a good name for a psychic or trance channeler.

Obsidian: obsidians, together with flints, were among the first rocks used by primitive people because they took on a sharp cutting edge when chipped. Obsidian is a glassy black extrusive rock (volcanic rock that solidified on the earth's surface). Obsidian is often called volcanic glass, but its hardness is not comparable to glass.

Dark stones are thought to be good for grounding, for connection with the earth energies. Apache tears (obsidian) are also thought to be good for ridding yourself of negative thoughts; transfer the thoughts to the stone, then toss it away with a spell to keep anyone else from ever picking it up. In this way, Apache tears act as a kind of emotional handkerchief for throwing away bad moods.

Obsidian is a good name for a sharp, tough, clear-thinking, and well-spoken activist. Obsidian is also good for getting in touch with the dark goddess aspects. This name suggests being deeply motivated by issues and quick condemnation of those who aren't in complete agreement. It is a name that brings the ability to see beyond tomorrow in terms of possible changes and their repercussions, although these forecasts are almost always gloomy. This is a good name for an environmentalist.

Ochre: when the bodies of priests and priestesses were laid to rest during the Stone Age, many cultures laid them out in the ground in the fetal position and painted their bodies with red ochre to represent blood. Virgil mentioned the beauty of certain red crystals in *The Aeneid;* these were a type of hematite in the same family as ochre.

Ochre is a marvelous magical name for a mother, a midwife, a healer, or a painter. It is one rich in humanity, earthiness, robust fertility, fire, and life. This could be a name for a redhead or a ruddy-cheeked individual. People who wish to increase their fertility might do well to choose Ochre.

Onyx: an agate with black and white bands (see Agate). Onyx is a good name for someone with the qualities mentioned in Agate (above), but who tends to see things in simple terms, either black or white. This might also be a good choice for those who seek less confusion in their lives.

Opal: the mysterious opal wraps us all in its subtle spell. It is said that it is unlucky for any but one born under the sign of Libra to wear opals. Despite this unlucky folklore, people began to use them early on in history. The earliest example of objects made from opal dates from 500 B.C.E. The Greek poet Onomakritos in the sixth century B.C.E. praised the inner fire of the opal. A Roman senator named Nonius owned a valuable engraved opal; rather than give up the stone to Marcus Antonius, he chose exile. Empress Josephine owned the famous "Trojan Fire" opal, which was part of the French crown jewels. It disappeared during the French Revolution.

Opals are as much as 34 percent water, and are often stored in water to keep the dryness of the air or changes in temperature from cracking the delicate stones. They form in cracks or in veins in rock and the amount of water in them determines the mix of colors present in the stone. The colors vary from the milky iridescence of delicate pastel hues of the precious opal, the brilliant fiery reds in a fire opal, to the dark reds, blues, greens, and purples emanating from a black opal. These stones captivate and fascinate like no other stone can do. They are indeed magical.

The name Opal brings a quixotic unpredictability. This is a name for bringing quicksilver intensity, sparkling beauty, milky softness, gentle but undeniable power, emotionality, intuition, and water energy.

Pyrite: the Greeks called this *par*, which means "fire," because when you break it, sparks fly. (I have a Manx cat by this name, and believe me, sparks do fly!) Throughout history it was thought to have magical healing powers and so was popular in amulets. Pyrite is believed to heal blood disorders. It was valued as a mirror to the Incas and they buried it with their dead. Pyrite occurs in coal seams. Its shiny gold appearance resembles gold, and its oxidized form is brightly colored with blue, red, and green. It decomposes and releases sulphuric acid. Since it oxidizes so easily, it is unsuitable for decorative purposes.

I would watch the buds swell in spring, the mica glint in the granite, my own hands and I would say to myself: "I will understand this too, I will understand everything."

—PRIMO LEVI
ITALIAN CHEMIST

Rocks crumble, make new forms, oceans move the continents, mountains rise up and down like ghosts yet all is natural, all is change.

—ANNE SEXTON
THE WALL

As a magical name, Pyrite is a name for a minx. This is a trickster name, one who is all stern fire and metal one moment then dissolving into rainbows of softness the next. This is a name for bringing unpredictability, mystery, changeable moods, twinkling fiery energy, humor, carefree abandon, and independence. The name also suggests the finer qualities of humanity, yet down deep isn't the gem it appears to be. Thus, it may be a good name for dealing with our social masks and true selves. This name is also for persons who get into trouble with addictive scenarios. Yet they are sparklers, unique and memorable tricksters. This is a good name for those who seek to loosen up and live less rigidly.

Quartz: (also see Amethyst, a variety of quartz; and Crystal.) The Greek word from which crystal was derived means "ice." Quartz was a popular medium in ancient times. The crystal ball into which the stereotypical mystic gazes is made from solid quartz. It is an excellent conductor of psychic energy.

Quartz crystals were used early in history due to their abundance, strength, and resistance to erosion by all external influences. The first tools were made of this mineral (in the form of flint), dating from the Paleolithic period to the Neolithic period. The popularity of the varieties of quartz continued to the present. In the Middle Ages, impressive goblets with magnificent carvings were made from quartz. It was used for jewelry and ornaments through the Renaissance; during the Victorian era, it became popular on lamps and chandeliers. The awareness of crystals as amplifiers of energy was renewed during the New Age movement. Quartz crystals are good for promoting clarity of thought, amplification of one's personality, and a variety of healing qualities.

Quartz is a name for bringing insight, strengthening one's intuitive abilities, honesty, clear thinking, cool and thoughtful actions in crisis, and for motivation of yourself and others.

Quicksilver: liquid mercury is formed from cinnabar decomposition. The ancient Greeks called it *hydragyrum,* from *hydor* (water) and *argyros* (silver). The word "quicksilver" is an Old English term. It is the only liquid mineral aside from water. Its name fits it, as you know, if you have ever handled it. It defies order and uniformity. You can't herd quicksilver where you want it to go; it will merely break up into a dozen smaller droplets and scatter.

As a magical name, Quicksilver is an interesting choice. It denotes someone who is quick to change; a shining, soft, liquid personality who easily melts from one attitude into another, leaving others breathless and intrigued. It is a name for a shimmering, glowing, energetic, effusive, enthusiastic, funny, and totally guileless human being. This is a name to choose for encouraging change in one's life or to become less rigidly controlling.

Ruby: the deep red ruby is of the corundum family, which also includes the sapphire. The ruby has long been a popular precious stone, especially in India. The ruby mines of India were known from as early as the sixth century B.C.E. The Bohemian crown of St. Wenceslas (1346) holds the largest ruby in history. The Indian princes and the shah of Iran possessed some of the largest rubies in the world. Rubies are believed to have the power to gather and enhance energy.

Ruby is a good name for a fiery, red-headed person; a clear and vociferous speaker; or a passionate, sexual, womanly female. This is a person who is sizzlingly sensual, tempestuous, fickle, sparkling, angry, vengeful, and (sometimes) heartless. This is a name to bring the fires of passion into your life.

Silver: there is nothing as beautiful as the luster of pure silver taken directly from the earth. Soon, however, oxidation occurs, creating a dark layer of silver sulphide. In the earth, silver occurs as a tangle of winding silver wires intertwined in a lump. Silver is created during the decomposition of silver sulphide ores, like galena.

Silver has been used as far back as the jewelry of the Chaldean kings in the fourth century B.C.E., and has never lapsed in its popularity. Silver is very soft and is unable to be used for ornamental work, except in compounds with stronger metals.

To each man, three measures of gold and nine measures of silver, one vessel each of onyx and alabaster; food and wine in plenty. All this and all honor shall each man enjoy in the second life. There we shall meet again, to stand side by side and serve. 'Til then, farewell. The Gods of Egypt have spoken.

—WILLIAM FAULKNER, HARRY KURNITZ,
HAROLD JACK BLOOM, HOWARD HAWKS
PHARAOH CHEOPS, LAND OF THE PHARAOHS

A harvest mouse goes scampering by,
with silver claws and silver eye;
And moveless fish in the water gleam,
by silver reeds in a silver stream.

—WALTER DE LA MARE

Begin again with a clean slate.

—TRADITIONAL

Into the sunset's turquoise marge
The moon dips, like a pearly barge;
Enchantment sails through magic seas,
to fairyland Hesperides . . .

—MADISON JULIUS CAWEIN
AT SUNSET

The cool, silvery color is symbolic of the lunar influence and hence the feminine aspect of the universe, the Goddess. Silver is seen as the Goddess' metal, whereas gold represents the sun or the God form.

Silver, because of the connection to the Goddess and the lunar influence, is an extremely popular and wonderful magical name. To differentiate yourself from the other Silvers out there, you might consider taking a second name in addition to Silver to more personalize the name. It is a name for a mysterious, cool, pale, intuitive, moon-driven, poetic, creative, goddess-oriented night owl who burns the midnight oil, perhaps writing of magic and moonlight. Silver is a dancer in the night; a hunter; a shining, bright, illuminating individual. This is a psychic, rhythmic, cyclic, turner-of-the-wheel-of-life kind of name. Silver is a good name to take for intuition, enlightenment, and for encouraging the lunar influence.

Slate: In the old days, slate was used to make school blackboards. Slate is a sedimentary, fine grained, clay-like stone that is made when deposits of sand, mud, calcium from seashells, and water are compressed under thousands of feet of earth deposited over millions of years. The heat and pressure compress the sandy, clay-like mixture and harden it to form slate, and in some combinations of deposits, sandstones. Slate is dark, smooth, and tightly compressed.

As a name, Slate indicates a plain, dark individual upon whom impressions can be easily left. This is a quiet person, better at writing than at speaking, perhaps tending toward shyness; this is a sometimes a poetic and romantic person in a very quiet way. This is an earthy person, a night owl, and very often a good writer. A good student's name.

Topaz: topaz may have been named from the island upon which it was found, yet some people think it was derived from the Sanscrit word *tapas*, meaning "fire." It is found in cavities in granite and in alluvial deposits associated with these granites. They are transparent crystals that are found in abundance all over the world. Topaz occurs in many colorful hues, including honey-blonde, smoky, pink, pale blue, yellow, gray, violet, and clear. Many large topaz stones have adorned the crowns and jewelry of the rich for thousands of years.

Topaz as a name evokes an image of smoky uncertainty. This is a name to bring subtlety and mystery to one's personality.

Turquoise: usually thought of as being worn by North American Indians in the southwestern United States, and indeed it is so. They combined native turquoise and silver into beautiful and distinctive jewelry that is still popular today. The Ottoman Empire sought this precious stone and the ancient Egyptians used turquoise in their artwork and jewelry. The sky-blue stone, which is often veined with the brown stains of iron compounds, tends to symbolize the joining of the sky and the earth. Turquoise is a great magical name for an air sign person. This balance of blue and brown, of sky and earth is a great stabilizer. It can add lightness to an earth-bound person and stability to an overly airy personality. Its pure blue is refreshing and uplifting; the brown marks are intricate and can inspire the imagination.

Velvet: another name for malachite. Because of its green color, it was called "rock green," then "the satin ore" and "the velvet ore." Velvet was believed to protect children from various misfortunes. The ancient Greeks and Romans used velvet in protective amulets. Its beautiful greenish layers form intricate patterns and lacy designs in the stone.

Velvet is a softly effective name. It suggests a soft, soothing, healing, protective, and maternal energy. This may be a good name for a teacher, nanny, nurse, mother, daycare worker, or social services worker. This is a name for learning the soft caress is better than the firm command. Velvet is a good name for softening one's style of human interaction, or for soothing that short temper.

Rock Meditation

Visualize yourself in a tranquil state. Do whatever relaxation techniques you need to get yourself there. See yourself at the base of a lovely mountain. Ahead of you is a cave. Walk toward it, noticing what stones, if any, are underfoot outside the cave. As you move into the cavern, a light comes from within you and lights the area. As you move through the caverns, examine the walls and the floors of the cave and look to see of what rock the cave is formed. Is it a luminescent and fiery opal with rainbows of color darting from within its core? Is it a brilliant diamond, ruby, sapphire, or emerald? Is the floor a different stone than the walls? Move to the very back of the cave where there is evidence of ancient cave paintings on the walls; read what it says. As you turn to leave, look for a rock that catches your eye. If there is one that does so, pick it up and take it with you. Return from whence you came.

The thing to notice with this meditation is how what is on the surface differs from what is below, how the floor on the cave differs from the walls, and what message is found in the cave paintings. If a particular stone speaks to you, you might try to find it at a crystal or rock shop and carry it in an amulet, as well as wear it as a magical name.

chapter sixteen

MAGICAL NAMES FROM
EXOTIC LOCALES

The names of distant places ring in our imaginations, conjuring up very personal images of what we imagine that place to be like. Everyone's image of a place name is unique. This is a name choice that can be exotic, unique, and inspire different images for everyone who hears it. These are good magical names for travelers, wandering spirits, adventurers, or those who long to be. They are unique names for unique people.

Not every place name mentioned here is a powerful place sitting squarely on a ley line radiating positive energy. Some I chose because of beautiful or exotic images that I associate with the places, or merely for the lyrical sound of the name itself. Because these places are not famous magical places doesn't mean that these names are without power. An important aspect to bearing a powerful name is to empower it yourself. I have a friend with whom I've circled many, many times. Each time I'm in circle with him he uses his magical name, a very short and simple one, to call the quarters and so forth, but as soon as the circle comes down, I cannot remember his magical name. He wanted it to be private. He wanted it used only in circle. "What's His Name" empowered the name for that purpose. You, too, can empower your names with whatever power you want them to hold.

These names have a magic of their own and do not need to be defined by location. Perhaps it would soil the image of a lovely, exotic-sounding name to know it was a polluted river near the Love Canal. Take the name and redefine it with your personality. Reclaim the name!

Adelaide
Africa
Ajax
Alabama
Albany
Albuquerque
Aldan
Alexandria
Algiers
Amarillo
Amazon
America

Amery
Amsterdam
Andorra
Angara
Anjou
Ankara
Antigua
Argentina
Ariel
Arizona
Aruba
Ashanti
Ashokan
Asia
Athabasca
Athens
Atlanta
Austin
Australia
Avalon
Azores
Babylon
Babylonia
Baden
Baffin
Baghdad
Bahama
Baja
Baku

Bali

Balkan

Baltic

Baltimore

Bangkok

Barbados

Barbary

Baroda

Bashkir

Basque

Bengal

Bergen

Berkshire

Berlin

Bermuda

Berwick

Bethany

Biloxi

Boise

Bolivia

Bombay

Borah

Borneo

Boston

Botswana

Bougainville

Bozeman

Brandon

Brazil

Brazzaville

Brea

Bristol

Britain

Britannia

Bronx

Brooklyn

Brunswick

Burgundy

Burma

Burundi

Byzantium

Cashmere

Calcutta

Caledonia

Calgary

Cambodia

Cameroon

Canterbury

Canton

Capri

Caracas

Carolina

Casablanca

Cayman

Celebes

Ceylon

Chaco

Chad

Where on earth did you get a name like that?
—COMMON SAYING

*Thrice happy he whose name has been
well spelt.*

—LORD BYRON

✡

Chaldea
Chambon
Charleston
Charlotte
Chatham
Cheyenne
Chicago
Chile
China
Chita
Cincinnati
Cody
Colorado
Columbia
Congo
Corfu
Cork
Cornwall
Corsica
Crete
Croatia
Cuba
Cumberland
Curaçao
Cyprus
Dacca
Dacia
Dakota

Dallas

Danube

Darien

Darling

Darwin

Dawson

Deccan

Delhi

Delos

Delphi

Denmark

Denver

Devon

Devonshire

Dixie

Djakarta

Donegal

Dresden

Dubuque

Duluth

Durango

Ecuador

Egypt

Elam

Elba

Elbe

Eleusis

Ellesmere

Ellis

El Salvador

Ely

Equator

Erebus

Esla

España

Essex

Estevan

Estonia

Ethiopia

Etna

Euphrates

Everest

Excelsior

Fargo

Fars

Fiji

Finland

Flanders

Flores

Florida

Fontana

Formosa

Franklin

Fraser

Fremont

Fresno

Fyn	Harvard
Gabbon	Havana
Gabon	Hawaii
Galapagos	Hebrides
Galatia	Helsinki
Galloway	Hobart
Gambia	Hobbs
Gander	Holland
Ganges	Honan
Gascony	Hondo
Gaul	Houston
Gaza	Hubbard
Geneva	Huron
Genoa	Iberia
Georgia	Idaho
Ghana	Illinois
Ghea	India
Gibraltar	Indiana
Glasgow	Indies
Granby	Indus
Greece	Inuvik
Greenwich	Inverness
Grimsel	Ireland
Guinea	Jaipur
Haiti	Jamaica
Halifax	Jandira
Hampshire	Jannali
Hannibal	Janula

Japan	Khiva
Japura	Kildare
Jasai	Kilimanjaro
Java	Kilkenny
Jersey	Killarney
Joplin	Kirby
Juneau	Kirin
Kalahari	Kiska
Kalambo	Kismet
Kalat	Klondike
Kalmuck	Kodiak
Kama	Kursk
Kamet	Lagos
Kanara	Lanae
Kansas	Lanai
Karafuto	Langley
Karelia	Laos
Kauai	Lapland
Kawara	Laramie
Kazak	Latvia
Kea	Lena
Kedah	Libya
Keeling	Lima
Kenora	Logan
Kent	Loire
Kentucky	London
Kenya	Lucania
Kerry	Macedonia

Mackenzie	Minneapolis
Macon	Mississippi
Madeira	Missouri
Madras	Monaco
Madrid	Mongolia
Majorca	Monrovia
Malacca	Montana
Malaga	Montenegro
Malay	Montreal
Mali	Montserrat
Malone	Morena
Malta	Morocco
Manchuria	Moscow
Manhattan	Myra
Manila	Nain
Manitoba	Nanaimo
Mankato	Nantucket
Marina	Nassau
Markham	Naxos
Marrakech	Nepal
Martinique	Nevada
Maui	Nevis
McKinley	Niger
Melbourne	Nigeria
Meru	Nile
Miami	Nippon
Miki	Nome
Milan	Oahu

Oceania	Philadelphia
Ohio	Philippine
Olympia	Phoenix
Once	Phoenixia
Orkney	Piedmont
Orlando	Pitcairn
Osaka	Pomona
Oskaloosa	Pompeii
Oslo	Pontus
Oswego	Portugal
Ottawa	Prescott
Oxford	Princeton
Ozark	Provence
Pacific	Prussia
Palermo	Quebec
Panay	Rainier
Papua	Ramos
Paraguay	Rangoon
Paris	Rawlins
Parma	Red Cloud
Pasadena	Reno
Pecos	Rhine
Pelée	Riviera
Pemba	Roanoke
Pennsylvania	Roswell
Penza	Russia
Perdido	Sacramento
Persia	Sahara
Perth	Sajama
Peru	Salem

Salinas	Sioux
Salvador	Skagway
Samar	Skitka
Samoa	Skye
Samos	Smithers
Santa Fe	Somalia
Santiago	Somerset
Sardis	Sonora
Saskatchewan	Spain
Saskatoon	Sri Lanka
Sava	Stonehenge
Savannah	Sumatra
Saxony	Sumer
Scotia	Summer
Seattle	Surrey
Selma	Sutherland
Senegal	Syria
Seward	Tacoma
Shanghai	Tagus
Shannon	Tahiti
Shasta	Taiwan
Sheridan	Tama
Shropshire	Tamara
Siam	Tamath
Sicily	Tamon
Sidney	Tamura
Sidon	Tanganyika
Sikkim	Tangier
Singapore	Tanis

Tarsus

Tasmania

Tehran

Tenedos

Tenerife

Tennessee

Texas

Thana

Thebes

Tibet

Tierra

Tigre

Tigris

Timbuktu

Timmins

Timor

Tipperary

Tisza

Tobago

Tobol

Togo

Tokyo

Tonga

Tonkin

Tortuga

Trinidad

Tripoli

Tripura

Troy

Tucson

Tunis

Turku

Tuscany

Tyre

Ulster

Utica

Valencia

Vegas

Vermont

Vernon

Vesuvius

Vienna

Volga

Wales

Wessex

Wexford

Weyburn

Wichita

Wiltshire

Windsor

Winnipeg

Wisconsin

Wisla

Wrangell

Xanthus

Xingu

Yale

Yangtze

Yukon

Zambezi

chapter seventeen

MAGICAL NAMES FROM
THE GREEN MAN'S
GARDEN

FLOWER NAMES

Floral names have been used since the Victoria Fera, but only a few names became popular. Here are dozens more to choose from, a beautiful bouquet of name ideas. Flower names invoke sweetness, beauty, freshness, youth, spring, new beginnings, and happiness, and they are some of the most beautiful feminine names. Boy's names can be found here too: Aster, Cosmos, or Larkspur, for instance.

Alyssum

Amaranthus

Asarina

Aster

Astilbe

He loves me.
He loves me not.

—DAISY LOVE SPELL
TRADITIONAL

The green Earth sends her incense up.
From many a mountain shrine;
from folded leaf and dewey cup
she pours her sacred wine.

—JOHN GREENLEAF WHITTIER

Balsam

Begonia

Bluebell

Calendula

Chicory

Chrysanthemum

Clover

Coleus

Columbine

Cornflower

Cosmos

Crocus

Daffodil

Dahlia

Daisy

Delphinium

Dianthus

Euphorbia

Foxglove

Fuchsia

Geranium

Hibiscus

Hollyhock

Honeysuckle

Hyacinth

Iris

Jasmine

Lady's Mantle

Larkspur

Laurentia

Lavender

Lupine

Marigold

Moonflower

Morning Glory

Nasturtium

Orchid

Pansy

Passionflower

Petunia

Poppy

Primrose

Rose

Sedum

Snapdragon

Starflower

Strawflower

Sunflower

Tithonia

Torenia

Tulip

Verbena

Veronica

Wildflower

Wild Rose

Windflower

Zinnia

TREE AND PLANT NAMES

Trees and plants have often been revered and held in awe by humanity. The early Celts devised a tree alphabet with each letter having a magical tree associated with it. Most gods and goddesses are associated with their sacred plants, flowers, or trees. It is extremely popular to choose one of these for a magical name. I have included the Old Celtic words for some of these trees (see the tree alphabet on page 200), as they might make a more interesting choice than the common name.

Acorn: not a tree, but the seed from the oak tree, the small, nut-like acorn is symbolic of great potential. This is why it would make a good student's name or a name for someone who is young, inexperienced, or just beginning on a new path. Acorn is a name for achieving one's potential.

Alder: one of the Druids' seven peasant trees and the fourth letter of the Celtic tree alphabet. Alder has a very distinctive perfume in spring. This tree is sacred to the Celtic God Bran. The alder is related to the element of fire and is prized as a raw material for charcoal by the Celts. Felling a sacred alder was once thought to bring about the burning down of one's house. The alder tree was used by the Celts to make milk pails and pilings for bridges and docks. They obtained fine red dye from its bark, green dye from its flowers, and brown from its twigs, relating to fire, water, and earth.

Alder is an excellent magical name for one who is secretive, changeable, a fire sign; one who loves color; a seamstress (or tailor) or an artist; one who loves incense, after-shave lotion, or perfume; a down-to-earth person who is a forest lover and a wise, experienced witch. This is the sort of person who loves the drama of ritual, who likes to dance skyclad in the shadows of the forest. Alder will bring out the hidden sensitivity and sentimentality lurking within you.

Apple: one of the Druids' seven sacred chieftain trees. The Celts used its bark for tanning. The secret inside the apple is a well-known bit of Pagan trivia. If you cut an apple in twain across the apple rather than down, a pentacle can be seen in the core. The sharing of an apple with a lover is a very old theme and part of the Gypsy wedding ceremony. The apple was seen as "the fruit from the tree of knowledge," and to the Christians it was considered a "sin" for a woman to eat of the fruit of knowledge. This didn't stop the fruit from becoming as popular and as "American as apple pie."

The name Apple brings to mind a rounded person, a ruddy (apple-cheeked), fertile, sweet, loveable (apple of my eye), alert, intelligent person who is thoughtful (apple for the teacher), funny, plump (juicy), happy, and generous.

Ash: one of the Druids' seven sacred chieftain trees and the third letter in their tree alphabet. The Celtic kings had their thrones made of ash. It was also used for the shafts of spears and arrows. Ash was considered sacred in many mythologies. Ash was sacred to the Sea God Poseidon; the mythical Norse world tree Yggdrasil was an ash tree. Odin's own runic alphabet was said to have been formed from ash twigs. Ash is attuned to the power of water.

As a magical name, Ash is an excellent choice. It is generally thought to be a male's name, but it would work well for women, too. It is a name for a leader, one who is a true warrior (not a mere limited soldier, mind you); one who has proven him/herself; a person comfortable with emotions and intuition; a strong, confident, brave, loyal, honorable, and decisive person. Ash is a good name for bringing leadership and teaching ability, both valuable qualities in a priest or priestess.

Aspen: the bark is used to make a remedy for fever. Aspens have white bark and large, broad leaves. This tree is also known as "quaking aspen" because of the fluttering movement its leaves make in the wind. Aspens are beautiful in the autumn. It is a common outing in the Colorado mountains to pack a lunch, drive into the mountains (aspens are most common in mountain areas), and "see the aspens turn." There are entire mountainsides covered with aspen, and when the leaves all turn golden, the effect is spectacular.

Aspen is a name for someone who is trying to face up to his or her own fears. It is a transformative name leading from fear into a fiery burst of courage. People who are shy, naive, or inexperienced could wear Aspen well. It could also be a good name for a dancer, a drummer, or anyone working with movement and rhythm. This is a mountain person's name. Aspens have a lot of potential.

Banyan: it is also known as the Indian god tree. This is a tree revered by the Hindus, Hawaiians, and the peoples of Polynesia. As a name it evokes mystery and an aura of the Orient. An exotic name for an unusual person.

Barberry: known in the Pacific Northwest as Oregon grape. It has yellow flowers and dusty blue berries. Its leaves often show autumn colors year round.

This may be a name for an artist. Barberry is a name for relating to one's own sexuality in a healthy way, for increasing one's confidence, self-esteem, motivation, strength, and stability.

Beech: writing tablets used to be made of beech; in fact, the word "beech" might be considered a synonym for literature. The English word "book" is etymologically connected to the word "beech."

Beech is a name for becoming more intellectual than physical, more cerebral than sexual. This is a name of introspection, philosophical contemplation, learning, seeking, and becoming less aggressive, more studious, and wise. Beech is a good name for a writer or a student.

Bilberry: this is part of the heather family, which includes huckleberries and blueberries. It is a very popular fruit among Native Indians in British Columbia.

Bilberry is an unusual name for a sweet, gentle person. This name brings to mind warmth, sweetness, generosity, caring, sharing, and love.

Birch: one of the Druids' seven peasant trees (Beithe or Beth) and the first letter in their tree alphabet. Birch is believed to drive off evil spirits. For this reason, the Celts used it to make cradles. It was used throughout Europe for flogging delinquents and lunatics. It was thought that birch would drive away the evil spirits that afflicted the victim.

Birch is a cleansing name, full of light and purity. It is a name for one who deals well with children, the sick, or the elderly. It is a name for a nurse, a teacher, a parent, a social worker, or one who seeks social or political change by gentle means. Birch invokes purification.

Blackthorn: this is one of the Druids' seven shrub trees. Blackthorn is a good name for a strong, dark person. A person with mighty shields and defenses might feel comfortable wearing this name. It is a place name that invokes a lot of protection, and so would be good for a house or covenstead.

Blueberry: a type of bilberry, part of the heather family. Blueberry is a magical name that suggests sweetness, purity, and a totally guileless human being. These are good traits to strive toward.

Bracken: a very common fern. The young shoots or "fiddleheads" are edible and were eaten by many Native Indian groups. The Indians made bread out of the starch obtained from bracken rhizomes.

Bracken is a good young man's name. It is a name for youth, inexperience, and great potential. This is a person who is very impressive, if a bit too brash and sometimes boastful. This is a lover, a drinker, and an energetic person. Bracken is the name for a passionate young drummer, or a shy fellow who wishes he were more outgoing.

Briar: one of the Druids' eight bramble trees. Briar is an excellent magical name. It is a protective and powerful name, not for the faint of heart or the untried youth. This is someone who has won the rewards of battle and is peacefully ensconced in his or her position. This is someone who does not like to move, and who usually does it very badly. Briar is a sharp, brilliant, quick-tongued, bright-eyed, prickly person who has a great deal of knowledge and expects you to appreciate that fact. This person is resourceful, cunning, smart, defensive, strong, confident, and harsh, but an extraordinary teacher. A good name for an older person.

Broom: one of the Druids' eight bramble trees. Broom belongs to the gorse family. Local variations on the name include basam, bisom, bizzom, breeam, browme, brum, and green broom. It is used in the construction of the Pagan besom or broom and also used to weave baskets, and to some extent, thatch. Its yellow flowers are in bloom from April to July. The broom was adopted as the badge of Brittany by Geoffrey of Anjou. Fulke of Anjou followed this tradition, and it was passed on to his grandson, Henry II of England. Henry used its medieval name of Planta Genista, which is how his family name came to be the Plantagenets. It first appeared in England on Richard I's Great Seal. Several other nobles used it as a symbol, including Richard II of England and Charles V and VI of France. It was considered a sign of plenty because of its long flowering season. Its flowering tops were used for house decoration at the Whitsuntide festival. It was considered unlucky to use the flowering tops for menial purposes when they were in full bloom. Before the introduction of hops, it was used to flavor beer. Its bark contains a large amount of tannin, which was used in tanning.

Broom is a wonderful witch's name. Of course, we jokingly refer to secretive witches as being "in the broom closet," and we have many old customs and uses for the magical broom in circle and out. Many a witch's wall is decorated with brooms dressed up with ribbons and dried herbs and flowers. The broom is the most famous tool of the trade for witches, and so would naturally make a great magical name. Broom is a good name for people of either sex, and is just as applicable to a youthful person as it is to a crone. Broom is a name that suggests fertility, cleansing, honor, protection, and freedom.

Bryony: a poisonous climbing and twining plant. Black bryony is in the same family of plants as yams. White bryony is in the cucumber family. The root of the black bryony is used to make rubefacients and diuretics, but an overdose can produce a very painful death. The roots of European white bryony are used to make one of the best diuretics in medicine. Both are used to treat gallstones. The roots of white bryony, also known as English mandrake, were used to make purgatives, but this is not common any longer because of the plant's powerful irritant properties.

Bryony is a great name, good for those who are (or want to be) balanced between their male/female or their light/shadow sides. This is a good name for one who is too sensitive, too emotional, and who wishes to become more balanced. This name can help you move from a water-dominated space into a more grounded place.

Candleberry: also known as bayberry. Its bark and wax are used to make astringents and stimulants, and is emetic in large doses. The greenish-white wax from its berries was in some places used as sealing wax. Bay-

berry candles are burned at New Year's to ensure good fortune for the following year in some Scottish folk traditions.

Candleberry or Bayberry are cleansing names that inspire the bearer to be more organized, cleaner, tidier, have more energy, more luck, and encourage silence.

Checkerberry: one berry bearing this name is also known as the partridgeberry or squaw vine. It has bright scarlet berries. It is taken by Native American women for weeks before childbirth to ease their labor pains. Another berry bearing this name was the wintergreen.

Expectant mothers, midwives, healers, and people going through difficult times would benefit from Checkerberry as a magical name. The healing and pain-reducing properties of Checkerberry work when you use the name as well as the plant itself. This is a nice-sounding name for a person that is friendly, well disposed to deal with life's situations, and possesses a fine sense of humor.

Chestnut: it is believed that chestnuts fed to a loved one ensure he or she will love you back. Chestnut is a good name for a brunette. It suggests warmth, home and hearth, and autumnal energy.

Chicory: is also known as succory. It is in the same family as dandelions. Its roots are used as a coffee substitute and its is cultivated in many places as a salad vegetable. It has lovely blue flowers.

Chicory falls off the tongue in an easy way and is memorable, yet not an overused, magical name.

Chocolate: the chocolate tree is known as the cacao or cocoa tree. Its seeds are used to make the popular confection called chocolate. It is a handsome tree, twelve to sixteen feet high with light-colored wood and reddish flowers.

Cocoa has long been a popular name for a dark-skinned or dark-haired person. Cocoa or Chocolate is a good name for anyone who is warm, sweet, soft, or who is one of the millions of people addicted to the joys of chocolate.

Drake: a grass also known as bearded darnel. Its seeds are used by herbalists to make a sedative. The word "darnel" comes from the French word *darne* (stupefied), and in France it was called *ivraie* (from *ivre;* "drunkenness"), because large doses cause all the symptoms of drunkenness. The Arabs called it *zirwan.* In some parts of England, it was called "cheat" because it was sometimes used to adulterate malt and distilled liquors.

Drake, Darnel, Cokil, Darne, Ivraie, or Zirwan all are good names for a person who is gregarious and loves his cups (and what's in them). It then would be a good name for someone who is trying to understand the motivations of a drinker. It might be a good choice for a drug and alcohol counselor.

Elder: one of the Druids' seven shrub trees. The dwarf elder was the twelfth letter in the Druids' tree alphabet, and the elder was the thirteenth. This tree is traditionally associated with Witches. It is a tree of doom in many Christian myths. It is often said that the tree on which Judas hanged himself and Jesus' cross were both made of elder wood. The word "elder" comes from the Anglo-Saxon word *aeld* (fire), as the hollow stems of the young branches were used to blow up a fire. Early names for it were eldrun, hyldor, and hyllantree. In Germany, it is called *hollunder.* In Low Saxon it is *ellhorn.* The pith is easily pushed out of the young branches and these hollow stems were used to make pipes, hence the elder was often called the pipe-tree, bore-tree, or bour-tree. This name survives in Scotland as burtree. Its Latin name, *sambucus,* is adapted from the Greek word *sambuca.* The ancient Greeks used elder to make pan-pipes. In Danish mythology, a dryad named Hylde-Moer (elder tree mother) was supposed to live in the branches of the elder. Should the tree be cut down and used to build a chair, she would haunt it. It was also believed in Denmark that if you stood under an elder on Midsummer Eve you would see the king of Fairyland ride by, attended by his retinue. An old spell is to take the pith and dip it in oil, light it, and float it in a glass of water on Christmas Eve. This was supposed to reveal the whereabouts of any sorcerers in the neighborhood. Up until recent times in England many people would not trim it lest they attract bad luck. In many parts of Europe, its wood is thought to drive off ill fortune. In England it was thought that elder trees were never struck by lightning. It was once cultivated near English houses as it was thought to drive off Witches. It was often used as decoration at funerals, and elder branches were placed in graves to ward off evil. Elder is a name that invokes versatility, sturdiness, mystery, musical ability, luck, and a serious attitude about magic.

Elm: one of the Druids' seven peasant trees. It is resistant to water and used for building ships. Its durability lead to its common use in lining carts and wheelbarrows.

Elm is a solid name that is versatile and easy to remember. It also works for either sex. Elm depicts a person who is dependable, secretive, solid, trustworthy, reliable, honest, sober, and believable. A Pagan elder.

Fabiana: also known as pichi. It is originally from South America. It bears white or purple flowers. Its dried leaves and twigs are used to make medicines to treat urinary and kidney disorders.

Fabiana and Pichi are lovely names for women. They suggest a feminine person, well versed in a captivating sexuality. These names are earth-oriented. This name may bring fertility, sexuality, femininity, a dancer's grace, and an appreciation of music.

Fern: one of the Druids' eight bramble trees. Ferns are thought to bring powerful protection to the home.

Fern is a quiet, earthy name. It suggests protection and a love of hearth and home. It is a good name for delicate but flourishing people who have their priorities straight.

Fir: the silver fir was the fourteenth letter in the Druids' tree alphabet. It is sacred to Artemis and the moon.

As a magical name, Fir is a cool, winter name for an older, wiser person. Fir suggests Yule and winter's cold, and one who possesses the knowledge gained in the turning of many seasons.

Goldenrod: a magical name is suggestive of a healer; a gentle, tender person who is better at healing the wounds than participating in the battle. It may be a name for a male or female, although the golden imagery that goes with the name is more suggestive of masculine energy.

Gooseberry: one of the Druids' eight bramble trees (Spin). It was formerly believed to cure all inflammations. Spin may be one of the most profound magical names I've ever heard. Spin is what we do. We spin among the webs of life when we weave our magic. It is a superb name for a weaver, a seamstress, or a teacher. Like Broom, Spin is an appropriate name for any witch. It is a name of action, motivation, change, growth, magic, and transformation.

Gorse: an evergreen shrub whose flowers have a strong scent and that blooms for a very long time (spring to late August). It is an old English custom to include a spray of gorse in the bridal bouquet because of

When gorse is out of bloom,
kissing's out of season.

—TRADITIONAL

The fair maid who, the First of May
Goes to the fields at break of day
And washes in dew from the hawthorn tree
Will ever after handsome be.

—TRADITIONAL

this. Gorse is in the same family as broom and furze. Gorse grows well near the sea. Its ashes are very alkaline and were used to make soap and an excellent fertilizer. The leaf buds have been used as a substitute for tea, and the flowers to make a strong yellow dye.

This is a romantic's name, a lover of love. This is the kind of person who likes to dance when he or she hears a romantic song, even if he or she is in a grocery store at the time. It is a name that suggests affection, sensitivity, creativity, imagination, tenderness, and love.

Hawthorn: It is also known as whitethorn, quick, thorn, haw, hazel, gazel, hagthorn, or May (from which the name of the month comes).

Hawthorn is sacred to the Goddess Maia. It is one of the Druids' seven peasant trees (Sceith) and the sixth letter in their tree alphabet (Uath). In general, considered an unlucky tree. In ancient Britain, Greece, and Spain, May was the month in which people went about in old clothes, a custom referred to in the old saying "ne'er cast a clout ere May be out" (meaning do not put on new clothes until the unlucky month is over). This is the origin of the current custom of buying new spring clothes (Easter bonnets). In Greece, all the temples were swept out and images of gods washed during the month of May. It was considered a very unlucky month for marriage. This is why more people get married in June than any other month. The hawthorn was the tree of enforced chastity. It was considered extremely bad luck to cut a sacred hawthorn down. This tree was used by the Turks as an erotic symbol because, to many men, the hawthorn blossom has a scent of female sexuality. There is an old poem that speaks of the hawthorn's ability to make one beautiful.

Hawthorn or any of its other names are wonderful names for a witch. They are steeped in craft custom and lore.

Hazelnut: the Druids considered white hazel to be one of their seven shrub trees (Fincoll). Hazel was the ninth letter in the Druids' tree alphabet. In Celtic myth, the nut was a symbol of concentrated wisdom.

Hazelnut is a good name for a wise, thoughtful, experienced witch.

Heath: one of the Druids' eight bramble trees. Heath is a superb name, and one that many Pagans have named their sons. The feminine version is Heather. Both names are good for magical names as well as mundane names. Heath is a name for a clean, honest, natural person who loves home and hearth, wife and family.

Heather: the sixteenth letter in the Druids' tree alphabet (Ur). Sacred to the Roman and Sicilian love Goddess Venus Eryncina.

Heather is a lovely woman's name. This is the name for a delicate, feminine, womanly, graceful, intelligent, quietly powerful person.

Holly: one of the Druids' seven sacred chieftain trees and the eighth letter in their tree alphabet. Holly is an evergreen with shiny green leaves and bright red berries. Its timber was used by the ancient Celts to make chariot shafts. It is a tree of the waning year and has been used by Pagans and Christians alike to decorate their homes at Yule.

Holly is a festive name for a sexy, attractive, sharp-witted person. This is also someone who has a temper and can be prickly when crossed. Holly brings an improved outward appearance and better defenses.

Ivy: one of the Druids' eight bramble trees and the eleventh letter in their tree alphabet. Ivy is sacred to the God Dionysus, and it was once believed that binding it around one's brow prevented intoxication. October was the season of the Bacchanal revels, during which people rushed wildly about with a roebuck tattooed on their right arms and waving fir branches wrapped with ivy. Plutarch said that the Bacchantes were intoxicated as much by ivy as by wine. Ivy is dedicated to resurrection because only it and vine grow in a spiral. English taverns used to have the sign of an ivy bush over their doors, to indicate the excellence of their liquor, giving rise to the saying "Good wine needs no bush." Also sacred to Artemis (or Ariadne). Its leaves formed the poet's crown. The Greeks presented a wreath of ivy to newlyweds as a symbol of fidelity.

Ivy is thought to be a symbol of a clinging person, but it is much more than that. Ivy is a sober name, a name to wear on the other side of the tunnel after having come through a battle with alcoholism. It is aligned with the passion of the Bacchanalian revels, but not without restraint. It reflects the power and mystery of the spiral path in its twining growth.

Ivy is a name for a faithful, stalwart, honest, poetic, humorous person who has walked a rocky path and who has learned well from that experience. This is the magical name of a person worthy of respect.

Juniper: leaves and berries were used in one of the earliest incenses. Juniper is thought to be a protective plant, and a necklace of the berries is thought to attract a lover. Juniper berries are used in the production of gin.

Juniper, as a magical name, is perfect for someone who is lively, spritely, excitable, vivacious, and protective. This is someone who longs to find his or her perfect mate and settle down and begin nest-building in earnest. Until then, Juniper enjoys a good party and lively society.

Linden: the flowers of the lime tree. In Lithuania, women once made sacrifices to linden trees.

Linden is a name that tends to be more for a male than a female. It is a name that signifies fertility, youth, male beauty, and the sweet flower of manhood.

Mahogany: Indians believed that mahogany protects against lightning. Mahogany is a good name for a brunette or a person with dark skin or eyes. This is a name for strength, durability, steadfastness, honor, and dignity.

Mandrake: used by herbalists to make emetics and purgatives. It was used in ancient times as an anesthetic. It was also believed to have the power to prevent "demonic" possession. Its roots often resemble human forms. Mandrake used to be placed on mantle pieces to avert misfortune and bring happiness and prosperity to the house. Ancient terms used to describe mandrake are phallus of the field, Satan's apples, hand of glory, and devil's testicles. It is very firmly entrenched in the ground and many customs have built up around the dangers involved in removing the roots.

Mandrake is a name steeped in sexuality for the male, and as such is a good name for improving (or perhaps advertising) male virility. Mandrake indicates a quiet man who is good with his hands, who is perhaps a sculptor or a painter. Mandrake is also a seer with a keen talent for telekinesis.

Mistletoe: venerated by the Druids and believed to protect the possessor from all evil. Youths were sent about with branches of mistletoe to announce the new year. It is from this custom that the modern one of including mistletoe in the Christmas decorations comes. In Norse mythology, Balder, the god of peace, was slain by a weapon made of mistletoe. He was brought back to life by the other gods and the mistletoe was placed in the keeping of the goddess of love. She ordered that everyone who pas-sed under it should receive a kiss, to show that the mistletoe had now become a symbol of love rather than of hate. To this day, lovers still kiss under the mistletoe. Druids considered the white berries to be drops of the Oak God's semen.

Mistletoe is a lover's name. This is someone who loves love, sex, and is a championship flirter. This name invokes the rites of courtship and love.

Myrrh: used for centuries as an ingredient of incense, perfumes, etc. In ancient Egypt, it was burned at noon to honor the sun God Ra and in the temples of Isis.

Myrrh is a noble name for a person who is a fire sign. This is someone who likes summer, the outdoors, and natural, aromatic scents. This is a mysterious person with exotic tastes.

Myrtle: the Druids considered the bog myrtle to be one of their eight bramble trees.

Myrtle is a very old name and a powerful magical name. Myrtle or Rait are names for an older woman, one who has the wisdom of silence and the will to keep it.

Oak: one of the seven chieftain trees of the Druids and the seventh letter in their tree alphabet. Oak is sacred to Zeus, Jupiter, Hercules, the Dagda, Thor, and all other thunder gods. It is also sacred to Janus in Greece and Llyr in Celtic myth. Our word "door" comes from the Celtic word for oak, *duir*, a wood favored for door construction due to its durability and strength. The sacred mistletoe grows in the branches of this tree of the waxing year. There is an old expression, "Fairy folks are in old oaks."

Oak is one of the best magical names for a male because of its qualities of strength, fertility, and majesty. An old oak is a thing that inspires great awe. As a name, Oak is good for one who would be a high priest.

Pine: one of the Druids' seven sacred chieftain trees.

The name Pine is one with clean, healthy connotations. It is a name for an athlete or a healer. It may be good in combination with a second name.

Poplar: white poplar (or aspen) was one of the Druids' seven shrub trees and the seventeenth letter in their tree alphabet. It was thought to be a shield maker's tree. It is a tree of the autumnal equinox and old age.

This is a good name for an older person, a warrior (of either sex) who is teaching young people the ways of Wicca.

Rowan: it is one of the Druids' seven peasant trees and the second letter in their tree alphabet. One of the ents in *The Two Towers* by J. R .R. Tolkien was a rowan. Rowan is used as a charm against lightning and ill fortune. Everybody and their dog is named Rowan these days. Why not try using some of the interesting folk names for rowan

I will pick the smooth yarrow that my figure may be more elegant, that my lips may be warmer, that my voice may be more cheerful; may my voice be like a sunbeam, may my lips be like the juice of the strawberries. May I be an island in the sea, may I be a hill on the land, may I be a star when the moon wanes, may I be a staff to the weak one: I shall wound every man, no man shall wound me.

—TRADITIONAL FOLK CHARM

instead? It is known as delight of the eye, mountain ash, quickbane, ran tree, roynetree, Thor's helper, whitty, wicken tree, wiggen, wild ash, witchbane, witchen, and witchwood.

Shamrock: the three-leaf clover known as shamrock was originally seen as representing the triple goddess, and was sometimes called "Three Morgans" or "Three Brigits." This triple goddess connection to the shamrock was common in Arabia and ancient India. Because of the connection to the Goddess, Christian authorities in Ireland were not comfortable with Ireland's fondness for the symbol. From this environment sprang the notion of the four-leaf clover being the lucky one (four being symbolic of the points of the cross).

Shamrock would be a good name for one who reveres the triple aspects of the Goddess.

Sycamore: the sycamore was thought to be a tree of the dead in which spirits lived. It was a tree long associated with the Goddess. In Greek myth, the sycamore was the tree under which Zeus lay with Hera.

Sycamore is a good magical name, as it is a tree sacred to the Goddess. It is a good name for a male or a female, and hasn't a specific age associated with it. It is an interesting name for a vital and earthy person.

Tamarisk: used for thousands of years in exorcisms. In Egyptian myth, the tamarisk tree was the one that enveloped Osiris' sarcophagus.

Tamarisk is a beautiful name. It embodies beauty, mystery, uniqueness, purity, and power.

Vine: the tenth letter in the Druids' tree alphabet. Sacred to Dionysus and Osiris.

Vine is a name that is indicative of a climber. This is someone of great potential, a hard worker, a networker, a go-getter.

Willow: it is sacred to Hecate, Circe, Hera, Europa, Persephone, and the Muses. This is definitely a lunar tree. The witch's besom is traditionally made of an ash stake, birch twigs, and osier binding. It is one of the Druids' seven peasant trees (Sail or Saille) and the fifth letter in their tree alphabet.

Willow is a wonderful name for a man or woman. It has more of a female feel to it, so it shouldn't be chosen as a name that will inspire masculine traits. This is a tree name of emotion, a water sign name; a liquid, moving, loving, moon-driven name.

Yarrow: also known as arrowroot, eerie, gearwe, knyghten, soldier's woundwart, and yarroway. Used for protection and courage.

Yarrow is an excellent magical name. It, or any of its other names, is for one who is a warrior. This is a good name for either sex.

Yew: one of the Druids' seven sacred chieftain trees and the eighteenth letter in their tree alphabet. The Celts used it to make household vessels and breastplates. It is sacred to the Goddess Hecate. In Ireland, wine barrels were made of yew. It is considered to be a tree of death in many European countries. Its seasoned and polished wood has an extraordinary power of resisting corruption.

Yew is unique. This is a name of honor, steadfastness, protection, lunar influence, and durability.

GREENWOOD MEDITATION

As with any meditation, begin by relaxation, deep breathing, and a well-grounded (or centered) mind set. Imagine that you are the mythical Norse tree Yggdrasil. You are ancient beyond reckoning. Your mighty branches reach up to form the sky and spread over the world. Humans live in your leaves and make their homes on your bark. Your trunk is as wide as the Earth and in your mighty roots snuffles the dragon Nidhug. Your breathing slows; your thinking slows. You are the solid, stable body of Earth itself. The mighty tree of life. Notice how slow and accepting of life you are as a tree. Notice how the comings and goings of the humans affect you. Observe the interaction of the elements and how they impact you. Draw in the strength and patience of Yggdrasil and let your human insecurities and fears drain unneeded into your roots. Become strength. Become one with all of nature. Listen to whatever comes to you. Return to being yourself when ready.

The thing to be aware of in this meditation is the slowness of trees. This is a good trait to have in today's crazy world. Learn to use it. It will help slow down the frenetic pace of life and put things into perspective. This is a great grounding meditation.

THE TREE ALPHABET

A relic of the ancient Druids, the tree alphabet was passed down orally through the centuries. It consists of five vowels and thirteen consonants, with each letter named after a tree or shrub thought to be sacred to the Druids. The months of the year, in the Celtic calendar, were named after these consonant trees. They reckoned time according to the lunar cycles, thus having thirteen months in a year. The Celtic months were Beth, Luis, Nion, Fearn, Saille, Uath, Duir, Tinne, Coll, Muin, Gort, Peith, and Ruis. The five vowel trees were assigned days that came thirteen weeks apart, on the solstices and equinoxes.

Brehon law in Ireland forbade the unlawful felling of certain trees or sacred groves. The law divided the trees into chieftain, peasant, shrub, and bramble, with the severity of punishment decreasing according to the category. The destruction of chieftain trees brought the severest penalty, sometimes even death.

SEVEN CHIEFTAIN TREES

Oak

Hazel

Holly

Yew

Ash

Pine

Apple

SEVEN PEASANT TREES

Alder

Willow

Hawthorn

Rowan

Birch

Elm

(unknown)

SEVEN SHRUB TREES

Blackthorn

Elder

White hazel

White poplar

Arbutus

(unknown)

(unknown)

EIGHT BRAMBLE TREES

Fern

Bog myrtle

Furze

Briar

Heath

Ivy

Broom

Gooseberry (Spin)

chapter eighteen

MAGICAL NAMES FROM
MYTHOS

A NAME QUIZ OF
MYTHIC PROPORTIONS

T his quiz is a tool to help you figure out which kinds of mythological characters you relate to. Taking names of a deity that is important to you will have much more resonance in your life. Some people shy away from taking a god's name. But that's the old god-in-a-cloud-somewhere kind of religion, the they're-up-there and we're-down-here kind of thing. Wiccan/Pagan religion isn't about that. I don't have a problem with taking a god name. After all, thou art God or thou art Goddess. So why not call things by their right names? And don't forget, we invented the gods to help us understand ourselves. We gave birth to them and we kept them alive through our myths and stories. We gave them their names. So it's fine to borrow them back again. You will find many likely names in this section. Circle the appropriate letter.

1. In a guided meditation, you are told to picture a goddess. She takes you by the hand and leads you to a place of silent reverie where you can let your mind think over the events of your life. Which of the following locations do you imagine you might like to go?

   A. A mountain top overlooking the world below.

   B. A castle turret with stained glass windows.

   C An ancient forest rich with the smell of loam.

   D. A beautiful flower garden with a babbling brook.

   E. A mysterious crystal cave.

2. If asked to visualize your ideal home, which would be yours?

   A. Tidy, practical, with everything well organized and substantial, strongly built. Big enough for all your stuff, but not bigger than that.

   B. In a safe neighborhood, good locks, doorman controlling security, a safe haven.

   C A log cabin in the woods with your own vegetable garden outside.

   D. A beautiful house with pretty vistas out the windows with a luxurious spa where you can hot-tub and get massages on your own table.

   E. A house with a big office/library with a brand new state-of-the-art computer system with all the bells and whistles . . . the works.

3. If you had to pick one kind of hobby, which would you be drawn to? Don't rule things out because of physical impairment. Not what can you do, but what would you like to do?

   A. Athletics, competitive sports. I'd like to play in a team sport and excel at it. I'd enjoy finding someone who challenges me and against whom I could engage in friendly competitions making us both better at what we do.

   B. I've always wanted to learn about herbs and oils and make potions, balms, ointments, and shampoos from natural ingredients.

   C. Bird watching, butterfly collecting, collecting wild flowers and pressing them into albums, backpacking above the tree line. Hobbies that get me out into nature.

   D. I'd be a dancer. I'd take classes and learn to move to music using my body to express myself.

E. I'd like to take yoga and have some quiet, meditational time to myself.

4. What kinds of movies do you enjoy?

A. I enjoy action films. I like war movies, dramas that pit human against nature, or dramas in which people achieve great things.

B. I like movies that show people in trouble finding their way. I like happy endings and I'm a little uncomfortable with blatant sex or violence.

C. I like animal movies or survival in the wild kinds of things. I like movies that explore the secrets of nature like wildlife documentaries.

D. I love love stories. I like romance, passion, sex and movies that explore these things.

E. I like foreign and art films.

5. What kind of books do you read?

A. Cop novels, horror, some action-oriented sci-fi.

B. Funny books. Cookbooks. I like self-help.

C. I like mythology.

D. Erotica.

E. Mysteries.

6. How do you deal with conflict?

A. Directly. I go to the person involved and state my case and let the chips fall where they may. I have to speak my peace. I'm an alpha beast.

B. I dislike conflict. I just like everyone to get along. I love feeling safe and protected. I stay away from fighting.

C. Conflict is natural. We are animals by nature. We will lock horns sooner or later. Best just to clash and get it over with.

D. I prefer to try healing all conflicts with love and compassion

E. Communication is the only way to solve disputes. If we could just talk to each other.

7. What kinds of guys / girls do you like?

A. Active. Adventurous. Physically fit. Ambitious. Hard working. Strong.

B. Sweet. Shy. Sensitive. Nice. Trustworthy. Kind. Compassionate.

C. Natural. Back to basics. Rustic. Outdoorsy.

D. I admire beauty. The person I am attracted to *has* to be good looking.

E. I am attracted to a person's mind. What they think. How they express themselves.

8. What do you think makes for success?

  A. Hard work. Planning ahead. Goal setting.

  B. Visualizing it. Meditating on it. Using affirmations and magic.

  C. There is enough prosperity for us all. It's a bountiful universe. You just tap into it.

  D. Marrying well. Being young and beautiful doesn't hurt either.

  E. Getting that degree.

9. If someone told you that you had bad breath, how would you deal with it?

  A. Make a note to brush my teeth more often, buy mints, and gargle more.

  B. Wonder why that person has a problem with bad smells. Send them love.

  C. Bad breath is natural. If you don't like how my mouth smells, stay out of it.

  D. Ack! Quick! Breath mints, toothpaste . . . this is *so* humiliating!

  E. You thank them for the input. You realize that sometimes breath odor can be a symptom of disease. You research the topic online.

10. You get to work and the boss is off sick. You are put in charge temporarily. Would you . . .

  A. Revamp how things are done so they will be more efficient. You've given this opportunity some thought and have just been waiting to get your shot at it.

  B. Hope you don't make any mistakes. You try to keep your head down and wish the boss would get back soon.

  C. Institute a walking club at lunchtime to get people outdoors during the day or a recycling program for office waste.

  D. Enjoy using the boss's big office with the executive chair and nice view.

  E. Act carefully, giving thought to each decision so as not to foul anything up.

11. You realize a large factory is doing something terribly wrong. How do you handle this social problem?

  A. You pull some strings and get in to see the head of the company and talk to him face to face.

  B. Send a nice but firm letter to their public relations department. Boycott their product.

  C. Get the gang together and picket the place raising the public's awareness of the problem.

D. Call their 800 number and have a nice chat about your concerns.

E. Whatever you decide to do, you must have the facts at hand. Do more research first.

12. What part of ritual do you particularly like?

A. The raising energy part.

B. I like wearing robes, seeing a beautiful altar. I like singing.

C. I like calling the quarters.

D. I love to be skyclad and participating in the great rite. I love to dance.

E. I like the words of a beautifully written ritual. Also the meditative part.

13. In which point of the pentagram do you belong?

A. South. Fire. Heat. Action. Danger. Firey feelings.

B. East. Morning. Dawn. Beginnings. Birds.

C. North. Moon. Midnight. Mystery. Antlered animals.

D. West. Emotion. Water. Tides. Moods. Cycles.

E. Center. Spirit. Underworld. Communion. Magic. Balance.

14. What part of romance do you like?

A. Winning her/his love. The moment they say "I love you" is huge.

B. Nesting, cuddling. Making a home for the two of you. Planning a future together. Dreaming lovely dreams.

C. Being yourself with someone. Feeling comfortable enough to show your vulnerable side. Trust.

D. Sex. Making Love. Physical affection. Being dazzled.

E. Communion with another person. Being soul mates. Agreement. Union.

If you answered mostly As

Perhaps you'd be drawn to the warrior gods and goddesses as they reflect aspects of your personality. The warrior aspect is not just fighting and warfare. We aren't talking Rambo here. The warrior is about honor, dedication, ambition, competition, getting the job done, being the best person you can be. The darker side of this archetype includes the death and trickster aspects. Some names for the warrior archetype are below. You can look under the section on warrior names in chapter 7 and also under Warrior Names in the Names by Their Characteristics for other ideas.

GODDESS NAMES / GOD NAMES

British (female)

Uther

Finnish (female)

Kalma

Kipu-Tytto

Kivutar

Tuonetar

Vammatar

Finnish (male)

Hisi

Greek (female)

Eris

Atalanta

Nike

Greek (male)

Ajax

Antaeus

Milanion

Zeus

Irish (female)

Anu

Anann

Macha

Medbh

Morrigan

Nemontana

Scathach

Irish (male)

Balor

Daghda

Lugh

Roman (female)

Bellona

Minerva

If you answered mostly Bs

You may be drawn to those mythic figures involved with protection, virginity, strength, households, and building. Usually home-bodies, young people, solitaries, or crafts-men are drawn to this archetype.

GODDESS NAMES / GOD NAMES

British (female)

Ratis

Egypt (female)

Bes

Greek (female)

Artemis

MAGICAL NAMES FROM MYTHOS 209

Chloris
Hestia
Greek
Achilles
Cadmus

India (female)

Hanuman

Irish (female)

Erin/Eire
Garbh Ogh

Irish (male)

Creidhne

Norse (female)

Jarnsaxa

Roman (female)

Befona
Fauna
Maia
Cardea
Cloacina
Cynthia
Diana
Jana

Roman (male)

Janus
Mars
Penates
Picunnus
Silvanus

Welsh (female)

Olwyn

If you answered mostly Cs

This is the realm of the nature gods. The seasonal, lunar, healing, fertility gods of nature. The nature gods are primal, nature oriented, animalistic, and basic.

Many people are drawn to this archetype as is evidenced by how many of them we humans have invented to illustrate that aspect of the human condition. If you find a nature god or goddess name is not right, try other areas to do with nature such as tree names and rock names, found in chapters 15 and 17.

GODDESS NAMES / GOD NAMES

British (female)

Belisma
Tamesis
Latis

British (male)

Herne

Llud

Nick

Tannus

Tinnus

Egypt (female)

Isis

Athtor

Mafdet

Tefnut

Egypt (male)

Aker

Akhnaton

Ra

Amun-Ra

Apis

Babi

Khepera

Nu

Osiris

Ptah

Finnish (female)

Annikki

Ilmatar

Luonnotar

Vellamo

Tuulikki

Finnish (male)

Ilma

Jumala

Nakki

Paiva

Pellervoinen

Tapio

Ukko

Vainamoinen

Greek (female)

Cybele

Delia

Demeter

Gaia

Pythia

Rhea

Selene

Brimo

Hera

Greek (male)

Achelous

Aeolus

Ares

Centaur

Centaurus

Helios

India (female)

Chanda

Anumati

Raka

Samdhya

Surya

Tamira

Tara

Devi

India (male)

Bhrigus

Brahma

Chandra

Indra

Varuna

Irish (female)

Brighid

Damona

Dana

Danu

Ernmas

Boann

Epona

Etain

Flindais

Sulla

Irish (male)

Borvo

Cernunnos

Diancecht

Mac Cecht

Maccuill

Macgreine

Miach

Pooka

Shoney

Norse (female)

Holle

Laufey

Nerthus

Rana

Rania

Norse (male)

Aegir

Balder

Donar

Farbauti

Frey

Heimdahl

Hoder

Hodur

Thor

Phoenician (female)

Baalat

Omicle

Annona

Ghe

Re

Sapas

Tanit

Adad

Adoni

Aleyin

Aleion

Aleyn

Baal

Phoenician (male)

Dagon

Elium

Eshmum

Esmun

Genos

Kolpia

Pontus

Salem

Roman (female)

Aestas

Annona

Ceres

Cerelia

Fides

Flora

Juna

Luna

Lucina

Nox

Salus

Terra

Tellus

Vesta

Roman (male)

Aeolus

Faunus

Jupiter

Mercury

Neptune

Saturn

Vertumnus

Welsh (female)

Cerridwen

Cyhiraeth

Don

Dwyvach

Morgan

Welsh

Amathaon

Beli

Dylan

Nwyvre

If you answered mostly Ds

This is the realm of the love gods. This area is involved with all things sexual, ecstatic, happy, and beautiful. This is the realm of beauty, youth, and perfection that we as humans honor because it so rarely appears amongst us. But don't worry if you'll seem full of yourself to choose this kind of name. It just shows that you honor perfection and seek to find it in yourself. It shows that you are comfortable with your own sexuality and are drawn to the ecstatic in life.

GODDESS NAMES / GOD NAMES

Egypt (female)

Bast

Hathor

Finnish (female)

Kyllikki

Egypt (male)

Min

Greek (female)

Aphrodite

Ate

Bendis

Cytherea

Delight

Suadela

Greek (male)

Adonis

Anteros

Cupid

Dionysus

Eros

Orion

Pan

Satyr

India (female)

Arani

Kundalini

India

Kama

Kamadeva

Krishna

Irish (female)

Blodeuwedd

Brighid/Bride

Irish (male)

Oenghus (Angus)

Daghdha

Diarmuid

Fergus

Norse (female)

Freya

Kara

Nix

Sjofna

Phoencian (female)

Astarte

Volupia

Venus

If you answered mostly Es

This is the realm of the underworld. These myths are about rebirth, communication, bards, inspiration, wisdom, and quests to the afterlife. These are archetypes of the wise woman, the sage, the psychics, and wizards. There are many god and goddesses of this ilk listed below. If you don't find your name here, try looking in chapter 7 under the heading of Names for The Magician on page 72.. Also check under Wizard Names in the Names by Their Characteristics on page 363.

GODDESS NAMES / GOD NAMES

British (female)

Launfal

Wayland

Egypt (female)

Maat

Egypt (male)

Anubis

Horus

Set

Thoth

Finnish (female)

Mielikki

Finnish (male)

Rot

Surma

Tuoni

Greek (female)

Astra

Athena

Calliope

Hecate

Irene

Iris

Melanie

Melusine

Greek (male)

Aeacus

Apollo

Glaucus

Hades

Hermes

Minos

Momus

Morpheus

Paris

India (male)

Budha

Ganesha

Irish (female)

Banshee

Cliodna

Morrigan

Irish (male)

Amergin

Donn

Luchtaine

Mider

Oghma

Norse (female)

Kara

Nanna

Saga

Norse (male)

Hoeni

Hoenir

Mimir

Njord

Niord

Njoerd

Odin

Roman (female)

Aradia

Pax

Roman (male)

Lares

Orcus

Summanus

Vulcan

Welsh (female)

Arianrhod

Branwen

Gwendydd

Rhiannon

"They were myths and they were real," he said loudly. "Both a wave and a particle."
—TERRY PRATCHETT
GUARDS GUARDS

Myths are the things that never happened but always are.
—SYNESIUS

Thy sister put forth her protecting power
for thee, she scattered abroad those who
were her enemies, she drove back evil Hap,
she pronounced mighty words of power,
she made cunning her tongue,
and her words failed not.
The glorious Isis was perfect in command
and in speech, and she avenged her brother.
—*THE EGYPTIAN BOOK OF THE DEAD*

Welsh (male)

Arawn

Belanus

Bran

Caswallawn

Gwydion

Taliesin

EGYPTIAN GODDESSES

Athtor: mother night, the primordial element covering infinity. A night or dark goddess name brings quiet power, respect for the darkness, a heightening of our other senses.

Bast: cat goddess. A kindly goddess of joy, music, and orgiastic rituals. A favorite name among cat fanciers. It is a happy, playful, sexual name. We have named our kitty condo Chateau Bast.

Hathor: goddess of beauty, love, and marriage. Represented as the sky. An air name that brings love and the power of self-love.

Isis: wife of Osiris, mother to Horus, known as mistress of charms or enchantments. A name of mystery, dedication, determination, and magic.

Maat: goddess who personifies honor, justice, truth, and steadfastness. A powerful name to bear when making a difficult decision.

Mafdet: cat goddess predating Bast. A name that conveys sleekness, skill, guile, mystery, wildness, and beauty.

Mert: lover of silence in Egyptian myth, another name of Isis. One of the most valuable lessons a Wiccan learns is when to be silent. This name brings the wisdom of silence and constraint.

Tefnut: goddess who carries away the thirst of the deceased, represented as a form of moisture. A water name bringing relief and attainment of one's dreams.

Finnish Goddesses

Annikki ("AHN-ikki"): nighttime goddess. Known as "she of good name." As a magical name, this would be appropriate for work involving the shadow side.

Ilmatar ("ILL-mah-tar"): mother of the waters. Creation goddess impregnated by the wind to give birth to the earth and stars and the first person (a bard). A good fertility name, or one for renewal and important beginnings.

Kalma ("KAHL-ma"): goddess of death. A croning name that brings the mystery of the dark goddess.

Kyllikki ("KEWL-likki"): means "beautiful island flower." Maiden goddess, equivalent to Persephone. She was abducted by a wanton and unlucky mate. This name suggests youth, beauty, and new beginnings.

Luonnotar ("LWOAN-oh-tar"): daughter of nature. A name to bond with the earth.

*And she jerked her knee
and she shook her limbs:
the eggs rolled in the water
sink into the sea's billow
the eggs smashed to bits
broke into pieces . . . .
The bits changed into good things
the pieces into fair things:
an egg's lower half
became mother earth below
an egg's upper half
became heaven above;
the upper half that was yolk
became the sun for shining
the upper half that was white
became the moon for gleaming;
what in an egg was mottled
became the stars in the sky
what in an egg was blackish
became the clouds of the air.*

—ELIAS LONNROT
THE KALEVALA

The ages go on
the years beyond that
as the new sun shines
as the new moon gleams.
Still the water-mother swims
the water-mother, air-lass
on those mild waters
on the misty waves
before her the slack water
and behind her the clear sky.

—ELIAS LONNROT
THE KALEVALA

Tiny forest wench
mead-mouthed maid of Tapio:
play a honey-sweet whistle
on a mead-sweet whistle pipe
in the ear of the kindly
the pleasant forest mistress
that she may hear soon
and rise from her bed
for she does not hear at all
hardly ever wakes
though I keep begging
with golden tongue beseeching!

—ELIAS LONNROT
THE KALEVALA

Mielikki ("MY-ay-likki"): Forest crone goddess. Creator of the bear. A fertility name that brings abundance and power.

Tuonetar ("TWOAN-etar"): goddess of the underworld. For delving into one's own depths seeking the shadow self.

Tuulikki ("TOO-il-eekey") forest goddess. Called upon to insure abundance of game. A name that brings abundance; especially powerful when used for animal rights and protection work.

Vammatar ("VAHM-mah-tar"): goddess of pain and disease. Helps to overcome and go through illness. Not a name to take unless the need is great.

Vellamo ("VAYL-ah-moe"): water goddess. For insight, true feeling, and clear meaning.

GREEK GODDESSES

Aphrodite: goddess of sexual love. Born of sea foam. A powerful name of beauty, sexuality, love, and desire. Especially powerful for work with building self-esteem.

Ariadne: using a thread, she helped Theseus find his way into the labyrinth to kill the Minotaur and get out again. She eloped with him but he abandoned her. She then became a lover of Dionysus. A name that brings recovery of a broken heart, healing after a failed romance.

Artemis: virgin, huntress. Protector of young girls. A strong, protective name for someone who has been victimized.

Aspasia: "the welcome." Mistress of Pericles, famous for her charm and intelligence. A noble choice for those who seek improved self-esteem.

Astra: goddess of justice and purity, seen in the constellation Virgo. A name bringing balance, fairness, and unswerving devotion to justice.

Atalanta: would only marry any man she couldn't outrun. A good name for a runner, surely, but also for anyone who seeks pride in her accomplishments.

Athena: goddess of wisdom and justice. Athena is a powerful name and a powerful force for change in our lives. To name yourself after the goddess of wisdom allows great transformation and learning to occur. It is a most worthy name.

Bendis: a moon goddess worshiped in orgiastic rites. A name that brings enlightenment, mystery, and seductive sexuality.

Brimo: fertility goddess. A good name for hopeful mothers.

Chloris: goddess of flowers. A good maiden's name, a name of springtime and youth.

Cytherea: title of Aphrodite; from the island Cythera, where she was born out of sea foam (see Aphrodite).

Calliope: muse of epic poetry. A lyrical name of whimsy, inspiration, poetry, and reflection.

Cybele: goddess of caverns, of the earth in its primitive state. Ruled over wild animals.

Start the chorus dancing,
Summon all the Graces
Send a shout to Artemis in invocation.
Call upon her brother,
healer, chorus master,
Call the blazing Bacchus, with his
maddened muster.
Call the flashing, fiery Zeus, and
call his mighty, blessed spouse, and
call the Gods, call all the Gods,
to witness now and
not forget
our gentle, blissful Peace:
the gift,
the deed of Aphrodite.

—ARISTOPHANES

Hither, huntress,
virgin, Goddess,
tracker, slayer,
to our truce!
Hold us ever
fast together;
bring our pledges
love and increase;
wean us from the
fox's wiles:
Hither, huntress!
Virgin, hither!

—ARISTOPHANES
LYSISTRATA

Muses, sweet-speaking daughters of Zeus
Kronides and mistresses of song,
sing next of long-winged Moon! From her
immortal head a heaven-sent glow
envelopes the earth and beauty arises under
its radiance. From her golden crown
the dim air is made to glitter as her rays turn
night to noon, whenever bright
Selene, having bathed her beautiful skin
in the Ocean, put on her shining raiment
and harnessed her proud-necked and
glistening steeds, drives them on as their
manes play with the evening, dividing
the months. Her great orbit is full and as
she waxes a brilliant light appears in the sky.
Thus to mortals she is a sign and a token.
Once Kronides shared her bed and her love;
and became pregnant and gave birth to
Pandeia, a maiden outstanding for beauty
among the immortal Gods. Hail, Queen
and white-armed Goddess, splendid Selene,
kindly and fair-tressed!

—HOMER
THE HOMERIC HYMNS

A wild and basic name, bringing an appreciation of primal instincts and natural wonders. I believe it is her voice that whispers in caves, caverns, and coal mines. I once worked in a coal mine, and this was where I first heard the voice of the Goddess. As the miners cut a new face into the rock, they would free ground water and tiny pockets of gases in the rock. As the gas moved through the wet face of the rock, it made an eerie, whispering song. I would work between shifts so I would be practically alone a mile or so below the surface of the earth, deep in the heart of the planet, listening to the song Cybele sang as I blessed and healed her wounds. I worked in the moist, cool, and companionable darkness.

Delight: daughter of Eros and Psyche. A happy and uplifting name.

Delia: moon goddess Artemis' name, from her birth place on the island of Delos (see Artemis).

Demeter: goddess of vegetation and fruitfulness. A name that brings maternal longing, worry, and sorrow, but also fruitfulness, joy, and bonding with her children.

Elara: the mother of a giant by Zeus. A name that brings greatness.

Eris: goddess of discord. An unusual name that may bring confusion, arguments, upset, and certainly a degree of humor.

Gaia: Earth goddess. A name that suggests fertility and plenty.

Hecate ("heck-AH-tay" or "HECK-ah-tay" *never* "Heck-ate"): goddess of the crossroads. Mysterious and powerful goddess of ghosts and witchcraft. A crone's name, or one who seeks the wisdom of the Dark Goddess, especially at a crossroad in one's life.

Hera: goddess of women and childbirth. Wife of Zeus. This name suggests healing and support, but Hera was also the most jealous and vindictive goddess in the Greek pantheon.

Hestia: goddess of the hearth, peace, and family. Of all Olympians, she is the mildest. A good name for a home, or bringing the feeling of home, security, warmth, comfort, and peace.

Iris: goddess of the rainbow, messenger of the gods. A name that brings color, enlightenment, beauty, treasures beyond expectation, and happy endings to stormy periods.

Irene: goddess of peace. A sweet, peaceful, serene, contented name.

Melanie: means "the dark one," one of Demeter's titles. A name to choose to delve into one's dark side.

Nike ("NIGH-key."): goddess of victory. For winning a battle or overcoming defeat.

Psyche: the wife of Cupid (Eros), she was the personification of the human soul. Zeus made her immortal.

I begin to sing of Pallas Athena,
defender of cities,
awesome Goddess; she and Ares
care for deeds of war,
cities being sacked and cries of battle,
and she protects an army going
to war and returning.
Hail, O Goddess, and
grant me good fortune and happiness.

—HOMER
THE HOMERIC HYMNS

Sing, O Muse, of Artemis, sister of the Far-
darter, arrow-pouring virgin, who was
nurtured with Apollo, she waters her horses
by Meles with its tall rushes and
thence on her golden chariot courses to Klaros,
rich in vineyards, where Apollo of
the silver bow sits waiting for the
far-shooting arrow-pourer. . . .

—HOMER
THE HOMERIC HYMNS

Of golden-throned Hera
I sing, born of Rhea, Queen of all the Gods,
unexcelled in beauty, sister and
glorious wife of loud-thundering Zeus.
All the Gods on lofty Olympus reverence her
and honor her together with Zeus who delights
in thunder.

—HOMER
THE HOMERIC HYMNS

. . . Mid hushed, cool-rooted
flowers, fragrant-eyed, Blue,
silver-white, and budded Tyrian,
They lay calm-breathing on the bedded grass;
Their arms embraced, and their pinions too;
Their lips touched not,
but had not bade adieu,
As if disjoined by soft-handed slumber,
And ready still past kisses to outnumber
At tender eye-dawn of aurorean love:
The winged boy I knew;
But who wast thou, O happy dove?
His Psyche true!

—JOHN KEATS
ODE TO PSYCHE

Pythia: serpent goddess. For sleekness, guile, mystery, and femininity.

Rhea: Earth. For fertility and abundance.

Selene: goddess of the full moon. Unlike Diana, not a huntress or virgin. One of the Pleiades. A fertility name.

Suadela: goddess of persuasion, an attendant of the goddess of love. A great name for a salesperson, a lawyer, or anyone who needs a handle on the art of persuasion.

GODDESS OF INDIA

Anumati: goddess of the waning moon. A name to use for ridding yourself of unwanted aspects of your personality (see section on naming rituals).

Arani: goddess of female sexual fire. For accepting one's own sexuality.

Chanda: one of the names of Devi, the great goddess. A unique and powerful name.

Kundalini: "coiled." The feminine serpent force, the life-force. Perhaps the most primal and elemental feminine aspect name. A profound name for enlightenment, fertility, all aspects of femininity.

Raka: goddess of the full moon. For attainment of fertility and success.

Samdhya: goddess of twilight. A nature goddess. A name that is for transition into darkness, a croning name, and a name rich in abundance and mystery.

Surya: goddess of the sun. A fire name bringing passion, warmth, and home energy.

Tamra: "copper-colored." Ancestress of birds. A name that brings freedom, flights of intellect, warmth, and merriment.

Tara: Hindu star goddess. A cool name for distancing one from trouble; a gentle teacher.

IRISH / CELTIC GODDESSES

Anu/Anann: Irish. Sex and war goddess. Part of the triple goddess Anu, Badhbh, and Macha, known collectively as the Morrigan. This is a powerful choice for a woman who must do battle on the battlefields of sexual discrimination or abuse. These are powerful names not to be chosen lightly. The empowerment potential from these names is impressive. One very frightened Pagan male of my acquaintance told me in a hushed voice that one never spoke these names aloud out of fear of this goddess. He was a wife-beater and a misogynist. He had reason to be wary. I hope his wife chooses this as her magical name. There is no goddess or god whose names we dare not utter. That is god-fearing hierarchical orthodox religion, not Wicca.

Banshee: "Woman fairy." Irish. Can be heard keening near a house in which someone is about to die. She is attached to certain families (she keens for members of my husband's family). A good crone name.

Blodeuwedd: a goddess of love made of flowers of the oak, broom, and meadowsweet as a wife for the God Lleu Llaw Gyffes.

Boann ("pboo ANN"): Irish. Goddess of the River Boyne. She mated with the Dagda on November 1 (a Samhain rite), and the Dagda also mated with the Morrigan on the same day. Boann gave birth to Aengus mac Og. A fertility-and-sexuality-enhancing name.

Brighid ("breed"): "Fiery arrow." Irish. Also Brigid, Brigit, Brid, Bride, or Bried. Goddess of fertility and inspiration. Daughter of the Dagda. The word "bride" is derived from this name. These names bring a fire of change to its bearer. They are for fertility, good fortune, inspiration, and new beginnings.

Cliodna: a goddess of the Irish otherworld. She was a beautiful woman who possessed three magical birds whose songs healed people.

Damona: Celtic. A cow or sheep goddess. A name for fertility and abundance.

Dana/Danu: Irish. The major mother goddess figure. Goddess of the Tuatha de Danann (which means "children of the Goddess Dana"). A powerful name for a woman seeking motherhood, coming into her own power, or becoming a teacher.

Epona: Celtic. Horse goddess of British and European Celts. A name symbolizing power, energy, and fertility.

Lady raven, fly. Black wings shadow falls over
battle fields, sacred fields and
bring the breath of Avalon, the peace of the
west. We have tried, warrior maid, we
have fought, we have died 'til the dolmens and
groves have run red with our blood.
Battle crone, are we lost as your standing
stones fall? Do our own Wicca ways go
for naught? Morrigan, Morrigan. Do not cry,
Wicca child, for your life or your
ways. Know the peace of the grave is a rest,
not an end. To my ways be reborn,
for the craft never died and my time comes
again, I am the Morrigan, Morrigan.
Lady raven, fly, black wing's shadow falls
over city lights, jeweled nights and
come to us from Avalon, come forth from
the west. See my black feathered cape
in the night, moonless night.
Know my wing's shadow falls not to hide,
but protect. For each wise one who calls,
never more shall they fall. And from Avalon
come I again. Morrigan, Morrigan.

—TEARA JO STAPLES
THE MORRIGAN

Erin/Eire: one of the three queens of the Tuatha de Danann. A daughter of the Dagda. She wanted Ireland to be named after her, and so it was. A name that brings the ancient call of Ireland with it. This aspect was representative of the maiden.

Ernmas: "She-farmer." Irish. The mother of the Irish triple goddess persona. A fertility name.

Etain: "Horse riding." Irish. Symbol of reincarnation. Very beautiful. A rejuvenating name to bring about shining renewal.

Flidais: Irish. Woodland goddess. Rode in a chariot pulled by deer. Married to Adammair, who was so lusty that when she was away he needed seven women to satisfy him. A name for increasing one's sexual appetite.

Macha: Irish. War and sex goddess. Part of the triple Goddess Anu, Badhbh, and Macha, known collectively as the Morrigan (see Anu).

Melusine: Irish/Scottish. Dark aspect of Lucina. One whose power lay in her secrecy and anonymity. A good name for a hidden child of the Goddess, one whose situation does not allow her to be public.

Morrigan ("MORE-ee-gan"): Irish. War and sex goddess. Pre-Celtic moon goddess whose symbol was the raven (see Anu).

Nemontana: Celtic. A British Celtic war goddess. A warrior's name that brings tenacity, courage, stamina, fortitude, and strength.

Scathach ("SKAH-hock"): Celtic. Warrior goddess who instructed Cuchulainn in martial arts on the Isle of Skye. A name for a teacher, a warrior, a strong and powerful person, one who desires to become fearless and skilled at combat.

Sulla ("silla"): Celtic. Also Sulis. Goddess of hot springs. For relief of arthritic complaints, a water element name that connotes healing, comfort, and energy. It would be appropriate to erect a shrine to Sulla near a hot tub to make it a safe and healing place.

Norse / Teutonic Goddesses

Freya: Norse. Goddess of love, beauty, and fertility. Another powerful name for building self-esteem, encouraging fertility, and increasing one's sexual appetite.

Holle: Teutonic. Also Holda or Holde. Moon/forest goddess. She bathed in streams in the forest in the summer, but in winter she showered herself in snow by shaking the trees. A name for cleansing and purifying.

Induna/Udun: Teutonic. The source of the magic apples that allowed the gods to be immortal. A name for rejuvenation, wisdom, cleansing, and healing.

Jarnsaxa: Teutonic. Wife of Thor. She was a giantess who gave birth to courage and might. A strong name, bringing realization of one's own power and unlocking great potential.

Kara: Norse. A Valkyrie, lover of Helgi. She charmed his enemies in battle by enchanting them with song, but in the end Helgi accidentally killed her. A name that brings the magic of music.

Laufey: Teutonic. Her name means "wooded isle." She gave birth to Loki, the trickster god. A name that brings tolerance, patience, maternal support, and the ability to laugh at one's troubles.

Nanna: Teutonic. Unfaithful wife of Balder. She was seduced by her husband's rival. She committed suicide on her husband's funeral pyre. A serious name bringing wisdom through folly, atonement through self-sacrifice, and the value of being true to one's word.

Nerthus: Teutonic. An early earth goddess. A fertility name bringing peace and plenty.

Nix: Teutonic. Sirens of great beauty who would sit and sing on the banks of rivers, combing their long hair and luring sailors to their doom. The sound of their singing drove people mad. A name of devastating beauty which has an alluring and sexual connotation. A name that also suggests the great power of music.

Rana/Rania: Norse. Goddess of the sea. She cast her nets upon the sea and set her alluring daughters to tempt sailors into her trap. Once drowned, however, the men were welcome at her feast. A name for bringing forth the inevitable, for working on capturing that which tries to elude you. It also suggests a reward for following the call of the Lady.

Saga: Teutonic. A giantess who is a seer. A name that brings insight and shows one the big picture. A good name for those who have trouble seeing the forest for the trees.

Skadi: Teutonic. She loved the mountains, but her husband favored the seashore. She eventually returned to the mountains. A name for following your bliss, being true to yourself, and learning to pay attention to your needs.

PHOENICIAN GODDESSES

Astarte: goddess of love. A name that brings us in touch with the most powerful human emotion.

Baalat: means "the lady." A generic name for all goddesses. A name that brings the coalition of many thoughts.

Ghe: means "Earth." Mother Earth Goddess, a derivation of Gaia. A fertility name with earth element properties.

Omicle: mother figure in Phoenician creation myth. She gave birth to everything. Her mate was "desire." A name for new beginnings, fertility, rejuvenation, and the fulfillment of desire.

Re: moon goddess. A name for gentle teaching and quiet enlightenment.

Sapas: sun goddess. Torch of the gods. For fire energy, passion, powerful enlightenment, harsh lessons, and quick growth.

Tanit: moon goddess. A fertility name bringing abundance, attainment of goals, growth, and fulfilment of desire.

ROMAN GODDESSES

Aestas: goddess of summer. A good seasonal name. A name that brings warmth, growth, nurturing, prosperity, and learning.

Annona: goddess of the harvest. A name bringing abundance, attainment of goals, prosperity, and success.

Aradia: goddess of witches. Daughter of Diana. In folklore she came to Earth to teach witches Diana's magic. A powerful name for a teacher.

Befona: also Befana. Italian. Witch fairy woman who flies down the chimney on Twelfth Night to bring presents to children. A good name for a good parent or teacher.

Bellona: goddess of war. A war goddess' name brings strength, power, courage, an overcoming of fear, and a respect for death.

Cardea: protection goddess for the home. She evolved into one who guards over children. A fierce name for defending children's rights and protecting the home.

Ceres: corn goddess. A name that brings abundance and fertility.

Cerelia: goddess of the harvest. A name bringing fertility, abundance, and success.

Cloacina: goddess of drains and sewers. This may seem amusing at first, but in any crowded, densely populated city it is important to keep this goddess happy. This is a good magical name for helping with house-hold plumbing problems but also for our own internal plumbing. This is a good name for those who suffer from colitis, ileitis, chronic diarrhea, constipation, or any other intestinal upset.

Cynthia: new moon version of Diana. A good name for new beginnings, for new projects, growth, and maturation. A name for a woman who has just come through her rite of passage.

Diana: goddess of the moon. A virgin huntress. A powerful, independent, strong, beautiful, and empowering name.

Egeria: an oracular water goddess who foretold the fates of newborn babies. A name for bringing foresight, enlighten-ment, and intuition to those who deal with children.

Fauna: also Bona Dea or Maia. Goddess of fertility, animals, farming, and chastity. Husband to Faunus. So faithful a wife she was made a goddess after death. A good name for fertility and earthiness. A good choice for working out marriage difficulties.

Fides: goddess of fidelity and honor. A good name to take to bring out these char-acteristics in you.

Flora: goddess of flowers and gardens. She enjoyed perpetual youth. A youthful name, appropriate for a maiden.

Jana: wife to Janus; guardian of doors and the turn of the year. A good name for

Queen and Huntress, chaste and fair,
Now the sun is laid to sleep,
Seated in thy silver chair
State in wonted manner keep:
Hesperus entreats thy light,
Goddess excellently bright.
Lay thy bow of pearl apart
And thy crystal shining quiver;
Give unto the flying hart
Space to breathe, how short soever:
Thou that mak'st a day of night,
Goddess excellently bright!

—BEN JONSON
"HYMN TO DIANA"

First she had a great abundance of hair,
flowing and curling, dispersed and
scattered about her divine neck;
on the crown of her head she bore many
garlands interlaced with flowers, and in the
middle of her forehead was a plain
circlet in fashion of a mirror,
or rather resembling the moon by the light
that it gave forth; and this was borne up on
either side by serpents that seemed to rise
up from the furrows of the earth.

—LUCIUS APULEIUS
THE GOLDEN ASS

initiation (opening of doors), movement, and growth; for dealing with aging and death.

Juno: supreme Roman goddess of marriage and childbirth. The month of June is named for her. A name for fertility and working out marital troubles.

Luna: goddess of the moon. Luna brings the power of the night, the illumination of insight, and the wisdom of the Goddess.

Lucina: midwife goddess of childbirth; her name means "light." A fertility name that brings the wisdom of the parent.

Maia: also Bona Dea or Fauna. Goddess of spring. One of the Pleiades. A good name for a maiden. A name conveying youthful energy, spring-like renewal, and hope.

Minerva: a war goddess who originally protected business, education, and industry. Goddess of wisdom and justice. Also called Athena in Greece. A strong name for achieving success in business, good grades in school, or in defeating an enemy of any description. A powerful name.

Nox: goddess of the night. A name for exploring one's shadow self, the dark goddess, or inner mysteries.

Pax: goddess of peace. A name that brings serenity, relief from stress, cool deliberation, and freedom from strife.

Salus: goddess of health. A good name for overcoming illness.

Terra/Tellus: Earth goddess. For fertility and abundance.

Volupia: goddess of pleasure. A feel-better name. One to take for increasing one's pleasure in life.

Venus: goddess of love (more sexual in nature than Aphrodite). A great name for self-esteem work, for increasing one's sexuality, for working with tantric energy.

Vesta: goddess of the hearth. A name for a home, surely, but also for bringing about hominess, safety, warmth, friendship, and family. A good name for people who need to feel more secure.

WELSH GODDESSES

In Wales, myths were very important. The Welsh word for mythologist or storyteller was *cyfarwydd*, which means "a seer and teacher who guides the souls of those who listen through the world of mystery." The Welsh word for story or myth comes from the root word that means "to see," and the word "story" means "guidance, direction, instruction, knowledge, and skill." The wise ones of Wales knew how to use their myths and the names found within them.

Arianrhod: means "silver wheel." Goddess of reincarnation. Mother of Llew by Gwydion. A transformational goddess whose name brings rebirth and acceptance of the cycles of life ("air-ee-EN-road").

Branwen ("BRAN-oo-win"): she was the wife of the king of Ireland, who mistreated her. Her brother, Bran the Blessed, came to avenge her but was mortally wounded. She took his head, which continued to talk for several years. It finally asked to be buried. A good name for one who seeks, to overcome oppression, leave environments of mistreatment, and listen to words of wisdom.

Cerridwen ("caer-EED-uin"): mother, moon, grain goddess. Mother of Creirwy (the most beautiful girl in the world) and Avagdu (the ugliest boy). Also the mother of Taliesin, the greatest of the bards. She is the owner of a cauldron called Amen in which she made a magic drink that gave inspiration and knowledge. A beautiful name that brings the cycles of life into focus; a rejuvenating name, a good crone's name. A name for knowledge, wisdom, and magic.

Cyhiraeth ("keh-HEAR-aeth"): water goddess who evolved into being a warning of impending death. This is a good name for bringing out one's awareness of death, and improving one's intuition and psychic abilities.

Don: equivalent to the Irish Danu. Mother goddess figure. Wife of Beliand mother to Arianrhod. A fertility name.

And she came, wearing a flame-red silken tunic, and a massive collar of red gold round the girl's neck, with precious pearls and rubies in it. Her head was yellower than the flowers of the broom; her flesh was whiter than the foam of a wave; her palms and fingers were whiter than the flowers of the melilot among thesmall pebbles of a gushing spring. No eye was fairer than hers, not even the eye of the mewed hawk nor the eye of the thrice-mewed falcon. Whiter than the breast of the white swan were her two breasts; redder than the foxglove were her cheeks. All who saw her became filled with love for her. Four white clover flowers would grow up in her footprints wherever she went; and hence she was called Olwen.

—WHITE FOOTPRINT

Dwyvach ("DWEE-vach"): husband to Dwyvan, with whom she built an ark to rescue many animals and escape a great flood in a pre-Christian myth. A name for an animal lover, a sailor, or a person who takes care of others, such as a mother or a teacher.

Gwendydd ("GWEND-eth"): also Gandieda, Vivienne, and Nimue. Merlin's sister, to whom he gave his gift of prophecy. A name for a powerful Witch, a strong woman who has considerable psychic talent.

Olwyn ("OLL-win"): an important character in the old king versus the new king struggle—seen in many myths, in which the winner becomes the consort to the Goddess. Olwyn is the daughter of Ysbadadden and the intended bride of Culhwch. If Olwyn marries Culhwch, then Ysbadadden must die. A sovereign goddess name that brings with it power, justice, wisdom, and fate.

Rhiannon ("hree-ANN-in"): fertility and underworld goddess. For the swiftness of a swift steed or fluttering bird. For overcoming punishment mistakenly laid upon one, or for recovering from abuse. A good name for one intent on self-healing, or a counselor of others who are healing. The birds of Rhiannon are said to have made such beautiful music that could "wake the dead and lull the living to sleep." This suggests an appropriate name for a singer or musician. There are a few very talented singers of Pagan music who share this name.

GODS

To call yourself "god" is an important and almost unparalleled act of self-acceptance and empowerment. To bear the name of one of the gods makes a man stand taller, feel braver, more confident, more in tune with his maleness, and more aware of the Goddess. These names are names accentuating the hero, the magician, the lover, the bard, and the warrior. These are very strong archetypal images that manifest powerfully in people who bear these magnificent names.

If your experiences with any deity speaks to you of different things than what I have written here then, for you, those things are what should be used to describe the deity and the deity's name. The bottom line is what does this name mean to you? You make the magic.

I have approached this from the perspective of women taking goddess names and men taking god names, but only because that is the most common connection.

Deity names work well for us, regardless of our current sexual affiliation. God names bring many good things to both sexes. Goddess names work well for men as well as women. Taking a deity name of the other sex, in fact, is a great way to understand more about the other sex. If you want to learn about men, who better to teach you than the God? What better female to lead you into the realm of womanhood than the Goddess?

BRITISH GODS

Herne: a hunter god. He bears a rack of deer antlers upon his head and races across the sky with his red-eared hunting dogs. He is associated with fecundity and usually portrayed with an enormous phallus. This is a particularly potent name for one who desires increased sexual fertility, virility, or ability.

Launfal: a knight of the Round Table. Tryamon, a fairy princess, loved him and gave him money, provided he did not reveal their love. He inadvertently did so, and instantly lost his wealth. He was put on trial and commanded to produce the object of his boasts. Trymon appeared, supported his boasts, and blinded Guinevere. A name that teaches the wisdom of silence.

Llud ("hleth"): British Celtic river god. Also Ludd, Nuda, or Nudd. Very similar to Nuada of the Irish pantheon. He also had a silver hand. This is a name for water energy and overcoming one's handicaps.

Nick: water god. Derived from the Nix, Teutonic water sprites. This is a good water energy name.

Tannus/Tinnus: British and French. Means "oak." He survived as a thunder god, but early Etruscan myth names him Tina. Gaelic words derived from his name mean "fire," and the word "tinder" comes from his name. This is probably more likely to be a lightning god involved with fire energy. This is a fire energy name, suggesting building energy, feeding the system, passion, fortitude, and self-sufficiency.

Wayland: British/Celtic. Also Weland or Weyland the Smith. A smith god. He was originally the Nordic God Volund. Son of Wade (Wada), king of the Finns. Grandson to Wachilt, a sea goddess. Wayland was abandoned by his wife, stolen from, abducted, lamed, imprisoned, and forced to work. He killed the two sons of his captor, made drinking cups from the dead son's skulls as a gift to his captor, raped the man's daughter, and escaped with wings he made during his captivity. This is a name of a victim who is sorely abused and who dreams of revenge. It is a name for one stuck in pain and unhappiness but who is thinking of ways to escape. This is also a name for a silversmith who seeks to create wonderful work.

EGYPTIAN GODS

Aker: god of the earth. A god who had the bodies of two lions with human heads, facing opposite directions. Aker ruled the underworld, guarding its gate. Aker is a name for

*The company of the Gods rejoiceth and is glad
at the coming of Osiris's son Horus, and firm of
heart and triumphant is the son of Isis, the heir
of Osiris.*

—*THE EGYPTIAN BOOK OF THE DEAD*

*Hail to thee, Osiris, lord of eternity, king of
the Gods . . . to thee are obedient the
stars in the heights . . . Thou art the Lord
to whom hymns of praise are sung in the
southern heaven, and unto thee are adorations
paid in the northern heaven . . . Thy
dominion is eternal, O thou beautiful Form of
the company of the Gods . . . Many
are the shouts of joy that rise to thee at the
Uak festival, and cries of delight ascend to
thee from the whole world with one voice.*

—*THE EGYPTIAN BOOK OF THE DEAD*

*[Ra said] I have made the heavens and the
Earth . . . I have stretched out the two
horizons like a curtain, and I have placed
the soul of the Gods within them. I am
he who, if he openeth his eyes, doth make
the light, and, if he closeth them,
darkness cometh into being. At his
command the Nile riseth, and the Gods
know not his name.*

—*THE EGYPTIAN BOOK OF THE DEAD*

those who are dealing with death or are undergoing any important new beginning.

Akhnaton ("auck-NAH-ton"): revolutionary king who worshiped Ra the sun god. Some say he has been reincarnated into the body of an ex-Las Vegas card dealer living in Denver, Colorado. The interior of this man's house is covered with beautiful hieroglyphics and decorated according to the tastes of an Egyptian king. He holds court there and tells his students the secrets of the universe, for a price. Akhnaton is a good name for one who desires to think for himself, to be a rebel, or to think about things in a new way.

Amun-Ra: also Ra. Sun god. A creation god from whose tears humanity sprang. Interestingly enough from a perspective of names, Isis tricked Ra into revealing his secret name to her and thus she acquired his magic powers. This is primarily a fertility name bringing warmth, insight, knowledge, and an awareness of the frailty of aging. This would be a good name to take if you are working on learning to keep secrets.

Anubis: god of embalming. Weighed the heart of the deceased against that of a feather to judge if the deceased was pure of heart. Like many underworld gods, this name is good for introspection and accepting the cycles of life and death. Also good for self-improvement.

Apis: a series of sacred bulls in which is believed to live the soul of Osiris. The name

Apis brings strength, fecundity, masculine prowess, and nobility.

Babi: baboon god. A fierce and phallic god who feeds on humans, yet could protect humans from snakes. This is a name for getting in touch with one's warlike aspects and for improving one's virility.

Bes: god who protects women during pregnancy and birth. A happy god who delights in music, merrymaking, families, children, married couples, and eroticism. Sort of a Pan with family values. This is a great name to take when one decides to become a father and to keep through the birth of the baby.

Horus: god of light. Son of Isis and Osiris. A name for enlightenment and understanding.

Khepera: god of the rising sun. The rising sun is seen as Khepera moving into the body of the sky goddess. He is a creation figure; in one myth, he was said to form the world. His symbology has to do with life and procreation. As a magical name, Khepera is a positive, hopeful, creative, and rejuvenating name for those beginning again.

Min: god of sexual potency. He was shaped like a phallus with a human or a lion's head. He protected desert travellers who offered him flowers to assure the fertility of the Nile Valley. This is a name for enhancing one's sexual drive, endurance, potency, and sexual capacity.

Nu: also Nun or Nunu. God of the primordial watery mass from which sprang the gods; known as the father of the gods. He and his wife were the first couple. This is a name for going back to the beginning and looking at your life. This is a starting over name. It is also a good name for new beginnings and the creation of new couples or groups.

Osiris: god of fertility, growing things (with his cycle of life, death, and rebirth), and the afterlife (he was a judge and caretaker of the dead). His reformation of the lands he touched was done without force, but with charm, music, and sound ideas. Husband of Isis. He was torn apart by Set and his body hidden all over Egypt. Isis had to find all the parts to restore him to life. The only part she couldn't find was his penis, which had been eaten by a fish. It was from this myth that the custom of eating fish on Fridays sprang. The sacramental imbibing of the flesh of deity began in this way and has persisted for thousands of years, thanks to the Catholics. This is a powerful name for those who seek to be in sync with the cycles of life, to accept death as part of life, and for those who seek to change the world in a gentle and profound manner. It is also a name for fertility, growth, intellect, charm, and balance.

Ptah: the opener. Called the father of fathers and the power of powers. A solar god. This is a name for creativity, craftsmanship, and skill.

Ra: the sun god of ancient Egypt (see Amun-Ra).

Set: originally a sun god. He ended up being a god of the powers of the deathly dryness in the Sahara. This is a name that brings an awareness of one's own dark side. It is a name for examining one's shadow self and dealing with it.

Thoth: god of divine intelligence and writing. A name to take as you write or study.

FINNISH GODS

Ilma ("ILL-mah") air god. Father of "Daughter of Nature" and "Mother of the Waters." An air energy name for creativity, fertility, power, and clarity of thought.

Ilmarinen ("ILL-mar-ee- nayn"): the Weyland Smith of the Finnish sagas. A smith god. He forged a talisman from a swan's quill tip, the milk of a barren cow, a small grain of barley, and the dawn of a summer ewe. This name is good for those who wish to create something new within themselves, and for those who seek to forge ahead despite setbacks. This is a building, changing, growing, and transforming name.

Jumala ("YOO-mah-lah"): supreme sky god. His symbol was the oak tree. An air elemental name bringing power, control, and creativity.

Nakki ("NAH-key"): shapeshifting water god. Bottomless lakes lead to the palace of Nakki. Swimmers must beware of him. He appears at the rising and setting of the sun. This is a water energy name, bringing immersion in one's inner emotions.

Paiva ("PIE-vah"): god of the sun. A name to take to bring about the flames of passion, will, and determination. A fire elemental name.

Pellervoinen: vegetation god. Protector of trees and plants. This is an vibrant name to take to do environmental activism work (protesting clear-cut logging, for example), or just to help you get in touch with the energy of plants while gardening ("PAYL-er-voi-nayn").

Rot ("roat"): god of the underworld. Underworld gods perform many functions. They are responsible for judgment, analysis, and understanding of one's inner self, synthesis, coming to terms with oneself, and rebirth or reward in a happier place. Thus, underworld names can help us do these things on our own. They can help us separate and identify aspects of our personality, analyze these aspects, synthesize this new awareness into our conscious mind, accept these aspects, and go through a rebirth of a new, improved person.

Surma ("SOOR-mah"): guardian of the gates to the realm of Kalma, goddess of graves. Surma is a frightening creature who represents fate and violent death. This name can acquaint us with death, the afterlife, and fate .

Tapio ("TAHP-pi-oa"): god of the forest realm of Tapiola. Husband to Mielikki. He is pictured as dark-bearded, wearing a fir hat and a moss cloak. A god's name to invoke abundance, safety, protection, and oneness with forest energy.

Tuoni ("TUOAN-ee"): god of the underworld. His daughters were the goddesses of death, disease, and suffering. This is a good name to take to work through an illness or sorrow. Sometimes you are given an unpleasant thing in order to learn from it and the only way to do that is to immerse yourself in it, work through it, then move on.

Ukko ("OOK-oh"): The supreme sky god (formerly Jumala). God of thunder and rain and he who supports the world. Husband to Akka, the Earth Mother Goddess. A creation name bringing supreme power, fertility, and expression. Especially good for dealing with enormous responsibility .

Väinämöinen ("VINE-am-moi-nayn"): the Finnish Adam. The son of the creator goddess and the east wind. His name is probably derived from an archaic word meaning "slow-flowing river." He is also called the "calm waters man." He is a bard/shaman/creator god with a powerful water name for creativity, fertility, and insight.

GREEK GODS

Achelous: a shapeshifting river god who, during a wrestling match, would change his form, but was eventually defeated and leapt into the river, which then bore his name. At one point he became a bull; when his opponent tore off his horn, it became a cornucopia. This name suggests a wily nature, a shifting person who is hard to pin down, water energy, and a person who attracts abundance and plenty.

Achilles: trying to make him invulnerable, his mother dipped him in the Styx when he was a baby. She held him by the heel and forgot to dip that as well, so it became his vulnerable spot. This name suggests a vulnerable person who is working on his weaknesses.

Adonis: a youth beloved by Aphrodite. When he was killed, Aphrodite begged Zeus to restore him to life, but Persephone had also become enamored of him and would not let him leave the underworld. Zeus decreed that he should spend half the year in the underworld and half in the upperworld. In the spring the festival of his rebirth was an occasion for wild celebrations, usually celebrated by women.

Aeacus: son of Zeus. A god of such great integrity that after his death, Zeus made him a judge of the underworld. A name that brings honor, reward, integrity, and respect.

Aeolus: father of the wind. An air name that brings to mind wisdom, flight, power, and freedom.

Mighty Ares, golden-helmeted rider of
chariots, stout-hearted, shield-carrying
and bronze-geared savior of cities, strong-
handed and unwearying lord of the
spear, bulwark of Olympus, father of fair
Victory, and succorer of Themis. You
curb the unruly and lead truly just men,
O paragon of manly excellence, wheeling
your luminous orb through the seven-pathed
constellations of the sky, where flaming
steeds ever carry you above the third
heavenly arch. Harken, helper of
mortals and giver of flourishing youth,
and from above shine a gentle light on my
life and my martial prowess, that I may
be able to ward off bitter cowardice from
my head, to bend wisely my soul's beguiling
impulse and to restrain the sharp
fury of my heart, whenever it provokes
me to enter chilling battle. But, O blessed
one, give me courage to stay within
the secure laws of peace and to escape
the enemy's charge and a violent death.

—HOMER
THE HOMERIC HYMNS

Ajax: a giant; the strongest of warriors. A name for those who wish to seem larger to others. A name that brings about increased body awareness and confidence about one's physique.

Anteros: son of Aphrodite, brother of Eros; represents mutual love. A name for those who seek affection, friendship, and love to be reciprocated.

Antaeus: a god who could defeat any opponent as long as he remained in contact with the earth. He was defeated by being lifted into the air and strangled. A name that brings a strong connection to the earth, a bonding of the bearer with the energy flows of the earth, and a grounding effect.

Apollo: god of intellect, music, art, healing, poetry, and light. He was expanded with the advent of patriarchy to encompass the former domains of many goddesses. This is a name that brings strength, male beauty, compassion, sensitivity, lust, passion, and talent.

Ares: also Aries. God of war. Lover of Aphrodite. Father to gods of terror, tumult, fear, panic, and goddesses of battle (Enos), discord (Eris), and fair victory. Sacred to him were the dog and the vulture. This is a warrior's name, bringing protection.

Cadmus: a builder god who gave the Greeks the alphabet. Husband to Zeus' daughter Harmonia. They became the rulers of Illyria and were associated with the snake god and goddess of Illyrian myth. A name for any snake fanciers or for those who have great ambition.

Centaur: means "those who round up bulls." Creatures with the body of a horse and the torso, arms, and head of a human. Originally Zeus thwarted a suitor of Hera by forming a cloud that resembled Hera. The suitor mated with the cloud, producing Centaurus. Centaurus mated with mares, creating the race of Centaurs. This name brings sexuality, fecundity, playfulness, swiftness, and power.

Dionysus ("dye-oh-NEE-see-us"): god of fertility, freer of emotions, remover of inhibitions. His rites were wild frenzies of female worshippers. This name is for overcoming shyness or inhibition.

Eros: son of Aphrodite. God of love. A name to be chosen carefully in this day and age because it brings eroticism, sexual potency, attractiveness, fecundity, and stamina. This name is male sexuality personified. Be careful how you use it.

Glaucus: a sea god who had the gift of prophecy given to him by Apollo. He appeared to sailors in warning of danger. A good name for developing psychic abilities, getting in touch with water energy, finding your one true love (Glaucus was loved by none but his true love), or for those who like to sail.

Hades: god of the underworld. He abducted Persephone, daughter of Demeter (corn goddess) and Zeus. Demeter was so distraught over losing her daughter that she refused to allow anything to grow upon the earth until her daughter was returned to her. In a compromise, Persephone was allowed to return to her mother for half the year but must return to Hades for the remainder of the year. This is symbolic of the cycle of growth of vegetation on the earth. Hades is a name for forceful energy, darkness, potency, faithfulness, wealth, and plenty.

Helios: sun god. The name brings travel, passion, sexuality, glory, and determination.

Hermes: messenger of the gods. His symbols are a winged cap and sandals. As a name, it brings increased acuity for intellect, communication, commerce, and a sense of freedom.

Melanion: husband to the nature and hunting goddess Atalanta, who vowed she would only wed the man who could beat her in a foot race. A name of competition, victory, guile, fleetness, and union with nature.

Minos: husband to Pasiphae and father to Ariadne. Poseidon caused his wife Pasiphae to fall in love with a white bull with whom she mated and gave birth to the Minotaur. After his death, Minos became a judge in the underworld. It is a name of sovereignty, honor, justice, and judgment.

Momus: god of mockery and spiteful criticism. This would be a good name for one who seeks to control his sarcasm, rudeness, cruelty, and overly critical nature.

His was a festive wedding, and inside the
house she bore to Hermes a dear son,
from birth monstrous to behold, with
goat's feet and two horns, boisterous and
sweet-laughing. His mother sprang up and
fled; the nurse in turn left the child
behind because she was afraid when
she saw his wild and well-bearded
visage. Helpful Hermes quickly received him
into his arms, and in his divine heart
the joy overflowed. He wrapped the child in
snug skins of mountain hares and
swiftly went to the abodes of the immortals.
He then set him down beside Zeus
and the other Gods and showed them his boy:
all of them were delighted in their
hearts and Bacchic Dionysos above all others.
They called him Pan because he cheered
the hearts of all.

—HOMER
THE HOMERIC HYMNS

I shall sing of Zeus, the best and the
greatest of Gods, far-seeing, mighty,
fulfiller of designs who confides his tight-
knit schemes to Themis as she sits
leaning upon him. Have mercy, far-seeing
Kronides, most glorious and great!

—HOMER
THE HOMERIC HYMNS

Morpheus: god of dreams. Dweller in the underworld. Son of death and nephew of sleep. An excellent name for bringing prophetic dreams, awareness, release, rest, and goal setting.

Orion: a hunter who loved the seven daughters of Atlas and pursued them. Zeus placed them in the sky to keep them from him. After death he was placed in the sky in endless pursuit of them. A name for bringing the essence of the hunt, pursuit, energy, determination, desire, and dealing with losing the object of your desire.

Pan: god of flocks. Body of a man but the horns, ears, and legs of a goat. He is playful, vigorous, lusty, and fertile. A powerful sexual name that brings lustiness, freedom, unabashed sexuality, eroticism, desire, longevity, and potency.

Paris: he was a prince of Troy who abducted Helen and began the Trojan war. This took place because he was challenged by the gods to choose who was the fairest—Hera, Athena, or Aphrodite. Hera offered him wealth and power, Athena offered wisdom, and Aphrodite offered love of the most beautiful woman in the world. Aphrodite won, and Helen of Troy was his reward. Paris died during the Trojan War. This name is a good one for bringing about change, making decisions, choosing wisely, and developing diplomacy.

Satyr: forest and mountain spirits who are crude, orgiastic, sexual, lusty, and wild.

A good name for developing more potent sexuality.

Zeus: a supreme deity. A name for developing power, omnipotence, fecundity, creativity, and authority.

GODS OF INDIA

Brahma: a creation god. Son of Kali. He divided himself into his male and female aspects. His wife was the goddess of music, speech, and the arts. One of his wives gave birth to the Universe. A creative, vital, balanced name evoking a balance between male and female.

Buddha: beautiful and radiant god. Son of Tara the star goddess and Soma the moon god. This is a powerful name with strong lunar influence.

Chandra: means "moon." Pre-Vedic lunar god. Married to Rohini, the cow goddess. A lunar influence name that brings about subtle change and gradual enlightenment.

Ganesha: god of good fortune, literature, and wisdom. He is a happy god. He has the head of an elephant and the body of a man. Husband to "intellect and intuition" and "achievement." He is worshiped before any new venture to ensure wealth and success. This is a success-oriented name that may bring wealth, wisdom, and respect.

By the sensual pleasures he gives them,
Krishna delights all women; at the
touch of his limbs, as dark and gentle
as a string of lotus-flowers, they know
the delights of love, while the beauties in
the heifer park kiss him to their hearts'
content . . . May the learned souls,
who seek ecstasy in Vishnu,
learn from the song of Govinda
awareness of what makes
the essence of love!

—GITA-GOVINDA

Hanuman: monkey god. He has incredible physical strength. He was virile, chaste, intelligent, and loyal. He was utterly devoted to Rama. This name suggests power through intellect and good intentions, a strong will, a strong body, a strong mind, and a strong set of ethics.

Indra: warrior and storm god. A name that brings about rapid change.

Kama/Kamadeva: god of love. A winged child who has a bow and arrow, like Cupid. Husband to "pleasure." A name to choose to bring eroticism into one's life; also love, romance, and renewal of passion.

Krishna: an avatar of Vishnu. Charming, erotic, strong, and impudent. This is a name that brings popularity with women, strength, and daring.

Varuna: a sky and water god. Also god of the dead, justice, and the moon. A good name for bringing justice, rewards, and fair compensation into one's life.

IRISH / CELTIC GODS

Amergin ("a-MORE-gin;" *g* as in "gone"): Irish. The bard and spokesman of the Milesians. Author of the traditional poem that begins, "I am a stag of seven tines." This is a good name for a poet, spokes- person, or a writer, for it brings poetry, inspiration, communication, and wisdom.

Balor ("BAIL-lore"): Irish. King of the Fomors. Husband to Danu. He possessed a magic eye that could kill just by looking at an opponent. His grandson Lugh killed him by throwing a rock into his magic eye. Balor is a good magical name for those who seek enlightenment, foresight, and the ability to see beyond the facades of others to their true motivations.

Borvo: Celtic. European Celtic god of hot springs. This would be a good name for a hot tub. It is also a name that is beneficial for inducing healing, comfort, relaxation, and letting go.

Bres: Irish. Husband to Brighid. He was king of the Tuatha but lacked the generosity and compassion that are necessary to rule. He was satirized, ridiculed, and labeled unfit to rule. This is a name to take to learn from your mistakes; for developing generosity, compassion, leadership abilities, and, most importantly, to listen to and learn from those around you.

Cernunnos ("ker- NU-nos"): Celtic. Horned nature god. Portrayed with animals. The details of the mythology of Cernunnos are lost, but from our experiences during drawing down this god, it can be assumed that he was a god of the basic wild forest energies, the running of the deer, and the chattering of the tiny creatures. He is of moss and lichen, antler and wood. He is of wild mating and valiant dying. This, then, would be a name for one who seeks the hushed tranquillity of the forest, knowledge of the cycles of life, and the fertility, longevity, and strength represented by an old forest.

Creidhne ("KREEN-nah"): Irish. Bronze worker who made the weapons with which the Tuatha de Danann defeated the Fomors. A name that works for any artesian, metal worker, sculptor, or smithy. It also speaks of skill, cunning, and victory.

Daghda ("dagda"): Irish. The good god. Main god of the Tuatha de Danann. He was a warrior, magician, artisan, and sage. He was a mighty warrior who possessed the cauldron of plenty from which no one left dissatisfied. His name brings strength, wisdom, fertility, sexual potency, abundance, protection, valor, hospitality, and rebirth.

Diancecht ("DIANE-kecked"): Irish. Healer god of the Tuatha de Danann. This name brings healing skill, artistry, compassion, and kindness.

Diarmuid ("dermut"): Irish. Hero of a love myth involving Grainne, who was betrothed to Fionn Mac Cumhail. She and Diarmuid fell in love and ran away. Diarmuid was eventually killed by a boar. The Celtic love god took pity on them and breathed life into Diarmuid's dead body. This is an excellent name to take when pursuing a love interest. The name brings romance, love, sexuality, passion, and desire.

Donn: Irish. Celtic god of the dead. A name for mourning the deceased and understanding death and rebirth.

Fergus: Irish. Lusty god of prodigious sexual appetites. A potent name for enhancing one's sexual capability.

Luchtaine ("luck-TAINE"): Irish. The woodworker master who helped make the weapons with which the Tuatha de Danaan defeated the Fomors. This is a name that lends skill, craftsmanship, artistry, and creativity.

Lugh ("looh"): Irish. Also Lugh Samhioldanach ("of many arts") or Lugh Lamhfhada ("of the long hand"). Young god who supplanted the old god (Balor). This is a warrior name bringing power, youth, strength, and victory.

Mac Cecht ("mac-KECKED") Irish. Tuatha de Danann god who represents the earth. Husband to Fodhla, the mother aspect of Ireland's trinity. This is an earth name bringing fertility, stability, and security.

MacCuill ("mack-QUIHL"): Irish. Tuatha de Danann god symbolizing the primordial water element. Husband to Banbha, the crone aspect of the trinity that symbolized Ireland. This is a name for new beginnings, or for going back and exploring your own.

MacGreine ("mack-GRAIN"): Irish. Tuatha de Danann god symbolizing the fire element. His wife, Eire, was the maiden aspect of Ireland's trinity. This name brings passion, youth, determination, and drive.

Miach ("mee-ACK"): Irish. A physician. When Nuada lost his hand, Miach made him a silver hand to replace it. Diancecht killed him for doing so. This is a name that brings healing powers, especially when suffering the loss of a limb.

Mider: Irish. Gaelic king of the underworld. Husband of the goddess of reincarnation. This name lends the bearer an appreciation of the cycles of life, the ability to cope with death, renewed hope in life, and rejuvenation.

Oghma ("OG-mah"): Irish. God of wisdom and writing. This name would be helpful to a writer, student, poet, philosopher, or someone who wished to become one of these.

Pooka: Irish. An ancient pre-Celtic god who degenerated into a malicious spirit. This name is suggestive of a deterioration of fortune. It is for overcoming such downfalls and learning from them.

Shoney: Scottish and Irish Celtic. Sea god. A water energy name bringing with it the power of the sea, which can awaken psychic abilities and bring insight, prophetic dreams, and wisdom.

NORSE / TEUTONIC GODS

Aegir: Scandinavian. Sea god. He lives with his wife and daughters in a palace under the sea lit by the gleam of sunken treasure. They work together to lure sailors to their doom. A water name. Also a name that brings a sense of working together as a team, an acceptance of death as part of the cycle, and working within that context.

Balder: Norse. Most beautiful of the Norse gods; god of the sun. A name to use for improving self-esteem, confidence, wisdom, and pride.

Donar: Teutonic. Thunder god. Known as Thunar to the Anglo Saxons and Thor to Scandinavians (see Thor).

Farbauti: Scandinavian. Fire god. He gave birth to fire and his wife was a wooded isle who fed the fire. A fire name that brings the warmth of the home fire, domesticity, the magic of the flame, and rewards for labor.

Frey: Norse. God of weather and fruitfulness. Protector of marriage. A name that brings fertility, solidity, and the power to weather the storm.

Heimdahl: Norse. Guardian of the rainbow bridge, Bifrost, which leads from Earth to the home of the gods. He is the son of many virgins and is tall, handsome, and fertile. This is a fertility name, a name for bringing safety on a trip, for travelling to extraordinary places, and for confidence in one's travels.

Hoder/Hodur: Norse. God of night. Blind son of Odin. A name for dealing with darkness and the unknown.

Hoeni/Hoenir: Norse. God who gave the first humans the ability to move and think. A name that suggests fleetness, intelligence, and the ability to bestow these traits in others. A good name for a physical therapist.

Loki: Scandinavian. Trickster god. A quick-witted, silver-tongued, cunning, crafty, and unpredictable god. A god who can be a great asset or painful liability, but always unique. A name to be used for breaking free of regimen, learning not to rely on routine, and accepting the crazy twists and turns in life and "lightening up." When you take on the name Loki, anything may happen. Just let it.

Mimir: Norse. The god of prophecy. Guardian of the meadow of poets, and streams, and lakes. A name for wisdom, prophecy, poetry, insight, inspiration, intuition, and water energy.

Njord: Norse. Also Niord or Njoerd. Husband to Skadi, who longed for her native mountains while she lived at Njord's seashore. She eventually left to return home. A name about allowing others the freedom to follow their bliss. A name for becoming less controlling, less commanding, and for no longer needing everything your way.

Odin: Norse. Supreme god. Warrior's god who also oversaw poetry, magic, and the underworld. A father name that brings fertility, creativity, power, strength, courage, and the poetic heart of the true warrior.

"Immortals are what you wanted," said Thor in a low, quiet voice. "Immortals are what you got. It is a little hard on us. You wanted us to be forever, so we are forever. Then you forget about us. But still we are forever. Now at last, many are dead, many dying," he then added in a quiet voice, "but it takes a special effort."

"I can't even begin to understand what you're talking about," said Kate, "you say that I, we—"

"You can begin to understand," said Thor angrily, "which is why I have come to you. Do you know that most people hardly see me? . . . It is not that we are hidden. We are here. We move among you. . . . You gave birth to us. You made us be what you would not dare to be yourselves. Yet you will not acknowledge us. If I walk along one of your streets in this . . . world you have made for yourselves without us, then barely an eye will once flicker in my direction."

—DOUGLAS ADAMS
THE LONG, DARK TEA-TIME OF THE SOUL

"Tonight I must go to Asgard," he said. "I must confront my father, Odin, in the great hall of Valhalla and bring him to account for what he has done."

"You mean, for making you count Welsh pebbles?"

"No!" said Thor. "For making the Welsh pebbles not worth counting!"

Kate shook her head in exasperation. "I simply don't know what to make of you at all," she said. "I think I'm just too tired. Come back tomorrow. Explain it all in the morning."

"No," said Thor. "You must see Asgard yourself, and then you will understand. You must see it tonight." He gripped her by the arm.

"I don't want to go to Asgard," she insisted. "I don't go to mythical places with strange men. You go. Call me up and tell me how it went in the morning. Give him hell about the pebbles."

—DOUGLAS ADAMS
THE LONG, DARK TEA-TIME OF THE SOUL

Sigmund: Norse. Warrior hero who pulled a sword from a tree, which Odin had placed there. He was thereafter a victorious warrior until Odin struck him down. Sigmund refused to be healed and chose to submit himself to Odin's will. This is a name for ridding oneself from being too controlling; for doing the best you can with the tools you have and leaving the rest to the gods. This is a name for an overachiever, a workaholic, or a perfectionist who wants to be less controlling.

Thor: Norse. God of thunder and the sky. Peasant's god. A name that brings power, authority, support for the working class; useful for letting out pent-up anger and expressing one's feelings.

Ull: Norse. God of skiers. A good name to take when you hit the slopes.

PHOENICIAN GODS

Adad: also Addu or Hadad. Storm god who brings fertilizing rain. A fertilityname. On a different level, a storm god name often brings rewards for dealing with one's stormy (or violent) emotions.

Adoni: vegetation god. Mate of Astarte. He has his cycle of growth, death, and rebirth. This name is an excellent one for grasping the cycle of life and death, for rejuvenation, growth, and coping with growing older.

Aleyin: also Aleion, Aleyn. God of springtime weather. Ruler of rainfall, clouds, and wind. A blustering, replenishing, fertility-causing name.

Baal: vegetation and storm god. A fertility name that brings the winds of change.

Dagon: sea god. A water elemental name.

Eliun: primordial Father God. Husband to Beruth, the Mother Goddess. Interms of a magical name, Eliun is one to bring fertility, the components necessary for new beginnings, and rejuvenation.

Eshmun/Esmun: healer god. Means "he whom we invoke." For use when healing is of paramount consideration.

Genos: means "race." He was the first person. His children were "first-born"and "life." His grandchildren were "light," "fire," and "flame." This is a name that suggests beginnings; going back to one's origins to work on old baggage.

Kolpia: wind god. To invite the winds of change to sweep through your house.

Pontus: means "sea." Sea god. Son of the Earth Mother. A water energy name involving creativity and new beginnings.

Salem: also Shalem or Shelim. Means "evening star." A name that brings a faint glimmer of understanding, a subtle enlightenment, and the attainment of your wishes.

ROMAN GODS

Aeolus: Roman and Greek. God of wind. He keeps the wind chained in deep caverns on a distant island. This is a powerful air name bringing insight, intelligence, change, and power.

Cupid: god of love. Son of Venus. He was the god of lovers. It was to him people came to ask for love and romance. This is a good name for a lonely man who seeks true love and romance to fill his empty life.

Faunus: god of forests and merrymaking. Means "the kindly one." He oversees the fruitfulness of the fields and of animals. He had psychic powers. This is a name of fertility, protection of the forests and the forest animals, and for learning to hear the whisper of the oracle in the depth of an old-growth forest.

Janus: god of beginnings. He watched over the doors and gates. He was seen as having two heads looking in opposite directions. Sacred to him were the first hour of the day, the first day of the week, and the first month of the year. This is an excellent name for new beginnings, new partnerships, business ventures, relationships, new jobs, or the beginning of anything to ensure it goes smoothly.

Jupiter/Jove: sky god. Supreme deity in Roman myth. Also known as Jupiter Lucetius (light-bringer). The full moon and the Ides were sacred to him. He is a god of thunder and lightning. His temples were erected upon places that had been struck by lightning. He acted as a conscience for his followers, being concerned with oaths, alliances, and treaties. He was also involved with protection and guardianship. This is a good name for a father to help guide, protect, guard, and teach the value of one's word.

Lares: protector and god of crossroads. A good name to take to bring safe and uneventful travel.

Mars: war god. Father of Romulus. Also an agricultural god protecting the fields from disease in times of peace. He was summoned in the spring with a shaking of his sacred spears and the cry *"Mars vigila!"* ("Mars, wake up!") when war was at hand. Laurel is sacred to him. His name can be used as a protective, powerful, and awe-inspiring name. It can be used to increase your assertiveness, strength of will, conviction, and resolve.

Mercury: god of trade. He insures good harvests and abundant trading. This is a good name for those who seek success in business or who are looking for a job. It is especially good for sales work.

Neptune: Sea god. Husband to Salacia, goddess of salt water. This is a powerful water name bringing the power of the sea, intuition, and a depth of emotion. This is a particularly good name for someone who is shut off from his emotions and unable to deal with his feelings.

Orcus: god of death. An underworld god, and the name of the underworld itself. He stole the living from the earth by force and took them to the underworld. This is a name for dealing with the seemingly meaningless and cruel aspects of death.

Penates: household gods. The domain of these protective gods is indoors, as opposed to the gods of the outdoors (Lares). The Penates protected the hearth and home, pantry and larder. There was a shrine honoring the Penates just inside the front door of a house so one might honor them as they entered. This is a name to charge with protection of one's hearth and family.

Picunnus: god of newborn babies. He and his brother Pilumnus are protectors of babies. They were made welcome in the bedrooms of hopeful parents. This is a fertility name or one to bring protection to infants.

Saturn: god of agriculture. He is a god of sowing seed. He is seen holding a sickle or ear of corn that symbolizes abundance. This name brings with it abundance, fertility, plenty, success, and prosperity.

Silvanus: god of uncleared land. He oversees the clearing and ploughing of wild land. This is a good name to take when one begins a new garden or builds a house on uncleared land.

Summanus: god of nighttime thunder. Brings change, energy, courage, and power. In addition, it also suggests mystery and dealing with that which is hidden (perhaps hidden fears?).

Vertumnus: shapeshifting god of gardens and orchards. Consort of Pomona. This name brings fertility, abundance, protection, fruitfulness, and growth. Great name for a gardener.

Vulcan: god of fire. Husband to Venus, goddess of love. He was a feared god, bringing fire when it wasn't wanted. To placate him, shrines were set up outside the walls of the city to ask protection of things that might readily burn, such as storage houses full of dry grain.

This is a name that brings fire energy, temper, rage, and destruction. Use it carefully; it can bring motivation, but it cuts both ways.

WELSH GODS

Amathaon ("am-ah-THAY-on"): a magician, son of the Goddess Don. *Amaeth,* the root word from which his name springs, means "ploughman" or "farmer." In *The Mabinogi,* the book of Welsh folk tales, it says "The only husbandman who can farm land or prepare it is Amathon son of Don, so wild is it." This suggests a name that is a combination of magician and farmer. Anyone who has gardened knows there is potent magic at work. This name would be

taken to understand more about the magic that causes plants to grow. It would also be for helping to tame wildness, increasing fertility, and for planting the seeds of self-transformation.

Arawn ("ah-ROAN") king of the Otherworld, Annwn ("ah NOOIN"). He rides a white horse in pursuit of a stag and is followed by his red-eared, white hunting dogs. This is a name for understanding or accepting death, for recovering from grief at losing a loved one, or for dealing with troubling transitions in life.

Beli ("BAY-ley"): father god. Husband to Don, father to Arianrhod, grandfather to Lleu. Seen as a great progenitor. This is a name that brings fatherhood and being the head of a large extended family.

Belanus ("bell-ANN-ous") Welsh/Roman. An underworld god. A name for a sage.

Bran: Welsh/Manx. Son of Llry and Iweridd, brother to Branwen. He was killed when avenging the death of his sister, but his head was brought back and it continued to speak, giving counsel for eighty years. Bran is a good name for one who likes to speak, or perhaps for endowing a shy person with the ability to speak comfortably (and at length). This is a name that brings strong communication skills.

Caswallawn ("cass-WHAH-hlaon"): a usurper of England. Uncle/ cousin to Bran and Branwen. He has a cloak of invisibility that he used to cause calamity. This name suggests slyness, sneakiness, deviousness, and guile. If you have need of these things, then this is the name for you.

Dylan: sea god. Son of Arianrhod and Gwydion. He married the Lady of the Lake, who bore him Vivienne (or Nimue), who became Merlin's lover. This is a name that brings magic, fertility, and magical children.

Gwydion ("gwid-E-ohn") bard and magician. Son of Don and brother to Arianrhod; together they parented Lleu Llaw Gyffes and Dylan. He was taught the secrets of magic by Math. Gwydion killed Pryderi. This is an-other of the many magical, mystical, and wizardly names in the Welsh pantheon.

Llyr ("hleer") Welsh, Manx, and Irish. Father to Branwen, Bran, Creiddylad, and Manannan mac Lir. His four eldest children were turned into swans by his second wife. Origin of Shakespeare's King Lear. A father name to bring responsibility, sound judgement, and fertility.

Mabon ("may-BON"): means "great son." Known as Maponus to the Romans. A hunter god, son of Modron (meaning "great mother"). He was kidnaped with he was an infant and rescued by Arthur. He is seen as a male version of Persephone. Gwair is another name of Mabon (the prisoner who must be released). This imprisonment aspect to the character is very strong.

It can be used for those who find themselves trapped (in a dead-end job, bad marriage, debt, etc.) and seek ways to escape. Taking the name of one who was trapped and rescued would help release the bonds.

Nwyvre ("new-EEE-vear"): means sky, space, or stars. Space god. Arianrhod's husband. He slipped into almost total obscurity. Since we know so little about his nature and his realm, we must assign our own meanings to him. He is a space god, dealing with that outside of the bonds of Earth. Perhaps he has disappeared until we take up space travel and have need of him. It may be time to bring him back.

Pryderi ("PREED-ahrie"): son of Pwyll and Rhiannon. Rhiannon was thought to have killed him when he was an infant and was punished for it, but he returned and revealed that he had been abducted. His name means "free from anxiety." He suffered misunderstanding and enmity of the gods. He was slain by the magician Gwydion. This is a name that describes a tolerance for abuse and an ability to wait out injustice and captivity to be free from anxiety. This is a good transitional name for someone who must suffer abuse while he plans the changes he must make to leave an abusive situation.

Taliesin ("tally-EE-sin"): means "radiant brow." Son of Cerridwen. The supreme seer poet who lives in the region of the summer stars. He is a harper, sage, seer, poet, initiate, and wizard. The name suggests these talents.

Ysbadadden ("ees-bah-DATH-ehn"): father of Olwyn. He was to die if his daughter married, and he was not able to prevent her marriage. The father, daughter, and husband represent the sacrificial trinity as in Holly King/Oak King and May Queen archetypes. The maiden is fought over by an old love and a young love, with the youthful one always victorious. These three represent the spring maiden, her winter lover, and her summer lover. Ysbadadden is the older, winter figure, a father or older man who is bowing to the younger man and forgoing the young woman. This is a good name to take at a saging ritual (a male equivalent of a croning).

chapter nineteen

MAGICAL NAMES FROM
OTHER CULTURES

I have included here a listing of names from a
variety of cultural sources. I have attempted
to omit any names that are biblical or derived
from other religions. I have also attempted to
omit any names that are merely feminine forms
of men's names. Women deserve names of their
own. While these names are good for naming
babies, they are also good choices for a magical
name. Pagans sometimes like to choose their
magical name from their culture of origin. Many
also choose names from the culture whose deities
and myths they work with in ritual. Feel free to
choose from other cultures. There is a
freedom for someone who has been brought up
enmeshed in their culture to take a name from an
alien culture. It says something about beginnings,
forming new traditions, being open to borrowing

wisdom and strengths from other cultures, and creativity. Many of these names are creative, unusual, beautiful, poetic even. I have gathered names from the following ethnic or cultural groups:

African

African-American

Armenian

Basque

Burmese

Cambodian

Celtic/Gaelic

Ethiopian

English/Welsh/Anglo-Saxon

Finnish

French

Greek

Hawaiian

Hispanic

Indian

Irish

Kenyan

Latin

Native North American

Teutonic

AFRICAN

Female

Abadi: comforter.

Adero: comes to make things better.

Adila: fair.

Ananda: bliss.

Anisa: joy.

Anukis: embrace.

Arawet: moon.

Aster: star.

Atum: accomplished.

Bahari: sea.

Besma: smile.

Dapo: brings together.

Davu: beginning.

Diketi: small girl.

Dukana: darkness.

Fanus: bright light.

Hasana: beautiful.

Hirsi: amulet.

Hoshoba: fancy.

Isabis: beautiful.

Iya: mother.

Janina: garden.

Kei: white.

Kileken: Venus.

Kione: comes from nowhere.

Kitoko: beautiful.

Kenda: December.

Lostris: daughter of the water.

Luam: calm.

Mabili: east wind.

Maha: beautiful eyes.

Malek: river spirit.

Malomo: don't go.

Mashava: red.

Mawu: queen of the universe.

Mo: substance of life.

Moke: little.

Morathi: seer.

Sadiki: believe.

Sarama: nice.

Shasa: precious water.

Shori: nightingale.

Tala: mirror.

Tarana: daytime.

Teshi: prone to laughter, cheerful.

Tiaret: lioness.

Tuli: silent person.

Ujana: youth.

Winta: desire.

Yalwa: abundance.

Zarina: golden.

Zena: fame.

Male

Borbor: small boy.

Cheelo: animal.

Cherif: noble.

Horus: hawk.

Issay: hairy.

Jumoke: everyone loves him.

Junza: tomorrow.

Kasim: controls anger.

Kerimu: liberal.

Kesho: future.

Khensu: moon god.

Kondo: fox.

Kunzi: electric.

Muchese: blade of a knife.

Mudashiru: cloaked one.

Mugesi: brave.

Murogi: magic.

Nafasi: good times.

Nasha: rain.

Niko: I am here.

Oburu: ash.

Pajonga: tall man.

Rabi: mystic.

Rahwa: better life.

Ramosa: friend.

Swahili: belongs to the coast.

Tai: eagle.

Taifa: tribe.

Yifter: craftsman.

Zo: spiritual leader.

Zuli: brilliant.

The Name is the Spirit.

—LALA OF ZAIRE

When a person is given a name,
his spirits accept it.

—IBO OF NIGERIA

Ancient things remain in the ears.

—ASHANTI OF GHANA

AFRICAN-AMERICAN NAMES

Many of these names were chosen by African-Americans from the 1600s to the mid-1940s as documented by Dr. Newbell Puckett. These are some of the best, most creative names I've encountered. A mix of antiquated names, surnames, and newly created names provides a refreshing list of unique and beautiful names. So many of these names had unknown origins that I chose not to provide meanings for the names in this list. Most of them were made up out of other names or place names. Not having a meaning does not reduce the name's effectiveness as we can imbue them with meaning in a naming ritual. Besides, once upon a time, we ourselves attached the meanings to our name words. They didn't come that way. If we could do it then, we can do it now. As many of the words are new, they aren't established as having specific meanings so there isn't any old baggage to overcome. These refreshing names are like a clean slate. I have long been a fan of the creativity and musicality of African-American and Southern name stocks.

Female

Abarena

Abba

Abriana

Addie

Adelaide

Adesta

Ailese

Airlessa

Aisey

Alabama

Alanza

Aldara

Alvira

Alzora

Amarillis

Amertine

Anaka

Ardella

Aretha

Arizona

Arnell

Arsula

Arva

Ashanta

Authertine

Avis

Azuba

Bellah

Belzara

Bemshi

Berit

Bertina

Bria

Brooklyn (-lynne)

Calandra

California

Camera

Casina

Cedrice

Chalina

Chanda

Chandra

China

Clementine

Comfort

Crecia

Dacia

Danula

Daya

Dearie

Deka

Delta

Desdemona

Dewonda

Dinora

Dixie

Dorcey

D'juna (JUNE-ah)

Egypt

Elester

Ellabelle	Hazel
Elmira	Hesper
Elza	Honey
Elzara	Hope
Emmaline	Inda
Enid	Isadora
Enola	Jada
Ensa	Jamaica
Ethiopia	Jamila
Etoria	Janel
Etta	Jannon
Eurcelyn	Jestine
Evora	Jewel
Fancy	Joella
Fanny	Joy
Fatima	Juda
Fatrice	Julet
Fawn	Kalina
Feeby	Kansas
Florida	Karma
Flossie	Kata
Fredonia	Katia
Galina	Keisha
Genora	Kendra
Geronda	Kinshasha
Haddie	Kizzie
Hallie	Laney
Hattie	Latiffah

Latrice

Laurice

Lavanda

Lenora

Leria

Lerona

Lestine

Letha

Lexie

Litha

Lorelei

Lorna

Lovie

Lucretia

Lura

Macedonia

Madena

Madora

Mahala

Mahogany

Maizie

Marlee

Marthena

Marva

Matoka

Mattiwilda

Maydelle

Maynell

Mayola

Melba

Memphis

Minta

Missouri

Montana

Myrtaline

Narcissus

Neala

Nedra

Nefertia

Nelta

Nerine

Nevada

Nodie

Nydia

Oprah

Orleans

Palmira

Paloma

Pandora

Patrina

Pepita

Petrina

Philomela

Philomina

Pink

Polly

Portia	Symora
Quandra	Synestine
Rain	Tabina
Ramona	Taffy
Raynoma	Taj
Riva	Tajama
Ruby	Talitha
Rudene	Tallulah
Rufina	Tatiana
Sabina	Tatum
Sadie	Teacake
Sage	Texanna
Samalla	Thulani
Saphronia	Tiny
Sarata	Treece
Savannah	Trese
Savory	Tulie
Scarlett	Ulyssandra
Sedonia	Ulystine
Seraphina	Undine
Shaba	Unis
Shanice	Utah
Sheena	Valenda
Shefroi	Valora
Sojourner	Vana
Sree	Vanity
Sula	Vanora
Surice	Velma

Velvet

Verda

Vermona

Vernice

Vesta

Virginia

Wanda

Westina

Whoopi

Willie Mae

Winna

Winona

Wonderful

Wyomia

Yasmin

Zelda

Zelma

Zenith

Zia

Zoa

Zora

Zura

Male

Adger

Augie

Aurven

Basie

Baz

Booker

Borel

Brimmer

Britus

Canada

Carvel

Carver

Cato

Cazzie

Chance

Chauncey

Chester

Chico

Clayborne

Clayton

Cleon

Clovis

Congo

Cornell

Craigory

Crispus

Cujoe

Darby

Darius

Darnley

Darwin

Dekovas

Delmar

Delwyn

Denzel

Derby

Devaughn

Dewey

Dexter

Dondre

Doyle

Duffy

Dupree

Durant

Early

Earvin

Edolphus

Elden

Eldridge

Eldzier

Elgin

Ellic

Elmo

Elmore

Elrick

Elton

Elvern

Elvert

Elvin

Emlen

Endris

Ennis

Errol

Erskine

Etheridge

Eubie

Eudell

Eulis

Evander

Evers

Eyton

Fairfax

Farris

Felder

Fenton

Finis

Flanders

Fletcher

Flint

Gaius

Galen

Gamaliel

Gardelle

Garrick

Gavil

Gayraud

Gevin

Gillance

Gilmore

Goffee

Grantley

Gylan

Hadley

Hamlet

Hamlin

Hampton

Hannibal

Hawthorne

Hayward

Haywood

Herschel

Hollis

Holmes

Homer

Horace

Howell

Hughlyn

Hulan

Huxley

Hyder

Innis

Ivory

Jarek

Jaron

Jarrell

Jarrett

Jarrod

Jasper

Jenkin

Jermaine

Jerrick

Juber

Judson

Kaream

Keane

Keenan

Kelby

Kelton

Kelvin

Kennard

Kentrell

Kermit

Kimball

Knoll

Knolton

LaBron

Lamar

Lambert

Lander

Larrimore

Larron

Lawanza

Lennox

Lenus

Levander

Lex

Liberty

Llewellyn

Lonzie

Lysander

MacArthur

Marlon

Marlow

Medgar

Mifflin

Mingo

Mookie

Mookinga

Morland

Mozell

Nat

Nayland

Nead

Needham

Neeley

Nesbit

Nimrod

Norvell

Novora

Octavious

Ollie

Olphin

Onando

Ornette

Orrin

Orson

Osborn

Otis

Ozzie

Paraway

Parlan

Parlett

Parry

Paxton

Perrin

Pervis

Pompey

Porter

Prescott

Primus

Putnam

Quade

Quinby

Quinn

Rafer

Ragis

Raleigh

Ramsey

Rance

Rand

Ransford

Ravell

Rayburn

Rean	Smith
Reggie	Stedman
Renny	Sterling
Rex	Swain
Rice	Tabor
Riddick	Taggart
Riordan	Tanton
Roarke	Tarleton
Rollin	Teague
Roman	Tedmond
Royd	Terrill
Rufus	Terris
Rylan	Thaddeus
Sabra	Tharon
Sandor	Thayer
Santana	Thurgood
Seafus	Thurman
Sebastian	Tibe
Selby	Tingo
Seldon	Titus
Selvin	Toby
Seneca	Tower
Sextus	Tremain
Shane	Trey
Shaw	True
Shim	Tucker
Sigh	Tunis
Sipeo (CPO)	Ulric
Sloan	Unis

Upton

Urban

Uthaw

Vallis

Vander

Varick

Vaughn

Veo

Visker

Wade

Walden

Waldo

Walker

Ware

Wayland

Weldon

Whitby

Whitney

Whittaker

Winton

Woodrow

Wycliffe

York

Zacko

Zango

Zanza

Zed

Zeno

Zindel

Zinka

Zoltan

Zuriel

ARMENIAN

Anahid: goddess of the moon.

Astrid: Persian. Star.

Nairi: land of canyons.

Siran: lovely.

BASQUE

Izar ("ee SAHR"): star.

Lur: Earth.

Nora: Greek. Light.

Pellkita: Latin. Happy.

BURMESE

Mima: woman.

Mya: emerald.

CAMBODIAN

Chan: sweet-smelling tree.

Chantrea ("CHAN-thee-ay"): moonshine.

Dara: stars.

CELTIC / GAELIC NAMES

Female

Aine: fairy queen at Knockany Hill.

Aislin: dream.

Alina: distant place.

Alyce: noble.

Ashling ("ais-LING"): dream.

Asthore: loved one.

Aurnia: historic name.

Avril: April.

Betha: life.

Bonnie: pretty.

Breeda: from Goddess Bried.

Brenna: raven maid.

Briana: the strong; powerful.

Bride/Brigid/Bridget: strong (from the goddess).

Brona: sorrow.

Caitlin: Kathleen.

Calum ("CAL-um"): dove.

Cara: friend.

Catriona ("KAT-ree-own-ah"): Catherine.

Daireen: literary name.

Darcy: dark one.

Deirdre: ("DEE-druh"): sorrow.

Devin ("dev-IN"): poet.

Doon: a landmark name.

Duvessa: dark beauty.

Eavan: fair form.

Edana: little fire.

Edwina: prosperous friend.

Enid: the spirit or soul.

Ennis/Erin/Erina: island.

Fenella: fair.

Finna: medieval Icelandic name from Fionn (fair).

Finola/Fiona/Fionnagh: fair or white.

Genevieve: magic sighs.

Glenna: valley.

Grainne: grain goddess.

Grania/Granna: love.

Guinevere/Gweneth: white or fair lady.

Hazel: tree.

Iseult: lover of Tristram in Arthurian legend.

Isolda/Isolde/Isolt: the fair.

Janel/Jannel/Jannell: darling.

Keelia/Keelin/Keely: beauty.

Kelly: female warrior.

Kerry: dark-haired.

Kyla/Kylia: lovely.

Mabbina/Maeve: intoxicating one.

Mavelle: Celtic. songbird.

Maili/Molly: bitter.

Margery: form of Maeve.

Morag ("MAW-rack"): princess.

Morrin: long-haired.

Neala: chieftainess.

Nessa: form of Agnes.

Niamh: Irish mythical princess of the land of promise.

Nola: noble.

Nora/Norah: honor.

Nuala: form of Fionnuala.

Onora/Ownah: lamb.

Peigi ("PAEG-ee"): pearl.

Ranalt: name dating from the twelfth century.

Rhona: rough island.

Riona: queenly.

Rona: sea.

Ronat: seal.

Rowena: Celtic. White mane.

Sabia/Sabina: goodness.

Saraid: excellent.

Shannon: little wise one.

Siobhan ("sha-VAHN"): ancient name.

Tara: tower.

Ula: jewel of the sea.

Vevina: Gaelic. Sweet lady.

Wynne: fair; light-skinned.

Yseult: the fair.

Male

Ahern: lord of horses.

Aidan: hearth fire.

Angus: from the love god.

Arlen: pledge.

Arthur: noble.

Baird: ballad singer.

Bevan: warrior's son.

Bowen: yellow-haired.

Brady: spirited.

Bram: raven.

Bren/Brendon/Brennon: little raven.

Brett: Briton.

Brock: badger.

Broderick: fertile flatland.

Brody: ditch.

Calhoun: warrior.

Callum: messenger of peace.

Camden: from the winding valley.

Cameron: crooked nose.

Campbell: crooked mouth.

Carlin: little champion.

Carson: son of the family on the marsh.

Casey: valorous, brave.

Cassidy: clever.

Cathal: great warrior; battle mighty.

Chalmers: son of the lord.

Chay: fairy place.

Cheney: from the oak forest.

Collin: child.

Conlan: hero.

Conway: hound of the plain.

Cormac/Cormick: charioteer.

Cory: mountain glen.

Cowan: hillside hollow.

Cullen: handsome.

Curran: hero.

Dacey: southerner.

Dagda: the good god.

Dallan/Dallas: wise.

Dane: after Goddess Danu.

Darby: free man.

Darcy: dark.

Daron: great little one.

Darren/Darrin: great.

Delaney: descendant of the challenger.

Desmond: man from Munster.

Devan: poet.

Diancecht: Irish god.

Dillon: faithful.

Donegal: dark.

Donnelly: brave dark man.

Donnovan: dark warrior.

Doyle: dark stranger.

Driscoll: interpreter.

Druce: wise man.

Duncan: dark-skinned warrior.

Edan: fiery.

Ennis: island.

Evan/Ewan/Ewen: young warrior.

Farrell: valorous.

Fearghus: strong man.

Ferrell: valorous.

Ferris: the rock; iron worker.

Finn: fair-haired (from Irish mythical giant Finn MacCool).

Forbes: prosperous.

Galen: intelligent.

Gallagher: eager helper.

Galvan/Galven: sparrow.

Gavin/Gawen: white hawk.

Gilroy: devoted to the king.

Glen/Glenn: valley.

Glendon: from the Glen Castle.

Grady: noble.

Hogan: youth.

Inness: from the river island.

Innis: river island.

Kane/Kayne: bright.

Kearney: victorious.

Keefe: cherished, handsome.

Keegan: ardent little one.

Keenan/Kienan: little and ancient.

Keene: handsome.

Keir: dark skinned.

Kele/Kellen/Kelly: warrior.

Kendrick: son of Henry.

Kennedy: helmeted chief.

Kennet/Kenneth: handsome.

Kenyon: fair-haired.

Kermit: free man.

Kerr: marshland.

Kerry: dark-haired.

Kevan/Kevin: loveable, gentle.

Kieran/Kiernan: little and dark-skinned.

Killian: little warrior.

Kyle: from the strait.

Laird: landlord.

Laughlin: a land in Irish legend.

Liam: Gaelic.

Logan: from the hollow.

Mackenzie: wise ruler's son.

Macnair: son of the heir.

Maddock: beneficent.

Mahon: bear.

Miach: son of Diancecht in Irish myth.

Morgan: sea's edge.

Morolt: brother of Iseult in Arthurian legend.

Muir: of the moors.

Murdoch: prosperous seaman.

Murray: sailor.

Murrough: sea warrior.

Neel/Nels/Niall: champion.

Nolan: famous.

Oren: pale-skinned.

Owen: young warrior.

Quinlan: very strong.

Quinn: wise.

Renan/Ronan: little sea

Rierdan/Riordan: king's poet.

Rory: red king.

Ross: promontory, headland.

Rowan: little red one.

Ryan: little king.

Shamus: supplanter.

Shay/Shea: fairy place.

Sheridan: wild man.

Skelly: storyteller.

Sloan: warrior.

Somerled: Scottish. Viking.

Synan: old.

Tadleigh: poet.

Teague: poet, bard.

Thorfinn: Norse chief.

Tiernan: lord.

Torin: chief.

Trahern: strong as iron.

Trevor: prudent.

Turlough: shaped like Thor.

Uileos: Ulysses.

Ultan: town of Ulster.

English, Welsh and Anglo-Saxon Names

Female

Afton: one from Afton.

Alodie: wealthy.

Arden: eagle valley.

Ashleigh/Ashley: from the ash tree farm.

Audrey: strength to overcome.

Avis: refuge in battle.

Billie: strong-willed.

Blake: one with a swarthy complexion.

Bliss: joy.

Blythe: joyful.

Brook: near the stream.

Chelsea: a port of ships.

Clover: clover blossom.

Cody: a cushion.

Dawn: break of day.

Dove: the bird.

Eadwine: valuable friend.

Eartha: the earth.

Edlyn: noble one.

Edmee: prosperous protector.

Edris: prosperous ruler.

Edwina: valuable friend.

Edyth/Edythe: rich gift.

Elfin: elf-like.

Ella: elf; beautiful fairy woman.

Ellette: little elf.

Elvina: befriended by elves.

Erlina: the elfin.

Esme: gracious protector.

Fancie: imagination.

Farra/Farrah: beautiful, pleasant.

Fleta: swift.

Genna/Gennifer/Guenna: white; fair.

Guinevere/Gwen/Gwendolen: white.

Gwenora/Gwyneth: fair.

Harley: from the long field.

Harper: harp player.

Hazel: commanding authority.

Holly: tree.

Isolde/Isolt: fair lady.

Jolene: she will increase.

Kendra: knowing woman.

Kimberlyn/Kimbra: from the royal fortress meadow.

Lane: from the narrow road.

Lark: skylark.

Leigh: from the meadow.

Lindsay/Lindsey: from the linden tree island.

Lynn: a cascade.

Maida/Mayda: a maiden.

Megan: strong or able.

Merry: happy.

Olwen: white track.

Ora: money.

Piper: pipe player.

Pixie: sprite.

Rae: doe.

Raven: like the bird.

Rhiamon: mythological; a witch.

Rhiannon: mythical name.

Robin: like the bird.

Rowena: famous friend.

Shandeigh/Shandy: rambunctious.

Shelby: from the ledge estate.

Skye: sky.

Skylar: sheltering.

Sorcha ("sor-kah"): bright.

Storm: stormy.

Summer: summertime.

Velvet: velvety.

Vivien: full of life.

Wallis: from Wales.

Wesley: from the western meadow.

Whitney: from the white island.

Wilda: willow forest dweller.

Willa: the desired.

Wilona: wished for.

Winnie: short form of Gwyneth.

Winter: wintertime.

Wynne: fair.

Yetta: to give.

English, Welsh, and Anglo-Saxon (male)

Aelfric: elf ruler.

Aethelweard: noble protector.

Aethelwine: noble friend.

Aethelwulf: noble wolf.

Aiken: oaken.

Ainsley: from the near meadow.

Alcott: from the old cottage.

Alden/Aldin/Aldis: old friend.

Aldrich: old wise ruler.

Aldwyn: protector.

Alfred: elf counselor.

Allard: noble and brave.

Archer: bowman.

Averell/Averill: born in April.

Aylwyn: old friend.

Bancroft: of the bean field.

Barclay: from the birch meadow.

Baron: nobleman.

Barton: from the barley farm.

Baxter: baker.

Bayard: having auburn hair.

Benton: of the moors.

Berwyn: bright friend.

Birch: of the birch tree forest.

Blake: fair-haired.

Bond: tiller of the soil.

Booth: from the hut.

Borden: from the valley of the boar.

Brad: broad.

Braden: of the wide valley.

Bradley: from the broad meadow.

Bradshaw: from the broad grove.

Bramwell: fierce. Willed.

Bran: raven.

Brand: fiery.

Brandon: from beacon hill.

Brenton: from the steep hill.

Broderick: from the broad ridge.

Bronson: son of a dark man.

Buachaill: sheep herder.

Burgess: castle dweller.

Burleigh: a field with knotted tree trunks.

Burne: from the brook.

Burris: of the town.

Burton: from the castle.

Calder: stream.

Caldwell: dweller by the cold spring.

Calvert: herdsman.

Carleton: farmer's town.

Carlisle: from the castle.

Carter: cart driver.

Chad: warlike.

Chadwick: from the warrior's town.

Chapman: merchant.

Cliff: steep rocks.

Clifton: from the town by the cliff.

Cody: a cushion.

Colby: from the black farm.

Collier: miner.

Cutler: knifemaker.

Darnell: from the hidden place.

Denver: green valley.

Dudley: from the people's meadow.

Dunstan: from the brown stone castle.

Eadgar: fortunate spearman.

Eadmund: rich protector.

Elden: protector.

Elton: from the town.

Elwin: friend of the elves.

Elwood: from the old wood.

Emlyn: winning.

Fairfax: fair-haired.

Falkner: falcon master.

Fenton: from the marshland estate.

Fleming: flemish.

Garland: from the battlefield.

Garrett: with a mighty spear.

Garrick: oak spear.

Garrnet: armed with a spear.

Garwin: comrade in battle.

Gladwin: cheerful.

Graham: the gray home.

Grayson: judge's son.

Harley: from the hare's meadow.

Hereward: army guard.

Hereweard: soldier protecting.

Hollis: from the holly grove.

Houston: from the hill town.

Kendall: from the bright valley.

Kenway: bold in battle.

Kingsley: from the king's meadow.

Landon: from the open grassy meadow.

Lane: from the narrow road.

Langdon: from the long hill.

Langley: from the long meadow.

Leland: meadowland.

Lowell: beloved.

Mabon: son.

Maddison: son of the powerful soldier.

Marlow: from the hill by the lake.

Merlin: falcon.

Merrick: ruler of the sea.

Newbold: from the new building.

Oakes: from the oak trees.

Perry: rock.

Ramsay: raven's island.

Rand: shield warrior.

Regenbeald: rainbow.

Sawyer: woodsman.

Sheldon: from the hut on the hill.

Shepard: sheep watcher.

Sherwood: of the bright forest.

Stanton: from the stony farm.

Taliesin: radiant brow.

Thackeray/Thatcher/Thaxer: roofer.

Thorley: Thor's meadow.

Tilden: from the liberal one's estate.

Tyler: tile maker.

Wade: from the river crossing.

Waite: guard.

Walden: from the woods.

Ward: guardian.

Waverly: from the meadow of aspens.

Wayland: from the land by the road.

Weston: from the western estate.

Weylon: from the land by the road.

Wildon: from the wooded hills.

Winslow: from the friend's hill.

Winston: from the friendly town.

Yale: from the corner of the land.

Yates: dweller at the gates.

Yul/Yule: born at yuletide.

ETHIOPIAN

Desta: happiness.

Fannah: fun.

Seble: autumn.

FINNISH

Ametisti ("ah-may-tis-tea"): amethyst.

Eeva ("eh-vuh"): life.

Haltijatar ("hahl-ti-yah-tahr"): fairy.

Haukka ("houk-kah"): hawk.

Joki ("yoa-key"): river.

Jumalatar ("you-mah-lah-tar"): goddess.

Kalevi ("kahl-ev-ee"): hero.

Kalwa ("kahl-wah"): heroic.

Kesa ("kay-sah"): summer.

Kevat ("kay-vaht"): spring.

Kunta ("koon-tah"): commune.

Kuu ("koo"): the moon.

Lahde ("lah-day"): spring.

Lilja ("leel-yah"): lily.

Linna ("lin-nah"): castle.

Luuta ("loo tah"): broom.

Maaginen ("maa-gi-nayn"): magic.

Meri ("may-ri"): sea.

Metsa ("mayt sa" [*sa* as in "sat"]): forest.

Metsikko ("mayt-sik-kur"): grove.

Noita ("noi-tah"): witch.

Moituus ("moi-tooss"): witchcraft, magic.

Onnellinen ("oan-nayl-li-nayn"): happy.

Onyksi ("oa-newk-si"): onyx.

Satu ("sah-too"): fairy tale.

Syksy ("sewk-sew"): autumn.

Talvi ("tahl-vi"): winter.

Timantti ("ti-mahnt-ti"): diamond.

Vesiputous ("vay-si-poo-toa-ooss"): waterfall.

FRENCH

Female

Blaise: Latin. Stammerer (also Blaize).

Candide: pure white.

Fantine: childlike.

Isidore: Greek. A gift of ideas.

Laure: crowned with laurels (also Laurel, Laura, Laurelle).

Morgance: sea-dweller (Morgane).

Natacha: born at Yule (also Nathalie, Natalie).

Sylvie: from the forest (also Sylvianne, Sylvette, Silvia, Silvaine).

Tatiana: Russian. Fairy queen.

Vivien: lively (also Vivienne, Viviane).

Male

Artur: Celtic. Noble, bear man.

Demitri: Greek. From Demeter, goddess of the harvest.

Denis: Greek. God of wine.

Gustave: Teutonic. Staff of gods.

Marlon: little falcon (also Marlin, Merlin).

GREEK

Female

Aileen: light.

Aldora: winged gift.

Aleris: ancient name.

Alexandra: helper of mankind.

Althea: healing.

Amara: unfading.

Amarantha: immortal.

Ambrosia: food of life.

Ambrosine: immortal.

Anastasia: one who will rise again.

Aretha/Arethusa: nymph.

Ariadne: daughter of sun god; goddess of spring.

Aspasia: woman famous for charm and intelligence.

Astra: starlike.

Athena: goddess of wisdom.

Calandra: the lark.

Calantha: blossom.

Cassandra: prophetess to whom no one listened.

Charis ("kahr-is"): love.

Chloe: flowering.

Clio: celebrate.

Cloris: goddess of flowers.

Corinne: a maiden.

Crystal: clear.

Cynara/Zinara: ancient name.

Cynthia: moon goddess.

Damara: gentle.

Damia: goddess of the forces of nature.

Delphine: derivation of Delphi, Oracle of Apollo.

Demeter/Demetra: goddess of the harvest.

Despoina: mistress.

Dorie/Dory/Dorissa: sea.

Emma: grandmother.

Hestia: goddess of the hearth.

Ilona: light.

Iona: purple jewel.

Irene: goddess of peace.

Iris: goddess of the rainbow.

Isadora/Isadore: gift of Isis.

Kalliope ("kahl-ee-o-pee"): beautiful voice.

Medea: part goddess, part sorceress.

Melaney: dark.

Moira: goddess of destiny.

Mona: solitary.

Nerissa: of the sea.

Nicole: people's victory.

Pandora: all gifted.

Panthea: of all the gods.

Pearl: the jewel.

Penelope: the weaver.

Phaedra: mythological figure.

Phoebe: brilliant; moon goddess.

Rhea: daughter of heaven and earth, mother of the gods.

Rue: plant used as an aspirilium in sacred ceremonies.

Selena/Selirra: moon goddess.

Terza/Tessa: the harvester.

Thaiassa: the sea.

Thalia: joyful.

Thea: goddess.

Theola: divine.

Tressa: the harvester.

Trina: pure.

Ursa: she-bear.

Vara: the stranger.

Vanessa: butterfly.

Vesta: goddess of the hearth.

Xena: distant place.

Zandra: helper of humankind.

Zoe: life-giving.

Male

Adonis: beautiful youth.

Aeneas: praiseworthy.

Ajax: eagle.

Alexander: great protector.

Ambrose: immortal.

Anatole: the east.

Apollo: manly.

Aristotle: the best.

Artemus: safe and sound.

Cletus: summoned.

Corydon: lark.

Cosmo: the world.

Cyril: lordly.

Damian/Damon/Daymond: constant.

Darius: wealthy.

Dorian: from the sea.

Erinys: angry.

Fabian: bean farmer.

Galen: calm.

George/Goran/Jorgan: farmer.

Homer: promise.

Jason: the healer.

Leander: lion-man.

Linus: flax.

Nicholas: victory of the people.

Orestes: mountain.

Orion: hunter.

Otis: hears well.

Saunders: son of Alexander.

Sebastian: majestic.

Silas: forest (also Silvanos).

Strephon: one who turns.

Ulysses: wrathful.

Xanthus: golden-haired.

Xenos/Zenos: foreigner.

Yurik: farmer.

Zeno: shining.

HAWAIIAN

Female

Kaili ("kah-ee-lee"): Hawaiian deity.

Kala: princess.

Konane ("ko-nah-neh"): bright as
moonlight.

Laka: goddess of the hula.

Lani: sky.

Leilani: sky child.

Luana: enjoyment.

Mahina: Polynesian. Moon.

Makani: wind.

Mapuana ("mah-poo-ah-nuh"): wind-
blown fragrance.

Male

Haimi: the seeker.

Kahoku ("kuh-hoh-koo"): the star.

Kaimi ("kah-ee-mee"): Polynesian.
Seeker.

Kala ("kuh-lah"): sun.

Kalama: Polynesian. Flaming torch.

Kali ("kah-lee"): spear carrier.

Kele: seahorse.

Keoki ("keh-oh-kee"): farmer.

Kika: from the forest.

Kolika: from the ocean.

Lono: god of peace and farming.

Lukela ("loo-keh-luh"): like a fox.

Mana: Polynesian. Supernatural power.

Nahele ("nah-heh-leh"): forest, grove of
trees.

Peni ("peh-nee"): weaver.

HISPANIC

Female

Adabela: happy and beautiful.

Adaluz: happy light.

Adamantina: diamond.

Adelfa: beloved sister.

Adelina: noble.

Adelinda: noble and pretty.

Adeltrudis: noble and beloved.

Adelrisa: noble sage.

Adriana: woman of the Adriatic.

Afra: form of Africana.

Afrodita: form of Aphrodite.

Aglaé: splendid, radiant beauty.

Ailen: the live coal from Chilian
Mapuche Indian.

Aire: purest air.

Bianca: white.

Bonita: pretty one.

Berlinda: bear.

Blanca: white, fair.

Caledonia: from Caledonia (Latin name for Scotland).

Caro: beloved.

Carina: cute.

Casilda: the fighter.

Celerina: quick.

Celmira: shining one.

Dafne: laurel tree.

Daira: knowledgable.

Dalinda: one of the names of Diana.

Delia: one of the names of Diana.

Dalin: one of the names of Diana.

Delicia: one who pleases.

Enid: life spirit.

Evelina: hazelnut.

Felicidad: satisfaction, pleasure.

Filis: leaves of the almond tree.

Flor: flower.

Florida: flowery.

Fortunada: fortune.

Gisela: arrow, lightning.

Heladia: born in Greece.

Hermosa: beautiful.

Hortensia: the gardener.

Indiana: of India or of Indias-America.

Isadora: gift of Isis.

Jenara: January.

Jovita: Jupiter.

Kora: maiden. Der. of Kore.

Liana: vine.

Lila: night.

Linda: pretty.

Luna: moon.

Maité: I love you.

Maya: mother.

Ninfa: young nymph.

Octavia: eighth.

Oliana: oleander.

Orquídea: orchid.

Perfecta: flawless.

Sabrina: from the area of the Severn River in Great Britain.

Selina: moon goddess.

Silvana: one who lives in the forest.

Siria: brilliant like the sun.

Tosca: of Tuscany.

Ubril: second month of ancient Roman calendar.

Úrsula: the bear.

Una: one.

Violeta: violet.

Víveca: alive.

Xaviera: new home.

Xenia: hospitable guest.

Xilma: helmet.

Yvette: yew wood.

Yvonne: yew wood.

Hispanic (male)

Abás: a centaur.

Abelard: Celtic. Der. of Abelard.

Acis: son of Faunus.

Agua: water.

Aldo: handsome.

Alfredo: peace.

Ali: sublime.

Arturo: noble bear.

Durante: the constant one.

Dante: der. of Durante.

Demetrio: belonging to Demeter.

Demetrius: belonging to Demeter.

Danto: constant.

Rante: constant.

Rantito: constant.

Eros: god of erotic love.

Fénix: phoenix.

Heraclido: Hercules.

Hercu: Hercules.

Hugolino: clear intellect.

Ugo: clear intellect.

Ugolino: clear intellect.

Igor: soldier.

Isadoro: gift of Isis.

Ivan: yew wood.

Jacinto: myth. Person Apollo turned into a flower.

Khalil: friend.

Jalil: friend.

Jorge: Earth.

Jovino: Jupiter.

Largo: Spanish for long.

León: lion.

Leopardo: leopard.

Leopoldo: being bold among the people.

Lino: Linus, Apollo's son who invented melody.

Luis: warrior.

Napoleón: lion of Naples.

Nereo: god of the sea.

Orestes: mountainous. Son of Agamemnon and Electra.

Orlando: man who comes from the glorious country.

Osmán: tender like a young pigeon.

Ponce: fifth.

Próspero: the fortunate one.

Quintin: fifth child.

Quinto: fifth child.

Quirino: Mars, god of war.

Randolfo: shield wolf.

Raúl: wolf.

Rocio: mist.

Renato: born again, a name of Pagan origin.

Renata: born again, a name of Pagan origin.

Sofanór: wise man.

Urbano: urbane. City dweller.

Vito: happy.

Xanto: blond.

Xavier: new house.

INDIAN

Female

Aditi: Hindu. Goddess.

Ambar: Hindu. Sky.

Ambika: Hindu. Goddess of power and destruction (also Sakti).

Amma: mother goddess (also Mata, Amba, Mahamba, Bimba).

Devi ("day-vee"): Hindu. Name of goddess Sakti.

Ellama: Hindu. Mother goddess.

Guri: Hindu. Goddess of abundance.

Hema: Hindu. Daughter of the mountains.

Matrika: Hindu. Mother.

Shashi: Hindu. Moonbeam.

Sita: Hindu. Mother Earth Goddess.

Soma: Hindu. Moon.

Male

Amritha: god.

Anala: fire.

Anila: Hindu. Wine god.

Chandra: Hindu. Moon; moon god.

Daru: Hindu. Pine or cedar.

Ganesha ("guh-nay-shuh"): god of good luck and wisdom.

Indra: Hindu. God of power.

Manda: Hindu. Saturn; god of the occult.

Mitra: Hindu. God of daylight.

Sesha: Hindu. Symbol of time.

IRISH

Female

Aideen: Irish legendary lover of the fairy man.

Banba: Irish goddess.

Briana: Celtic. Strong.

Bride: Celtic. Strength (also Briget, Bridget, Brighid, Brid, Breed).

Caitlin ("kat-leen" or "kate-lin"): pure.

Erin: Gaelic. Peace.

Fiona ("fee-oh-nah" or "fee-nah"): Celtic. White, fair.

Glynis: Gaelic. Valley.

Grainne ("groh-nyuh"): grace.

Ide ("eed-uh"): old Irish. Thirst.

Ismenia: Irish name.

Izett: Irish name; a form of Iseult.

Kelly: Gaelic. Warrior.

Kennocha ("ken-oh-kuh"): Celtic. Beauty.

Kerry: Gaelic. Dark-haired (also Keriann).

Kinnat/Keenat: traditional name.

Maiti (pronounced "mat-tee"): Irish name.

Mave: mirth.

Mavelle: Celtic. Songbird.

Meara: Irish. Merry.

Morgan: Celtic. Sea dweller.

Moya: Celtic. Great.

Rowena: Celtic. White mane.

Sheena: god's gift.

Sorcha: old Irish. Clear, bright.

Tara: Celtic. Tower.

Una ("oo-nuh"): unity.

Zaira: Irish name.

Male

Aidan: Celtic. Flame, fiery.

Aindreas ("ahn-dree-ahs"): manly.

Artur: Celtic. Noble, bear man.

Baird: ballad singer.

Bevan: Celtic. Youthful warrior.

Brenainn ("breh-neen"): Celtic. Sword.

Brendan: Gaelic. Raven.

Brett: Celtic. From Brittany.

Broin ("bree-ahn"): raven (also Brennan).

Carlin: Gaelic. Little champion.

Cian ("keen"): ancient name (also Cein, Kian, Kean).

Cillian ("keel-yan"): war (also Killian).

Colla: ancient Irish name.

Conary ("koh-ner-ee"): ancient Irish name.

Conroy: Celtic. Wise man.

Conway: Gaelic. Hound of the plain.

Corey: from the hollow.

Cullan: Celtic. Handsome one (also Cullin, Cully, Collin).

Dagda: good god.

Daibheid ("deh-vid"): beloved (also David, Daibid).

Daire ("deh-ruh"): old Irish. (Also Dary, Darragh).

Dallas: Gaelic. Wise.

Daray: Gaelic. Dark.

Derry: Gaelic. Red-haired.

Devin: Celtic. A poet.

Donagh: brown warrior, high king; son of Brian Boru.

Donahue: Gaelic. Dark warrior.

Donovan: Celtic. Dark warrior.

Duncan: Celtic. Dark man.

Erin: Gaelic. Peace.

Evan: young warrior.

Faolan ("feh-lahn"): wolf (also Felan).

Farrell: Celtic. Courageous.

Ferris: Greek. The rock (also Farris).

Fionan ("fin-ee-ahn"): fair.

Gannon: Gaelic. Fair of face.

Glen: Celtic. Valley.

Innis: Celtic. Island.

Kearney: Celtic. Warrior.

Keegan: Gaelic. Little and fiery one (also Kegan).

Keir ("care"): Celtic. Dark-skinned (also Kerr, Kern, Kearn, Kerry).

Lochlain ("lokh-lan"): home of Norsemen.

Logan: Gaelic. From the hollow.

Maghnus ("makh-nus"): great.

Mahon: bear; brother of high king Brian Boru.

Mannix: monk.

Morven: Celtic. Mariner.

Nealon: Celtic. Champion (also Neal).

Nolan: Gaelic. Famous.

Padraig ("pah-dreek"): Latin. Noble (also Patric, Padraic).

Rory: Teutonic. Famous ruler.

Scully: Gaelic. Town crier.

Seamus ("shee-a-mus"): the supplanter (also Shemus).

Sean/Shawn: Hebrew. God's gift (also Seaghan, Shane, Shan).

Searlas ("shar-las"): full-grown; manly (also Charles).

Torc: Irish. Boar.

Uaine ("oon-yuh"): old Irish.

Wynne: Celtic. White, fair.

KENYAN

Barika: Swahili. Bloom.

Dalila ("dah-lee-lah"): Swahili. Gentle.

Machupa ("mah-choo-pah"): likes to drink.

Makalani ("mah-kah-lah-nee"): one skilled in writing.

Mwasaa ("m-wah-sah"): Swahili. Timely.

Paka: Swahili. Pussycat.

Pili ("pee-lee"): Swahili. Second-born.

Sadiki ("sah-dee-kee"): Swahili. Faithful.

Sanura ("sah-noo-rah"): Swahili. Kitten.

Shani ("shah-nee"): Swahili. Marvellous.

Sikudhani ("see-koo-than-nee"): a surprise; unusual.

LATIN

Female

Adora: beloved.

Adrienne: dark, rich.

Allegra: lively.

Almeda: pressing toward the goal.

Amabel: loveable.

Amanda: deserving of great love.

Andra/Andrea/Andreanna: womanly (also Andriana, Aundrea).

April: opening.

Arda/Ardelle: warmth.

Ardis/Ardra: enthusiasm.

Auerelie/Aurelia/Aurora: golden.

Austin: majestic.

Autumn: fall.

Averyl/Avril: opening.

Belinda: beautiful serpent.

Bellona: goddess of war.

Brina: from the boundary line.

Cerelia: goddess of the harvest.

Chantal: song.

Delcina/Dulce/Dulcinea: sweetness.

Dia: goddess.

Diana: goddess of the hunt.

Diva: goddess.

Emily/Emmaline: hard-working.

Enid: quiet.

Ermin: regal.

Fabula: myth.

Faline: catlike.

Fawn/Fawna/Fawne: young deer.

Felicity: happiness.

Flora: goddess of flowers.

Gelsey: jasmine.

Gemma: jewel.

Ginger: the spice.

Grace: charm.

Hilary/Hillair: full of cheer.

Imogene: image.

Ivory: made of ivory.

Julia/Juliet: youthful.

Justine: just.

Laura: crown of laurel; honor.

Lauralee/Laureen/Laurel: honor (also Laurette).

Lauren/Lauyrn/Lorrin: laurel crown.

Leandra: lioness.

Lelia: lily.

Lena: temptress.

Leola/Leona/Leoni: lion.

Lorelle: little.

Lucina: goddess of childbirth.

Lucretia: riches.

Lumen: star.

Luna: moon.

Magice: magic.

Maia: goddess of springtime.

Maris/Marris/Meris: of the sea.

Melena: canary-yellow colored.

Merle/Merril/Merryl: blackbird.

Miranda: admirable.

Monica: counselor.

Natalie: born at yule.

Nona: one of the three Fates.

Nova/Novia: newcomer.

Nydia: from the nest.

Ondrea: womanly.

Oona: one.

Oriana/Riana: golden.

Pomona: goddess of fruit trees.

Portia: offering.

Renata: reborn.

Risa: laughter.

Sabina: Sabine woman.

Sabrina: from the boundary line.

Saga: witch.

Season: sowing, planting.

Selena: salt.

Serena: calm.

Stella: star.

Sybil: prophetess.

Terra: goddess of the earth.

Tertia: the third.

Tessa: essence.

Valene/Valery/Valora: strong.

Valentine: healthy.

Venus: goddess of love.

Vesta: goddess of the hearth.

Zia: type of grain.

Male

Adrian: seacoast.

Alban: pure heart.

Ardan/Arden/Ardin: fiery.

Ardere: fire.

Austen/Austin: great usefulness.

Bard: bearded.

Basil: magnificent.

Blase: stammerer.

Branch: claw.

Calvin: bald.

Cash: vain.

Cervus: stag.

Clark: scholarly.

Corbett/Corbin/Corvin: raven.

Cornelius: horn-colored.

Deus: god.

Dex/Dexter: dexterous.

Divus: god.

Drake: dragon.

Emlen/Emlyn: charming.

Felix: prosperous.

Forrest: woodsman.

Foster: keeper of the woods.

Griffin: mythical beast.

Hadrian: seacoast.

Jarl/Jarlath/Jarlen: man of control.

Justin/Justinian: just.

Linus: flax-colored.

Lombard: long-bearded.

Magnus: great.

Magus: magician.

Max/Maxim/Maximillian: most
  excellent.

Montgomery: hill.

Myer: great.

Myles: soldier.

Oliver: olive tree.

Orson: bear-like.

Paganus: Pagan.

Paine: country peasant.

Patten/Paxton/Payton: nobleman.

Quentin/Quincy/Quintin: fifth.

Quercus: oak.

Remus: mythical founder of Rome.

Rex: king.

Romulus: mythical founder of Rome.

Ross: rose.

Rufus: redhead.

Sebastian: majestic.

Silvanus: the forest god.

Sumner: summoner.

Sylvester: woods.

Torin: tender.

Trenton: torrent.

Turner: one who works the lathe.

Ursa: bear.

Vassily: magnificent.

NATIVE NORTH AMERICAN

Aleshanee: one who coos. She plays all
  the time.

Amitola: rainbow.

Aponi: butterfly.

Awenasa: Cherokee. My home.

Awenita: fawn.

Ayita: Cherokee. First in the dance.

Elsu: falcon flying.

Enola: alone.

Gaho: mother.

Hakan: fiery.

Hinto: Dakota. Blue.

Hinun ("hee-noon"): god of clouds and
  rain.

Ilia: meaning unknown.

Iye ("ee-yeh"): smoke.

Jacy: Tupi-Guarani. Moon; creator of
  all plants.

Jolon: valley of dead oaks.

Kachina: sacred dancer.

Kai: Navaho. Willow tree.

Karmiti: Inuit. Trees.

Kaya: Hopi. My elder sister.

Kimama: Shoshone. Butterfly.

Leotie ("leh-o-tee-eh"): prairie flower.

Litonya: Miwok. Hummingbird
  darting.

Lulu: rabbit.

Luna: Zuni. Moon.

Macawi: Lakota. Motherly.

Macha: Lakota. Aurora.

Mahal: woman.

Mahkah: Lakota. Earth.

Mamid: Chippewa. The star dancer.

Mascha: Navaho. Owl.

Masou ("mah-so-oo"): fire deity.

Meda: prophet.

Miakoda: power of the moon.

Migina: Omaha. Returning moon.

Mimiteh: Omaha. New moon.

Nahimana: Lakota. Mystic.

Nasnan: carrier. Surrounded by a song.

Nata-akon: Chippewa. Expert canoeist.

Niabi: Osage. Fawn.

Nidawi: Omaha. Fairy girl.

Nita: Choctaw. Bear.

Nokomis: Iroquois. White or fair woman.

Nova: Hopi. Chasing a butterfly.

Nuna: land.

Omusa: Miwok. Missing things when shooting with arrows.

Onatah: Iroquois. Corn spirit, daughter of the earth.

Orenda: Iroquois. Magic power.

Pelipa: Zuni. Lover of horses.

Raini: Tupi-Guarani. Deity who created the world.

Satinka: magic dancer.

Sedna: Inuit. Goddess of food.

Snana: Lakota. Jingles like little bells.

Tadewi: Omaha. Wind.

Taigi: Omaha. Returning new moon.

Taima: crash of thunder.

Taini: Omaha. Coming new moon.

Tala: wolf.

Tama: thunderbolt.

Tateeyopa: Lakota. Happy hostess, her door.

Tuwa: Hopi. Earth.

Waitilanni: Laguna. Wonder water.

Wakanda: Lakota. Inner magical power.

TEUTONIC NAMES
Female

Ailsa/Alyssa: of good cheer.

Alda: rich.

Amelia: industrious.

Ara: eagle maid.

Ardith: rich gift.

Audris: wealthy.

Bianca: white.

Blenda: dazzling.

Dagna: fair as the day.

Dena: valley.

Emera: industrious.

Ethelind: nobly wise.

Farica: peaceful ruler.

Felda: a field.

Garda: protected.

Gisela: pledge.

Griselda: gray heroine.

Gudrun: daughter of the king of the Nibelungs.

Haldis: stone spirit.

Hazel: commander.

Hertha: Mother Earth (after the goddess of fertility).

Ida: happy.

Ilsa: gaiety.

Lorelei: destruction.

Marelda: famous battle maid.

Melisande: industrious, strong.

Minetta/Minna: loving memory.

Raina: mighty.

Ramona: wise protectoress.

Vedis: sacred spirit of the forest.

Velda: of great wisdom.

Wanda: the wanderer.

Wandis: lithe and slender.

Male

Abelard: resolute.

Adalard: brave and noble.

Alaric/Alarick: ruler of all.

Aldrich: wise ruler.

Allard: resolute.

Archaimbaud/Archambault: bold.

Archibald: truly bold.

Arvin: friend of the people.

Aubrey: elf king.

Axel: father of peace.

Baldwin: bold friend.

Ballard: bold.

Baron: noble warrior.

Barret: mighty as a bear.

Bevis: archer.

Bond: farmer.

Chalmers: lord of the manor.

Charles: manly.

Conrad: honest counselor.

Crosby: dweller near the crossroad.

Derek/Derrick/Dirk: great ruler.

Derwin: friend to the animals.

Dustin: brave fighter.

Dwight: fair one.

Garner: guardian warrior.

Goddard: divinely firm.

Graham: from the gray house.

Haines: vined cottage.

Hardy: bold, daring.

Humphrey: man of peace.

Ingram: angel raven.

Kirby: Norse. From church town.

Lombard: long beard.

Loring: famous in war.

Merrill: famous.

Meyer: farmer.

Paxton: pack man.

Roscoe: deer forest.

Sprague: lively.

Talbot: valley bright.

Tate: cheerful.

Thayer: of the nation's army.

Thorp: hamlet.

Tyson: son of the German.

Ulrich: wolf ruler.

Waldron: mighty raven.

Warner: armed defender.

Warren: defender.

Warrick: defending ruler.

Wayne: wagon.

Wolfe: wolf.

chapter twenty

MAGICAL NAMES FROM
FICTION

I have consulted a wide variety of texts to create the following listing, which includes
names from science fiction, fantasy, ancient
texts, poetry, novels, children's books, and modern historical novels. I have included names from
several Arthurian works to illustrate some of the
differences in characters' names involved for any
Arthurian buffs who may be interested. I have
included the works of the science-fiction and
fantasy genres because of the remarkably creative names in such works. I have attempted to
include names from many different eras, exclud-
ing works whose characters bore strictly Christian names. I have also included some names
from the popular phenomenon of Harry Potter
and the marvelously inventive world of the novels of Terry Pratchett.

When choosing a name from something that already exists, one must be sensitive to what is called the universal or collective unconscious. This is a stock of symbols universally understood by almost everyone. To become part of the collective unconscious, a symbol must be understood by a large part of the world to mean a certain thing. To choose such a symbol and try to redefine it as something else is very difficult. It is nearly impossible to swim against the tide of collective understanding—ask Richard Nixon's PR people. The media has a lot to do with putting ideas into the collective unconscious, regardless of whether the ideas are based in reality or not. Many people connect into this when they say "I don't know why I think such as thing is true, but it's everywhere, on television, in the papers; it must be true."

A small-scale example is the Pagan use of the pentagram, which is understood by many Westerners to be a symbol of Satanism. You can tell people that you define the pentagram differently, that it doesn't mean Satanism to you, but the stigma is persistent. Most of the time people won't give you a chance to explain, they don't want to talk to you. You can't reason with people if they won't talk to you. Many Pagans have come to realize they can't overcome their own aversion to the symbol, despite how the symbol is redefined by Pagans. Another example would be to say that the very ancient symbol of a swastika is an appropriate Pagan symbol based solely on its antiquity. Much of the world knows that to be a symbol of the Nazis, and it is so ingrained with this meaning in the collective unconscious that it would be impossible to use the symbol without the emotional and societal stigma associated with it.

The same idea works in the choosing of names. Most literary names would work well when taken as a magical name, because there isn't a universally understood definition involving such names. If you have read the particular book, you have an idea about what one author meant the name to be, but one name can be used by many authors for many different characters, thereby muddying the collective understanding of the name. The same holds true for geographic place names; there are many rivers that share the same name. These sorts of names are easily chosen, cleansed, and used by people.

However, the more popular the book is, the more ingrained in the collective unconscious. That is why biblical names are are so difficult to redefine. What those names symbolize is far from reclaimable. If you compare a name from the Bible and a name from a science-fiction novel, the biblical name has a great deal of energy attached to it from centuries of use by millions of people. It was often used in times of trauma or upset. The science-fiction name, on the other hand, has very little "feeling" or "energy" attached to it. What little there is comes from relaxed reading for pleasure and a fleeting association with a particular character, if you happen to have read the novel. Of course, the better known the book, the more ingrained it is in the collective consciousness. Scarlett O'Hara, for example, could never be used to indicate shyness and modesty; it is too well understood as selfish, beautiful, greedy, and bold.

You do not have to have read the particular books listed in this section to get a feeling for the name listed. Remember that when the author named the character (often by invention) the chosen name had no meaning attached to it, but the author breathed life into it by attaching it to the character. Breathe life into these names yourself and redefine them. If you like a particular name, take it off the shelf, check it out, and wear it home. It's a good read. Fiction names are from the following books:

Acts of King Arthur

Aeneid

A Midsummer Night's Dream

Beowulf

Bevis of Hampton

Castle of Wizardry

Celtic Miscellany

Crusade

Crystal Shard

Crystal Singer

Darkling Hills

Darkover novels

Death Gate Cycle

Death's Master

Deryni novels

Discworld novels

Dragonriders of Pern

Dune

Epic of Gilgamesh

Faerie Queen

Fall of Atlantis

Far Pavilions

Firelord

Grettir the Strong

Gulliver's Travels

Guy of Warwick

Harry Potter novels

Heart of the Fire

Horse Goddess

House of Dreams

Ivanhoe

Jungle Book

Kalevala

Le Morte d'Arthur

Lion of Ireland

Lord of the Rings

Mabinogi

Macbeth

Masters of Solitude

Merlin novels

Mists of Avalon

Nibelungenlied

Song of Hiawatha

Song of Roland

Storm Lord

Story of Burnt Njal

The Tempest

Tristan and Isolde

Wizards' World

Wolves of the Dawn

THE ACTS OF KING ARTHUR AND HIS NOBLE KNIGHTS

By John Steinbeck

Accolon

Alardine

Alyne

Anguyshaunce

Arthur

Balan

Balin

Bawdewyn

Bors

Brastias

Carados

Clarivaus

Claudas

Colombe

Cradilment

Ector

Elaine

Ettarde

Ewaine

Fergus

Galahad

Garlon

Gawaine

Gilmere

Grastian

Gryfflet

Guinevere

Hugh

Igraine

Kay

Ladynas

Lamorake

Lancelot

Launcelor

Lodegrance

Lyle

Lyonel

Lyonse

Margawse

Marhalt

Merlin

Mordred

Naram

Nentres

Nyneve

Outlake

Pelham

Pellinore

Percival

Phariance

Placidas

Raynold

Royns

Sanam

Tarquin

Torre

Ulfius

Uryens

Uther Pendragon

AENEID
(17 B.C.E.)

By Publius Vergilius Maro
(By order of Augustus Caesar)

Acestes

Aeneas

Amata

Anchises

Anius

Anna

Aruns

Ascanius

Camilla

Celaeno

Creusa

Dido

Evander

Latinus

Lavinia

Nautes

Nisus

Opis

Palinurus

Pallus

Turnus

BEOWULF
(725–750 C.E.)

Aeschere

Beowulf

Brosing

Ecglaf

Ecgtheow

Ecgwela

Eormenric

Finn

Fitela

Folcwalda

Freawaru

Frisian

Gotar

Grendel

Halga the Good

Hama

Healfdene

Heorogar

Heorot

Hnaef

Hrothgar

Hunlaf

Hygelac

Naegling

Offa

Oslaf

Sigemund

Unferth

Waels

Waelsing

Wealtheow

Weder

Weohstan

Wulfgar

BEVIS OF HAMPTON
(1200–1250 C.E.)

Ascapard: giant.

Bevis: hero and knight.

Bradmond: king.

Ermyn: Saracen king.

Guy: prince.

Inor: king.

Josyan: heroine; lady fair.

Miles: prince.

Sir Murdour: murderer.

Saber: knight.

CASTLE OF WIZARDRY
By David Eddings

Adara

Aldur

Aloria

Ariana

Barak

Belar

Beldaran

Belgarath

Belgariad

Brand

Ce'nedra

Cherek

Ctuchik

Durnik

Garion

Gorek the Wise

Gorim

Issa

Kharel

Lelldorin

Mandorallen

Nedra

Olban

Polgara

Poppi

Relg

Rhodar

Riva Iron Grip

Salmissra

Silk

Torak

Tupik

Ulgo

Valgon

Vordai

Xantha

Zakath

Zedar

Zelik

A CELTIC MISCELLANY

By Kenneth Hurlstone Jackson

Aeron: place name.

Ainnle: brother of Noise.

Arianrhod: Lugh's mother.

Arran: place name.

Arthur: mythical king.

Athairne: poet.

Balar: legendary Fomorian chieftain.

Bassa: place name.

Bedwyr: Sir Bedivere of Arthurian legend.

Beli: legendary British king.

Berwyn: place name.

Boadhagh: mythical king of the happy otherworld.

Boann: nymph of the River Boyne.

Bron: ancient name.

Cadwalader

Cailidin: a wizard killed by Cu Chulainn.

Cailte: one of Finn's chief heroes.

Camlan: King Arthur's last battle.

Caradawg

Cashel: chief place of the early kings.

Celyddon: forest in Scotland.

Conall: one of the early Ulster heroes.

Conn: legendary ancient king of Tara.

Connaught: place name.

Cork: place name.

Cu Chulainn: the hound of Culann.

Drem

Edain: fairy woman.

Elfan (Elvan): brother of Cynddylan.

Emhain (Evin): place name.

Emlyn: place name.

Ethal Anbhuail: one of the kings of the fairies.

Finn: legendary Irish hero.

Galway: place name.

Gwaddn: sole.

Llanddwyn: place name.

Llew: sun god, Welsh equivalent of Lugh.

Morann: a mythical wise judge.

Moy: river.

Muirinn: imaginary midwife.

Olwen: daughter of the ogre Ysbaddaden.

Sedanta: Cu Chulainn's childhood name.

Tara: place name.

CRUSADE
By James Lowder

Alusair

Azoun

Balin

Brunthar

Brunthar Elventree

Chanar

Cyric

Dargor

Farl

Filfaeril

Fonjara

Jad

Kiri

Koja

Lugh

Lythrana

Mourngrym

Myrmeen

Rhigaerd

Salember

Susail

Tanalasta

Torg

Torm

Tuigan

Tymora

Tyrluk

Vrakk

Winefiddle

THE CRYSTAL SHARD
By R. A. Salvatore

Agorwal

Akar

Beorg

Beornegar

Biggrin

Bruenor

Cassius

Dineval

Dorim

Drizzt

Dualdon

Eldeluc

Errtu

Glensather

Heafstaag

Jensin

Kemp

Kessell

Konig

Luskan

Mithril

Moradin

Morkai

Regis

Rumblebelly

Shander

Targos

Telshazz

Termalaine

Tirith

Torga the Orc

Wulfgar

CRYSTAL SINGER
By Anne McCaffrey

Andurs

Borella

Borton

Carigana

Carrick

Enthor

Falanog

Gorren

Jezerey

Killashandra

Rimbol

Shillawn

Tukolom

Valdi

THE DARKLING HILLS
By Lori Martin

Adrell

Armas

Ayenna

Baili

Bainne

Boessus

Carden

Dalleena

Desja

Ditta

Envy

Ferra

Forlas

Gharei

Heila

Inama

Kellstae

Kentas

Lilli

Lindis

Lissor

Nesmin

Nialia

Nichos

Nilsor

Phenna

Pillyn

Proseras

Raynii

Rena

Rendell

Sanlin

Seani

Shandel

Sillus

Simsas

Teleus

Telph

Temhas

Traehi

Valtah

THE DARKOVER NOVELS
By Marion Zimmer Bradley

Alanna

Aldaran

Aleki

Alexis (Lexie)

Alida

Allart

Allira

Anjali

Ann'dra

Annelys

Aquilara

Ardrin

Arielle

Arilinn

Auster

Avarra

Aven

Barak

Bard

Barron

Bethany

Brynat

Byrna

Calinda

Callista

Carlina

Carolin

Caryl

Cathal

Chandria

Chieri

Cholayna

Clariza

Cleindori

Colin

Colryn

Coryn

Cressa

Cyrillon

Dalereuth

Damon

Danilo

Danvan

Darill

Darissa

Darnack

Deonara

Desideria

Devra

Dezi

Donal

Donell

Dorilys

Dyan

Again and again the great blue-white, green-white bolts ripped and flamed down on Dead Man's Peak, and Dorilys shrieked with hysterical laughter.

Kyril stared at her, his eyes wide with awe and dread, "Sorceress," he whispered, "Storm queen . . . "

—MARION ZIMMER BRADLEY
STORMQUEEN!

Edric

Eduin

Elhalyn

Ellemir

Ellers

Elorie

Felix

Ferrika

Fianna

Fiona

Garin

Garris

Gwynn

Hali

Hilary

Idriel: a moon.

Irmelin

Jaelle

Jandria

Janetta

Janine

Javanne

Jerana

Kadarin

Karinn

Kennard

Ker

Kermiac

Kerstal

Kerwin

Kieran

Kilghard

Kindra

Kyntha

Kyril

Kyrrids: a moon.

Laurens

Lauria

Laurinda

Lella

Leominda

Leonie

Lerrys

Li

Linnea

Linnell

Liriel: a moon.

Lisarda

Loran

Lorenz

Lorill

Luciella

Lyondri

Magda

Magdalen

Mallina

Mallinson

Margali

Margwenn

Mariel

Marius

Marsiela

Marya

Maura

Mayra

Melisendra

Melora

Merelie

Merryl

Mhari

Mikhail

Millea

Mirella

Montray

Mormallor: a moon.

Neskaya

Neyrissa

Nira

Orain

Rafaella

Rafe

Ragan

Rakhaila

Rannath

Rannirl

Rannvil

Rayna

Reade

Renata

Rezi

Ria

Rima

Rohana

Romilly

Rory

Rumal

Sharra

Shaya

Sherna

Stefan

Sunstar

Taniquel

Tella

Thyra

Valdir

Varzil

Wolf

Yllana

Zandru

DARKOVER NOVELS WITH THE FRIENDS OF DARKOVER

By Marion Zimmer Bradley and the Friends of Darkover

Alais

Alar

Alaric

Alessandro

Allira

Amara

Amaury

Amrek

Anya

Ariane

Arielle

Artros

Asharra

Auster

Avarra

Belloma

Beltran

Bredan

Brigid

Bronwyn

Bruna

Buartha

Caelly

Caillean

Caitlin

Caitrin

Caltus

Cara

Carolin

Casilda

Cassalina

Catlyn

Catriona

Cerdic

Chimene

Clea

Colryn

Coryn

Corys

Cullen

Cyril

Cyrilla

Damrys

Danilys

Danla

Danlyn

Darla

Darriel

Dawyd

Denita

Deonara

Derik

Dione

Donal

Dorata	Keithyl
Dorian	Kell
Eadar	Kennard
Edric	Kennet
Elena	Kiera
Elholyn	Kyla
Elinda	Kyria
Elorie	Larissa
Elys	Lauria
Enid	Liane
Erharth	Linnet
Farren	Lionora
Finn	Lira
Gabriela	Liriel
Gaelan	Lisandra
Garrik	Lora
Garris	Loran
Harkspell	Lori
Jamilla	Macrae
Janella	Maellen
Janetta	Maol
Janna	Mara
Jaqual	Margatta
Jemel	Margolys
Jharek	Mari
Julana	Marissa
Kadi	Marji
Katria	Marna
Kayeta	Mhari

Mikhael

Millim

Mirrei

Morag

Naella

Nemma

New Skye

Nyal

Peidro

Rabharty

Rael

Raghall

Raimon

Ramhara

Rannan

Ranwyn

Ranyl

Reva

Rima

Robard

Roualeyn

Ruyven

Sabrynne

Sarena

Seanon

Shandra

Shilla

Stelle

Tani

Tarisa

Temora

Terel

Torayza

Torcall

Toria

Valaena

Valentine

Vardis

Verdis

Veynal

Wellana

Xiella

Ysabet

Zhalara

THE DEATH GATE CYCLE

By Margaret Weis and Tracy Hickman

Abarrach: the Realm of Earth.

Alake: a human princess.

Aleatha Quindiniar: a beautiful elf who is the sister of Calandra.

Argana: a powerful sorceress of Chelestra.

Arianus: the realm of air.

Bane: a male child who has magical powers.

Baltazar: the necromancer of king of Karin Telest.

Bothar'in: an elven lieutenant.

Calandra Quindiniar: an elven matriarch.

Callie: a nickname for Calandra.

Carfa'shon: "At harmony with the elements," the name of an elven airship.

Chelestra: the Realm of Water.

Daidlus

Darral: the high froman of the Island of Devlin.

Delu: a human queen of Chelestra.

Devon: Alake's boyfriend.

Drakar: a dwarven leader.

Drugar: a male dwarf warrior.

Dumaka: a human king of Chelestra.

Durndrun: an elven lord.

Eliason: elven king of Chelestra.

Elixnoir

Equilan: the Realm of Fire.

Hugh the Hand: an assassin.

Gareth: a knight of Ke'lith.

Gregor: a human merchant trader.

Griffith

Grundle: a dwarven princess.

Haplo: a Patryn sorcerer.

Hartmut: lover of Princess Grundle.

Jarre: a female dwarven rebel.

Jerra: a duchess of Abarrach.

Kevanish

Kleitus: the king of the Necropolis of Abarrach.

Lenthan Quindiniar: a male elf who was an inventor.

Limbeck Bolttightner: a dwarven inventor and rebel.

Lucillia

Magicka: a wizard of Arianus.

Marabella: a female friend of Sabia.

Orla: a Sartan sorceress of Chelestra.

Orn: a god of Arianus.

Paithan Quindiniar: Calandra's brother, a merchant.

Patryn: a race of sorcerers.

Peytin

Pons: the high chancellor of the Necropolis of Abarrach.

Pryan: the Realm of Fire.

Pundar: a trader.

Reesh'ahn: an elven prince.

Rega: a human female who is the sister of Roland Redleaf.

Rogar: a lord of Ke'lith.

Roland Redleaf: a male human adventurer.

Sabia: elven princess of Chelestra.

Samah: a Sartan leader of Chelestra.

Sartan: a race of sorcerers.

Sigla: the magical tattoos of the Patryn.

Sinistrad: a black monk of Arianus.

Terncia: a kingdom of Arianus.

Thea: a nickname for Alethea.

Thillia: one of the kingdoms of
Arianus.

Trian: a magicka who is an advisor to
one of the kings of Arianus.

Ulaka: a trader.

Yngvar Heavybeard: a dwarven king of
Chelestra.

Zankor'el: an elven captain.

Zifnab: a Sartan sorcerer.

DEATH'S MASTER

By Tanith Lee

Azhrarn: master of night.

Beyash: priest.

Drin: dwarves.

Druhim Vanashta: city.

Eshva: dark angels.

Gornadesh: king of Mehr.

Hhabaid: princess.

Kassafeh: beautiful woman.

Lylas: witch.

Narasen: leopard queen.

Simmu: shapeshifter (Shell).

Uhlume: lord of death.

Vazdru: elite Eshvas.

Yolsippa: rogue.

Zhirem: princess.

THE DERYNI NOVELS

By Katherine Kurtz

Alaric

Alroy

Alyce

Arilan

Barrett

Bennett

Bethane

Bradene

Bran

Brendan

Brion

Bronwyn

Burchard

Camber

Cara

Cardiel

Carsten

Charissa

Conall

Conlan

Coram

Cordan

Coroth

Corrigan

Corwyn

Creoda

Culdi

Danoc

Davency

Davis

Dawkin

Deegan

Deforest

Derryd

Derry

Dobbs

Donal

Duncan

Elas

Elsworth

Elvira

Eric

Ewan

Fathane

Fianna

Garon

Giles

Godwin

Graham

Gryphon

Gwydion

Gwyllim

Hort

Hugh

Ian

Istelyn

Jared

Jatham

Jehana

Kelson

Kevin

Kirby

Kyri

Laran

Lewys

Liam

Loris

Mal

Malcolm

Marluk

Mclain

Medras

Merritt

Moira

Morag

Morgan

Nigel

Payne

Ralf

Ralson

Rhafallia

Rhemuth

Rhodri

Rhydon

Rhys

Rimmell

Rogier

Rolf

Ronal

Royston

Selden

Shannis

Thorne

Tolliver

Torin

Torval

Vera

Vivienne

Wencit

DISCWORLD NOVELS

By Terry Pratchett

Abraxas the Agnostic: a philosopher struck by lightning at least fifteen times.

Achmed the Mad: necromancer, wrote the *Necrotelicomnicon (Liber Paginarus)*.

Alfonz: sailor with a good build, lots of scars, and very instructive tattoos.

Alohura: goddess of lightning.

Amber: troll love story heroine.

Angua Delphine von Öberwald: a werewolf.

Annaple, Nanny: a witch.

Aristocrates: philosopher.

Astoria: goddess of love. A complete bubblehead.

Azaremoth: the stench of dog breath, a demon.

Beano: clown.

Beedle, Granny: witch.

Belafon: druid and computer specialist.

Beryl: a troll.

Bibulous: god of wine. Drunk all the time.

Bilious: god of hangovers.

Billias, Skarmer: a wizard.

Binky: Death's horse.

Black Aliss: witch.

Blenkin: manservant.

Bluejohn: a troll in the City Watch. Used as a riot shield.

Bobby, Most Holy Saint: a donkey.

Boffo: doorkeeper at the Fool's Guild.

Boggis: a family of thieves

Borgle, Nodar: a canteen owner in Holy Wood.

Bottler, Violet: the tooth fairy.

Breccia: troll.

Brezock the Barbarian: hero.

Brunt, Ossie: xenophobic maniac.

Bunu: the goat-headed god of goats.

Bylaxis: kind-hearted lady whose leg falls off.

Cake, Evadne: a medium and landlady for the undead.

Cake, Ludmilla: a werewolf daughter of Evadne.

Carbonaceous: troll.

Carding, Marmaric: wizard head of the Hookwinkers.

Caslong: dwarf printer.

Catbury: geneticist.

Chalky: troll.

Chance: a female anthropomorphic personification.

Changebasket, Skrelt: wizard.

Cheesewaller: wizard.

Chert: troll.

Chidder: assassin.

Chondrodite: troll god of love.

Chrysophrase: troll godfather.

Chume: the notorious herring thrower.

Clay: troll kid or "pebble."

Coalface: troll criminal.

Cohen, Genghis: barbarian hero.

Crag: troll.

Cripslock: engraver.

Critchley: baker.

Cubal: fire god.

Cuddy: dwarf member of the Night Watch.

Cumberbatch, Silas: crier turned Watchman.

Cutangle: archmage.

Cutwell, Igneouos: wizard.

Dafe: apprentice.

Declivities: philosopher.

Destiny: god/goddess.

Detrius: troll member of the Night Watch.

DeVice, Amanita: junior witch coven member. Has a tattoo.

Diome, Witch of the Night: adventuress.

Dismass, Gammer: witch who goes through time at random.

Drumknott: clerk.

Dykeri: philosopher who wrote *Principles of Navigation* then got lost in his bathroom.

Eerie: pet rabbit.

Endos: a listener (for money).

Errol (Goodboy Bindle Featherstone of Quirm): a swamp dragon.

Expletius: philosopher.

Febrius: messenger of the gods.

Filter, Goodie: old sharp-tongued witch.

Flannelfoot, Zlorf: assassin with a troll somewhere in his family tree.

Flatulus: god of winds.

Fondel: composer.

Foorgol: god of avalanches.

Fresnel: wizard.

Furgle: dwarf.

Galena: troll actor in Holy Wood (screen name Rock Cliffe), later on Night Watch.

Garhartra: wizard.

Garlick, Magrat: witch. New Agey, wears a lot of occult jewellery.

Gaspode, the Wonder Dog: mongrel dog who can talk.

Gavin: a wolf from the "Clan That Smells Like This is Öberwald."

Gern: an apprentice to an embalmer (*gern* means "gladly" in German).

Gigalith: troll god of wisdom.

Gimlet: dwarf owner of a cafe.

Glodsson, Glod: dwarf horn player.

Goatfounder, Hilta: witch who dresses like a Gypsy.

Gogol, Erzulie: voodoo priestess and cook.

Goodmountain, Gunilla: dwarf printer.

Goriff: restauranteur.

Gorper: an undead.

Gortlick: dwarf songwriter.

Grateful, Lady Sara: pupil at Quirm College for Young Ladies. Likes horses.

Greebo: Nanny Ogg's very smelly cat.

Grim Squeaker: Death of rats.

Grodley, Sister: witch.

Grune: god of unseasonal fruit.

Hacknee: a dwarf and City Watch member.

Hammerthief, Agi: dwarfish demi-god of mischief in mines.

Harebut, Nijel: apprentice barbarian.

Harridan, Herrena: the henna-haired swordswoman. Lots of common sense.

Hammerjug: dwarf songwriter.

Hamstring, Ammeline (Goodie): an old witch who had a young spirit.

Harga, Sham: restauranteur.

Hashimi: prophet.

Hat: vulture-headed god of unexpected guests.

Hex: A magical computer built with ants, clocks, beehives, a mouse nest, etc.

Hong, Long: warlord.

Hogfather: god of winter solstice. Rides in sleigh pulled by four giant pigs.

Hoki the Jokester: god of tricks and jokes.

Hollow, Desiderata: fairy godmother and witch.

Hotaloga Andrews: god of voodoo.

Hwel: dwarf writer.

Hyperopia: goddess of shoes.

Ibid: authority on everything except geometry and interior decorating.

Igneous: a troll, a potter, and a wall.

Igor: a class of assistants all named Igor. They all lisp.

Io, Blind: god of thunder.

Iodine: pupil at Quirm College for Young Ladies.

Irexes: a philosopher.

Irnia: one of the three sisters who live by the cherry orchard.

Ironfoundersson, Carrot: a hero. Member of the Night Watch. Raised by dwarfs.

Ironhammer: dwarf hero. Baker of the Scone of Stone.

Jasper: troll love story protagonist.

Jimi: god of beggars.

Jones, Sweeney: barber arrested for manslaughter with a razor.

Juf: cobra-headed god of papyrus.

Ket: ibis-headed god of justice.

Khefin: two-faced god of gateways.

Koomi, Hoot: high priest. Looks like a crocodile.

Kwartz: troll.

Lemon, Satchelmouth: musician.

Littlebottom, Cheery: Night Watch's dwarf alchemist.

Longfinger, Dozy: captain of candles in charge of illumination in dwarf city.

Lully: an alchemist.

Lupine: a reverse werewolf. Each full moon he turns into a person.

Magma: king.

Malachite, Tubal de: wizard student of dracology (dragons).

Marrowleaf: wizard inventor of theory of Thaumic Imponderability.

Mazuma: high priest.

Meggelin: keeper of the door in Holy Wood.

Modo: Odd job dwarf.

Monolith: troll folk hero.

Mooty, Zebbo: thief.

Morraine: troll.

Mort: Death.

Nivor, Grunworth: tutor in assassin's school.

Nobbs, Cecil Wormsborough St. John (Nobby): crossdressing, ape-like Watchman.

Nutley, Grammer: a witch.

Octavo: most powerful book of magic. Kept in a welded iron box in a deep shaft.

Offler: six-armed crocodile god.

Ogg, Gytha (Nanny): witch. Owns a sinister cat.

Orm, Great: god of strict authorized ormits.

Palm, Rosemary: owns a house of "negotiable hospitality."

Patina: goddess of wisdom.

Pediment: gargoyle and constable of the Watch.

Petulia: goddess of "negotiable affection."

Piloxi: farmer.

Poldy, Champett: one-time guard.

Poons, Windle: wizard.

Put: Lion-headed god of justice.

Pyjama, Hrolf: man of the Watch.

Quoth: a raven, likes eyeballs.

Reg: god of club musicians.

Ridcully, Mustrum: archchancellor of the Unseen University. Wizard.

Rincewind: wizard who is often unwillingly abducted by adventures.

Rust, Lord: nobleman.

Safe Way, Mister: voodoo god.

Sandelfon: god of corridors.

Sarduk: goddess of caves.

Scrofula: Death's assistant.

Sessifet: goddess of the afternoon.

Skazz: student at Unseen University.

Silicarious: troll god of good fortune.

Skinner, Inigo: clerk assassin.

Sleeps, Wando: ambassador in Überwald.

Smith, Eskarina: first female wizard.

Sniddin: four-inch-high gnome actor in Holy Wood.

Squeak: talking mouse from Holy Wood.

Stride, Wide Man: voodoo god.

Stripfettle: wizard author of *Believe It Or Not Grimoire*.

Stronginthearm, Abba: dwarf community leader and in the City Watch.

Swires, Buggy: gnome. Later member of the Watch.

Talonthrust of Ankh, Lord Mountjoy Gayscale III: pedigree swamp dragon.

Tazikel: a man who owns twenty elephants.

Teatar, Prissal: wizard who liked practical jokes.

Teg: god of agriculture.

Tento: keeper of the door in Holy Wood.

Tightbritches, Bjorn: dwarf baker.

Thighbiter, Hrolf: constable in the City Watch.

Thumpy, Mr.: a rabbit.

Thunderaxe: dwarf printer.

Thunderfoot: dwarf actor.

Thundergust, Grabpot: dwarf cosmetics manufacturer.

Topsy, Washable: laundry woman in assassin's guild.

Truckle the Uncivil: member of Cohen's Silver Horde.

Trymon: Wizard. very organized.

Tugelbend, Victor: student wizard.

Tumult, Grammer: witch.

Turnipseed, Adrian: student wizard.

Vyrt: assassin.

Weatherwax, Esmerelda (Esme, Granny): witch.

Wheedown, Blert: a guitar maker.

Whemper, Goodie: Magrat's tutor and a research witch. Experimented with magic.

Windpike: maker of soap.

Woddeley: wizard.

Wrangler, Senior: wizard. Philosopher who looks like a horse.

Zephyrus: god of slight breezes.

THE DRAGONRIDERS OF PERN
By Anne McCaffrey

Brand

Brekke

Celina

Dunca

Elgion

Fandarel

Fanna

Fax

Felena

Gemma

Groghe

Jaxom

Jora

Kern

Kylara

Lessa

Lidith

Lytol

Manora

Menolly

Merika

Moreta

Nadira

Piemur

Rannelly

Sanra

Sharra

Talina

Toric

Wansor

Yanis

Zurg

DUNE
By Frank Herbert

Alia: psychic sister to hero.

Arrakis: planet name.

Atreides: clan name.

Bene Gesserit: priesstesshood of psychics.

Caladan: planet name.

Chani: hero's wife, desert warrior.

Fedaykin: fremen warriors.

Fremen: desert warrior tribe.

Gurney Halleck: troubador warrior.

Harkonnen: evil clan.

Jessica: priestess.

Kwisatz Haderach: male seer.

Leto: hero's father.

Maud'dib: hero's magical name (means mouse).

Melange: spice drug.

Mentat: human computer.

Sandrider: fremen who ride giant sandworms.

Shari

Stilgar: fremen leader.

Thufir Hawat: warrior.

Usul: nickname of hero.

Vladimir Harkonnen: evil leader.

Weirding: witchcraft.

THE EPIC OF GILGAMESH THIRD MILLENIUM B.C.E.

Adad: storm, rain, weather god.

Anunuki: gods of the underworld.

Anshan: a bow-making location in Persia.

Antum: wife of Anu.

Anu: father of the gods.

Apsu: primeval waters under the earth.

Aruru: goddess of creation.

Aya: the dawn; wife of the sun god.

Belit-Sheri: scribe to the gods.

Dilmun: Sumerian paradise.

Dumuzi: god of vegetation and fertility, husband to Inanna.

Ea: god of the sweet waters and wisdom; patron of the arts.

"It's . . . water," Chani said.

Jessica marveled at the way she said it. "Water." So much meaning in a simple sound. A Bene Gesserit axiom came to Jessica's mind—"Survival is the ability to swim in strange waters."

And Jessica thought, Paul and I, we must find the currents and patterns in these strange waters . . . if we're to survive.

FRANK HERBERT
DUNE

Egalmah: home of the Goddess Ninsun; a great palace.

Enlil: god of earth, wind, and space.

Ereshkigal: goddess of the underworld; once a sky goddess.

Gilgamesh: son of Goddess Ninsun and a priest.

Gizzida: see Ningizzida.

Hanish: one who forewarns of storms.

Humbaba: guardian of the cedar forests.

Igigi: collective name for the gods.

Ishtar: goddess of love and fertility; also of war. Patroness of Uruk.

Ki: Earth.

Lugulbanda: a shepherd god, protector of Gilgamesh.

Magan: land of the dead.

Mammentum: goddess of fate or destiny.

Mashu: the mountain where the sun goes at night.

Nergal: underworld god. Was once an air god who "fell" to being an underworld plague god, much as the Christian Satan.

Neti: underworld gatekeeper.

Ningal: wife of the moon and mother of the sun.

Ningizzida: fertility god called "lord of the tree of life." Later a healer god of magic.

Ninhursag: mother goddess; also called Nintu (meaning lady of birth).

Ninki: mother of enlil, god of earth.

Ninsun: mother of Gilgamesh. Goddess of wisdom.

Ninurta: warrior and wind god.

Nisaba: goddess of grain.

Samuquan: god of cattle.

Shulpae: god of feasting.

Siduri: goddess of winemaking and brewing. She lives in the garden of the sun.

Silili: horse goddess.

Sin: the moon god, father of the sun and of Ishtar.

Tammuz: dying god of vegetation.

Uruk: town in southern Babylonia between Fara and Ur (Gilgamesh was king of Uruk).

THE FAERIE QUEENE (1590)

By Edmund Spenser

Acrasia: Circe-like temptress in her bower of bliss.

Adonis

Amoret: Scudamour's bride.

Archimago: evil wizard.

Arthur: prince.

Atin: servant.

There, whence that Musick
seemed heard to bee,
Was the faire Witch her selfe now solacing,
With a new Lover, whom through sorceree
And Witchcraft, she from farre
did thither bring—
There she had him now layd a slombering,
In secret shade, after long wanton joyes—
Whilst round about them pleasauntly did sing
Many faire Ladies, and lascivious boyes,
That ever mixt their song with light
licentious toyes.

—EDMUND SPENSER
THE FAERIE QUEENE (1590)

Belphoebe: virgin huntress reared by Goddess Diana.

Diana

Duessa: Diana's seductive assistant.

Error: monster in the wandering wood.

Faunus: satyr.

Florimell: loveliest and gentlest lady in Faerieland.

Gloriana: faerie queene.

Ireana: victim.

Kirkrapine: church robber.

Mammon: god of riches.

Marinell: son of a sea nymph.

Merlin: wizard.

Mollana: nymph.

Neptune: sea god.

Panope: an old nymph.

Phaedria: coquette.

Scudamour: knight skilled in lovemaking.

Snowy Florimell: made a witch.

Timias: Prince Arthur's squire.

Una: daughter of the king and queene.

Venus: goddess of love.

THE FALL OF ATLANTIS
By Marion Zimmer Bradley

Arkati

Arvath of Alkonath

Cadamiri

Chedan

Demira

Deoris

Domaris

Elara

Elis

Isarma

Karahama

Lissi

Lydara

Maleina

Micail

Micon of Ahtarrath

Nadastor

Ragamon

Rajasta

Rathor

Riveda

Simila

Talkannon

Tiriki

THE FAR PAVILIONS
By M. M. Kaye

Anjuli: princess of Gulkote (Kairi-Bai).

Ashton Hilary Pelham-Martyn: (Ashok) British soldier.

Belinda Harlowe: British girl.

Biju Ram: the scorpion.

Dunmaya: nurse.

Gobind: doctor.

Gul Baz: servant.

Hawa Mahal: house of winds.

Jhoti: prince.

Koda Dad: master of horse.

Kulu Ram: syce.

Lalji: prince of Gulkote.

Mulraj: uncle to Anjuli and Shushila.

Nandu: prince of Gulkot.

Shushila: princess of Gulkot.

Sita: wet nurse.

Tuku: mongoose.

Zarin Khan: adopted brother of Ashok.

FIRELORD
By Parke Godwin

Agrivaine

Ambrosius

Arthur

Avalon

Bedivere

Bedwyr

Belrix

Bors

Bredei

Cador

Caius

Carline

Cerdic

Coel

Cradda

Cunedag

Dafydd

Dorelei

Drost

Druith

Eleyne

Fhain

Flavia

Gareth

Gawain

Geraint

Gryffyn

Guenevere

Imogen

Kay

Lancelot

Maelgwyn

It's an insult to freeze men like Bedivere and Trystan, Gareth, Geraint and Lancelot into a legend . . . we were never that still or complete. Guenevere wouldn't sit still while Time painted her in serenity, and God knows— Morgana? Catch the lightning, friend. Chain the wind . . .

PARKE GODWIN
FIRELORD

Melga

Merlin

Modred

Morgana

Nectan

Nectin

Peredur

Prydn

Rhian

Trystan

Uredd

Urgus

Uther

Ygerna

GRETTIR THE STRONG (1200s)

Aesa: wife of Onund.

Asmund Longhair: father of Grettir.

Atli: Grettir's brother.

Bjorn: jealous man.

Einar: farmer.

Glam: shepherd.

Grettir the Strong: Icelandic hero.

Grim: outlaw.

Illugi: Grettir's brother.

Karr the Old: father of Thorfinn.

Ofeig: father of Aesa.

Ogmund: raider.

Onund: Viking ancestor of Grettir.

Redbeard: outlaw.

Skeggi: killed by Grettir.

Thorbjorn Slowcoach: enemy.

Thorfinn: Norwegian landlord.

Thorir of Gard: father.

Thorodd: kinsman of Oxmain.

Thrand: hero.

GULLIVER'S TRAVELS (1726)
By Jonathan Swift

Calin

Clumglum

Clustril

Drunlo

Flimnap

Galbet

Golbasto Momaren Evlame Gurdilo Shefin Mully Ully Gue

Grildrig

Gulliver

Hurgo

Island of Blefuscu

Lalcon

Laputa

Lilliput

Limtoc

Lustrog

Mildendo

Nardac

Reldresal

Skyresh Bolgolam

Slamecksan

Tramecksan

GUY OF WARWICK (1200s)

Anlaf: king of Denmark.

Athelstan: king of England.

Colbrand: giant.

Ernis: emperor of Greece.

Felice La Belle: heroine.

Guy: knight.

Loret: Ernis' daughter.

Morgadour: knight.

Otous: duke of Pavia.

Reignier: emperor of Germany.

Rohaud: earl.

Segyn: duke of Louvain.

Segyn: prisoner.

Tirri: knight.

HARRY POTTER NOVELS
By J. K. Rowling

Agrippa: wizard on a card.

Animagi: wizards who can transform into animals.

Animagus: individual wizard who can transform into animals.

Aragog: spider.

Bane: a centaur.

Binns: Professor of the History of Magic.

Black, Sirius: a wizard and Harry's godfather.

Bloody Baron: ghost.

Bludgers: a ball.

Bode: unspeakable.

Boggart: a dark creature.

Buckbeak: a hippogriff.

Circe: witch on a card.

Cliodna: witch on a card.

Crabbe: Malfoy's friend.

Crookshanks: Hermione's cat.

De Mimsy-Portington, Sir Nicholas: (nearly Headless Nick): ghost.

Dippet, Professor: Hogwarts teacher.

Dobby: a house-elf.

Dudley: mean cousin.

Dumbledore, Albus: headmaster at Hogwarts.

Dursley: mean relatives.

Emeric the Evil: historical figure.

Errol: an elderly owl.

Fang: Hagrid's dog.

Fawkes: a phoenix.

Filch, Argus: caretaker.

Firebolt: a broom.

Firenze: a centaur.

Fletcher, Mundungus: wizard.

Flintwick, Professor: charms teacher.

Fluffy: giant three-headed dog.

Fudge, Cornelius: Minister of Magic.

Goyle: Malfoy's friend.

Granger, Hermione: friend of Harry and Ron.

Griffindor: school house.

Grindlewald: a dark wizard defeated by Dumbledore.

Grindylow: a dark creature.

Griphook: a goblin.

Grubbly Plank, Professor: temporary care of magical creatures teacher.

Grummion, Alberic: wizard on a card.

Gryffindor, Godrick: great wizard.

Hagrid, Rubeus: groundskeeper at Hogwarts.

Hedwig: Harry's owl.

Hengist of Woodcroft: wizard on a card.

Hinkypunk: a dark creature.

Hippogriff: magical animal.

Hootch, Madam: flying teacher.

Howler: an angry wizard message.

Hufflepuff, Helga: great witch.

Hufflepuff: a Hogwart's house.

Kappa: a dark creature.

Krum, Viktor: quidditch player.

Lestrange

Welcome! Welcome to a new year at Hogwarts! Before we begin our banquet, I would like to say a few words. And here they are— Nitwit! Blubber! Oddment! Tweak!

—PROF. DUMBLEDORE
J. K. ROWLING'S
*HARRY POTTER AND
THE PHILOSOPHER'S STONE*

It was one of my more brilliant ideas, and between you and me, that's saying something. . . . My brain surprises even me sometimes."

—PROF. DUMBLEDORE
J. K. ROWLING'S
*HARRY POTTER AND
THE PHILOSOPHER'S STONE*

Lockhart, Gilderoy: wizard gardener.

Longbottom, Neville: student.

Lupin, Professor: dark arts teacher.

Malfoy, Draco: student.

McGonagall, Professor: transfiguration teacher.

Mermish: language of merpeople.

Miggs, Martin: the Mad Muggle (a comic book).

Moody, Mad-Eye: retired dark wizard catcher.

Morgana: witch on a card.

Mortlake: wizard.

Muggle: non-wizard folk.

Nagini

Nifflers

Nimbus: a broom.

Norbert: Norwegian ridgeback dragon.

Nott

Padfoot

Paracelsus: wizard on a card.

Peeves: a poltergeist.

Pigwidgeon: a tiny owl ("Pig").

Pomfrey, Madam: school nurse.

Potter, Harry: a wizard.

Ptolemy: wizard on a card.

Quirrell, Professor: defense against the dark arts teacher.

Ravenclaw: school house.

Ronan: a centaur.

Rowena Ravenclaw: great witch.

Scabbers: magical rat.

Sinistra, Professor: astronomy teacher.

Slytherin, Salazar: great wizard.

Slytherin: a house at Hogwarts.

Snape, Severes Professor: potions teacher.

Sprout, Professor: herbology teacher.

Trelawney, Professor: divination teacher.

Uric the Oddball: historical figure

Veela: enchanting dancers.

Voldemort: evil wizard.

Warbeck, Celestina: singing sorceress.

Wattlebird: a password.

Weasley, Ron: Harry's best friend.

Winky: a house-elf.

Wormtail

THE HEART OF THE FIRE
By Cerridwen Fallingstar

Amergin

Anu

Ashtara: sexual goddess of passion.

Avalon

Bearhearth

Blouwedd: goddess of beauty and flowers.

Briget

Cailitie: the cat.

Cailleach: a dark aspect of the goddess.

Cernonus

Cerridwen

Chanda

Copper

Crosby

Druaderia: Gypsy tantra (sex magick).

Elana

Eostre

Ewan

Fiona Mcnair

Galen

Grizelda Greediguts the Cat

Ian

Jesses

Jonet

Kelpie: sea or lake monster.

Kyairthwen

Leman: lover.

Lindsay

Litha

Lizbet

Lochlan

Magpie Maiden

Mairead

Malcolm

Mannanon MacLir

Mari

"Thu," he said gently, "I saw your face in the oil three months ago. I was divining for Pharoaoh, my mind upon him, and as I bent over the bowl you were there, the blue eyes, the sweetly curving mouth, the sultry black hair. Your name whispered through my mind, Thu, Thu, and then you were gone. I do not need to read for you. Fate has presented us to each other, for reasons that are as yet unknown. My name is Hui, but you will call me Master. Would you like to learn?"

PAULINE GEDGE
HOUSE OF DREAMS

Marianna: goddess of the sea.

McTavish

Mina

Minstrel

Mist the Cat

Moonsock the Cat

Morrigan

Myrrhiana

Nimue

Oberon the Cat (Obie)

Orrin Argyle

Peat Moss the Cat

Ragni: spider goddess.

Sari Snowflower

Scotia Cailleach

Sean

Sooktart Machlana

Staghorn

Taliesin

Verado

Violet

Wind Mare

Winter

Drui

Epona

Esus

Goibban

Kazhak

Kelti

Kernunnos Shapechanger

Kolaxis

Kwelon

Mahka

Nematona

Okelos

Poel

Rigatona

Ro-An

Suleva

Talia

Taranis

Tena

Toutorix

Tsaygas

Uiska

Vilma

THE HORSE GODDESS
By Morgan Llywelyn

Basl

Brydda

Dasadas

HOUSE OF DREAMS
By Pauline Gedge

Ahmose: village woman.

Ani: scribe.

Ast-Amasareth: royal wife.

Benemus: general.

Disenk: body servant.

Harshira: teacher.

Hatia: concubine.

Hui: seer.

Hunro: concubine.

Kaha: scribe.

Kenna: steward.

Mersura: chancellor to the Pharaoh.

Nebnefer: trainer.

Pa-ari: priest of Wepwawet.

Paiis: Hui's brother.

Pentu: scribe of the Double House of Life.

Ramses: Pharaoh, the Great Bull.

Ramses: prince.

Thu: healer, beautiful concubine.

Twosret: a queen.

Wepwawet: jackal god of war.

Wia: overseer.

IVANHOE
(1820)
By Sir Walter Scott

Athelstane of Coningsburgh: a descendant of ancient Saxon kings.

Aymer: lazy prior captured by Robin Hood.

Cedric the Saxon: master of Rotherwood.

Gurth: Cedric's jester.

Lady Rowena: beautiful, young ward of Cedric.

Reginald Front De Boeuf: savage.

Ulrica: Saxon hag.

Waldemar Fitzurse: Prince John's wily follower, banished by Richard.

Wilfred of Ivanhoe: chivalrous hero, son of Cedric, Rowena's husband.

THE JUNGLE BOOK
By Rudyard Kipling

Akela: a wolf.

Bagheera: the black panther.

Baloo: brown bear.

Chuchundra: the muskrat.

Darzee: the tailorbird.

Hathi: the white elephant.

Ikki: the porcupine.

Kaa: the rock snake.

Kala Nag: the elephant.

Lungri: the lame one.

Mang: the bat.

Mao: the peacock.

Mowgli: the frog.

Mysa: buffalo.

Nagaina: the cobra.

Raksha: the demon.

Rann: the kite.

Rikki-Tikki-Tavi: the mongoose.

Shere Khan: the tiger.

Tabaqui: the jackal.

Toomai: the boy.

THE KALEVALA
(PRIOR TO 1000 C.E.)
By Elias Lonnrot (oral)

Ahti: matchless boy.

Aino: Joukahainen's sister, wife to Vainenoinen.

Annikki: she of good name, girl of the night, maid of dusk.

Ilmarinen: the smith.

Joukahainen: the young bard.

Jack Frost: the evil one, a trickster.

Karelia: ox.

Kullervo: Kalervo's son.

Kylli: an island maid; island flower.

Kyllikki: an island maid; island flower.

Lemminkainen: wanton, luckless one.

Louhi: mistress of the northland.

Marjatta: nice young maid.

Mieliki: forest daughter.

Nyyrikki: Tapio's son.

Osmo: the brewer woman.

Pellervionen: the field's son.

Piltti: tiny wench.

Sampsa: tiny boy.

Tellervo: Tapio's maid.

Tiera

Tuoni: river.

Tuulikki: forest girl.

Utamo: fisherman.

Väinämöinen: the timeless old bard.

LE MORTE D'ARTHUR
(1469)
By Sir Thomas Malory

Agravaine: Gawain's brother.

Arthur: king of Britain.

Balan: brother of Balin.

Balin Le Sauvage: knight.

Brangwaine: Isoud's maid.

Breunor Le Noire: knight.

Dodinas Le Sauvage: knight.

Ector De Maris: knight.

Elaine Le Blanc: the fair maid of Astolat.

Gaheris: Gawain's brother.

Galahad: Launcelot's son.

Gareth: brother of Gawain.

Gawain: Arthur's nephew.

Gouvernail: Tristram's tutor.

Isoud: Irish princess, lover of Tristram.

King Evelake: ancient ruler.

Launcelot du Lake: knight, lover of the queen.

Linet: damsel.

Lionel: knight.

Liones: Linet's sister, Gareth's wife.

Meliogrance: kidnapper of Guenevere.

Merlin: wizard.

Mordred: Arthur's son.

Morgan Le Fay: Arthur's half-sister.

Numue: lady of the lake,
   Merlin's mistress.

Palamides: valiant Pagan knight.

Pellinore: knight who continuously
   pursues the Questing Beast.

Percival: knight.

Queen Guenevere: queen of Britain.

Sagramore: knight.

Sir Kay: Arthur's foster brother.

Tristram: knight.

LION OF IRELAND
By Morgan Llywelyn

Ailill

Amlaff

Anluan

Aoife

Ardan

Bebinn

Benin

Brian Boru

Brigid

Brodir

Cahal

Callachan

Camin

Carroll

Cashel

Cennedi

Cet

Conall Cernach

Conn

Connlaoch

Conor

Corc

Cuchullain

Cullen

Damon

Deirdre

Dermott

Donncuan

Donogh

Echtigern

Emer

Ferdiad

Fiacaid

Fiona

Fithir

Flann

Gilli

Gormlaith

Guaire

Ilacquin

Ivar

Kernac

Kian

Kincora

Lachtna

Leti

Liam Mac Aengus

Macliag

Maelmordha

Mahon

Malachi Mor

Mangus

Marcan

Molloy

Muiredach

Murrough Mac Brian

Nessa

Niall

Olaf Cuaran

Ospak

Padraic

Sabia

Sigurd

Sitric

Svein

Teigue

THE LORD OF THE RINGS AND THE SILMARILLION

By J. R. R. Tolkien

Aerin

Aglon

Ainur

Aldaron

Aldor

Almaren

Aman

Amandil

Amlach

Amras

Amrie

Amroth

Anach

Anarion

Aragorn

Arathorn

Arien

Arthad

Arwen Evenstar (Undomiel): elvish princess.

Atani

Avallone

Avari

Azaghal

Bain: dwarf lord.

Balar

Baldor

Balin: dwarf lord.

Balrog

Barahir: warrior of Gondor.

Bard the Bowman

Barliman Butterbur: innkeeper in Bree.

Beechbone: an ent (tree creature).

Beleg

Belfalas: place name.

Beorn: a warrior of the Mark.

Bereg

Beregond: a warrior of Gondor.

Beren

Bergil

Beruthiel

Bifur: a hobbit.

Bilbo Baggins: the finder of the ruling ring; a hobbit.

Bombadil, Tom: the oldest creature in Middle Earth.

Borlach

Borlad

Boromir: a warrior prince of Gondor.

Brand: a legendary warrior.

Brandir

Bregalad: an ent.

Brego

Brodda

Cardolan

Carnil

Celeborn

Celebrimbor

Celon

Ceorl

Cirdan: the ancient shipwright.

Ciryon

Daeron

Dagnir

Dagorlad: a battle plain.

Dain: a dwarf lord.

Dairuin

Deagol: an ancient hobbit, brother of Smeagol.

Denethor: steward of Gondor.

Dernhelm: a warrior of the Mark.

Dimbar

Dior

Dolmed

Dori: a dwarf lord.

Doriath

Dorlas

Draugluin

Drengist

Dunadan: man of the west.

Durin: a dwarf lord.

Dwalin: a dwarf lord.

Dwarrowdelf: place name.

Ea

Earendil

Earnur

Ecthelion

Edain

Elbereth Gilthoniel (Varda): an elvish princess.

Eldar

Elendil: a king of westernesse.

Elenna

Elerrina

Elessar

Elfhelm: a warrior of the mark.

Elfstone

Elladan: an elvish warrior.

Elrohir: an elvish warrior.

Elrond Halfelven: an elvish king.

Elwe

Elwing

Emeldir

Eomer: heir to the throne of the Mark.

Eomun

Eorl: legendary warrior king of the Mark.

Eothain

Eowyn: warrior princess of the Mark.

Erkenbrand: a warrior of the Mark.

Fangorn (Treebeard): leader of the ents.

Faramir: a captain of Gondor.

Feanor

Fimbrethil: an ent.

Finglas (Leaflock): an ent.

Fingon

Finrod

Floi: a dwarf lord.

Forlong: a lesser king of Gondor.

Fredegar Bolger: a hobbit.

Frodo: the hero of the story; a hobbit.

Fundin

Galadriel: elvish queen of Lorien.

Galdor

Gamling

Gandalf the Grey (Mithrandir): a wizard.

Garulf

Gildor: an elvish warrior.

Gimli: a dwarf, Frodo's companion.

Gladden Fields

Gloin: a dwarf lord.

Glorfindel: an elvish warrior.

Goldberry: Tom Bombadil's wife.

Goldwine

Gorlim

Gram

Grimbeorn

Grimbold

Guilin

Guthlaf

Gwindor

Hador

Haladin

Halbarad

Haldir

Halflings: hobbits.

Hama

Harding

Helm

Herefara

Hirgon

Hirluin

Horn

Hurin

Iarwain Ben Adar

Idril

Imrahil

Ingold

Ioreth

Iorlas

Isengrim

Isildur: legendary warrior king.

Legolas Greenleaf: an elf.

Lindon

Lorien: an elvish land.

Luthien Tinuviel: an elvish princess.

Magor

Mahal

Malbeth the Seer

Mauhur

Melian

Meneldil

Meneldor

Meriadoc Brandybuck (Merry):
  Frodo's companion.

Mim

Miriel

Mirkwood: place name.

Mordor: Sauron's realm.

Nandor

Narvi: an elvish smith.

Narya: an elvish ring.

Nenya: an elvish ring.

Nimrodel: a river.

Noldor

Nori

Ohtar

Oin: a dwarf lord.

Olorin

Ori: a dwarf.

Orome

Orophin

Peredhil

Peregrin Took (Pippin): a hobbit,
  Frodo's companion.

Quenya

Quickbeam: an ent.

Radagast the Brown: a wizard.

Ragnor

Rian

Rumil

Salmar

Slimbirch: an ent.

Strider

Taras

Targon

Tauron

Telchar

Thengel: a legendary king of the Mark.

Theoden: king of the Mark.

Theodred

Thingol

Thistlewood: an ent.

Thorin Oakenshield: a legendary warrior dwarf.

Thrain: a dwarf lord.

Thranduil

Thror

Turgon

Turin

Ulfang

Valandil

Vana

Vanyar

Vorondil

Wandlimb: an ent.

Widfara

Yavanna

THE MABINOGI (900s)

Annwen

Aranrhod

Arawn

Arberth

Arthur

Bendigeidfran

Branwen

Bres

Cei

Ceridwen

Cigfa

Coraniaid

Diaspad: cry.

Dyfed

Dylan

Efnisien

Elphin

Formorian

Garm: shout.

Gawain

Gilfaethwy

Glewlwyd

Glyn Cuch

Goewin

Gwaeth: worse.

Gwaethaf Oll: worst of all.

Gwales

Gwion Bach

Gwydion

Gwynedd

Hafgan

Harlech

Lleuelys

Llew

Lludd

Llwyd

Llyr

Lugh

Maelgwn

Manawydan

Matholwch

Nisien

Nuadha

Olwen

Owaen

Pendaran Dyfed

Pryderi

Pwyll

Rhiannon

Sefwlch

Silver-Hand

Taliesin

Teyrnon

Twrch Trwyth

Ywain

MACBETH
By William Shakespeare

Angus

Banquo

Caithness

Donalbain

Duncan

Fleance

Hecate

Lennox

Macbeth

MacDuff

Malcolm

Menteith

Ross

Seyton

Siward

ALL WITCHES *(Dancing in a ring)*
> *The weird sisters hand in hand,*
> *Posters of the sea and land,*
> *Thus do go about, about*
> *Thrice to thine, and thrice to mine,*
> *And thrice again to make up nine.*
> *Peace! The charm's wound up.*

> WILLIAM SHAKESPEARE
> *MACBETH*

TITANIA
> *First rehearse your song by rote,*
> *To each word a warbling note.*
> *Hand in hand with fairy grace*
> *Will we sing and bless this place.*

> WILLIAM SHAKESPEARE
> *A MIDSUMMER NIGHT'S DREAM*

THE MASTERS OF SOLITUDE
By Marvin Kaye and Parke Godwin

Arin

Bern

Bowdeen

Callan

Callee

Charzen

Deak

Echo

Elin

Gannell

Garrick

Hoban

Holder

Janny

Jay

Jenna

Karli

Kon

Korbin

Lams

Loomin

Lorl

Magill

Maysa

Moss

Mrikan

Myudah

Samman

Sand

Shalane

Shando

Sidele

Singer

Suffec

Thammay

Tilda

Uhian

Wengen

The Merlin Novels
By Mary Stewart

Branwen

Cadal

Camlach

Cei

Cerdic

Dyved

Gwydion

Igraine

Kevin

Lancelet

Lot

Merlin

Morgaine of the Fairies

Morgause

Niniane

Pellinore

Taliesin

Uriens

Uther Pendragon

Viviane

Galapas

Keridwen

Merlin

Merlinus

Moravik

Myrddin Emrys

Niniane

Ulfin

Uther

Vortigern

Ygraine

A Midsummer Night's Dream
By William Shakespeare

Cobweb: fairy.

Egeus: Hermia's father.

Francis Flute: a bellows master.

Helena: in love with Demetrius.

Hermia: Egeus's daughter.

Hippolyta: queen of the Amazons.

Lysander: loved by Hermia.

Moonshine: Robin Starveling in the interlude.

Moth: fairy.

Mustardseed: fairy.

Nick Bottom: a weaver.

Oberon: king of the fairies.

Peaseblossom: fairy.

Philostrate: Theseus's master of the revels.

Prologue: Peter Quince in the interlude.

Puck: or Robin Goodfellow.

Pyramus: Nick Bottom in the interlude.

Snug: a joiner.

Theseus: duke of Athens.

Thisbe: Francis Flute in the interlude.

Titania: queen of the fairies.

THE MISTS OF AVALON
By Marion Zimmer Bradley

Ambrosius

Arthur

Avalon

Balan

Balin

Caerleon

Cai

Galahad

Gawaine

Gorlois

Gwenhwyfar

Gwydion

Igraine

Kevin

Lancelet

Lot

Merlin

Morgaine of the Fairies

Morgause

Niniane

Pellinore

Taliesin

Uriens

Uther Pendragon

Viviane

The Nibelungenlied
(1203)

Alberich: a dwarf, warden of the treasure.

Aldrian: Father of Hagen and Dankwart.

Alzei: a town northwest of Worms.

Amelrich: brother of the ferryman on the Danube.

Amelungland: country in northern Italy.

Arras: a city in France famous for its tapestries.

Astolt: lord of the castle in Medelick.

Azagouc: a mythical land somewhere in the orient.

Balmung: Seigfried's sword.

Bechelaren: town in Austria.

Bern: Dietrich's home. Capital of Amelungland.

Bloedel: Etzel's brother.

Botelung: Etzel's father.

Brunhild: queen of Isenland, Gunther's wife.

Dankrat: Ute's husband.

Dankwart: Hagen's brother.

Dietrich: king of Amelungland.

Eckewart: Margrave of the Burgundian kings.

Else: ruler of the border province.

Gelfrat: Else's brother.

Gere: Margrave in Burgandy.

Gernot: son of Ute and Dankrat.

Gibeche: a king.

Giselher: a king.

Gotelind: wife of Margrave Rudeger of Bechelaren.

Gran: city in Hungary.

Gunther: a king.

Hadeburg: mermaid.

Hagen of Troneg: son of Aldrian.

Hawart: Danish prince.

Helca: Etzel's first wife.

Helfrich: one of Dietrich's vassals.

Helmnot: one of Dietrich's vassals.

Hildebrand: Dietrich's teacher and armor bearer.

Hildegund: fiancée of Walther of Spain.

Hornboge: one of Etzel's vassals.

Hunolt: chamberlain of the Burgundian kings.

Irnfried: Landgrave of Thuringia.

Isenstien: Brunhild's castle in Isenland.

Kriemhild: daughter of Ute and Dankrat, wife of Siegfried and Etzel.

Liudegast: king of Denmark.

Liudeger: king of the Saxons.

Natwin: father of Herrat.

Nibelungs: possessor of the Nibelung treasure.

Nudung: kinsman of Gotelind.

Ortlieb: son of Etzel and Kriemhild.

Ortwin: son of Hagen's sister.

Ramung: duke from the land of the Walachs.

Rudegar of Belchelaren: Margrave of Bechelaren, Gotelind's husband.

Rumolt: master cook.

Schrutan: participant in tournament.

Siegmund: king of the Netherlands.

Sindolt: cupbearer.

Spessart: hilly forestland northeast of Worms.

Swemmel: minstrel.

Troneg: Troja.

Ute: Dankrat's widow.

Vergen: town on the Danube.

Volker: a minstrel.

Walther: hero from Spain.

Waske: Iring's sword.

Werbel: minstrel.

Witege: warrior.

Witchart: one of Dietrich's vassals.

Wolfhart: one of Dietrich's vassals.

Xanten Castle: capital of the Netherlands.

Zazamanc: mythical land in the orient.

THE SONG OF HIAWATHA (1855)

By Henry Wadsworth Longfellow

Bemahgut: grape vine.

Bena: pheasant.

Ishkoodah: the comet.

Kahgahgee: raven.

Keewaydin: northwest wind.

Kwo-Ne-She: dragonfly.

Maskenozha: pike.

Meenahga: blueberry.

Minnehaha: laughing water.

Mudgekeewis: west wind.

Nahma: sturgeon.

Nepahwin: spirit of sleep.

Nokomis-moon: mother goddess.

Odahmin: strawberry.

Okahahwis: herring.

Opechee: robin.

Owaissa: bluebird.

Pah-Puk-Keena: grasshopper.

Sebowisha: brook.

Shahbomin: gooseberry.

Shawgashee: crawfish.

Shuh-Shuh-Gah: heron.

Subbekashe: spider.

Wawonaissa: whippoorwill.

Wenonah: first-born daughter.

The Song of Roland
(1050–1096)

Acelin

Aelroth

Apollin

Aude: damsel engaged to Roland.

Balagant: emir of Babylon, leader of the Saracens.

Basan

Basilie

Blancandrin: the wisest of the Pagans, he plots with Ganelon.

Bramimond: widow of King Marsilion. Charlemagne takes her to France where she is baptised and named Juliana.

Canabeus

Capuel

Charlemagne: two-hundred-year-old emperor (King Charles or Carlon); possessed a militant zeal for Christianizing Pagans.

Clarin

Climborin

Durendal

Esprieris

Estamarin

Eudropin

Ganelon: traitor knight who conspires with Pagans.

Gefrey

Gerer

Gerin

Grandonies

Guarlan the Bearded

Jouner

Jozeran

Jurfaret the Blond

Maheu

Malbien

Malduit

Malprimis

Marsilium: Saracen king.

Milun

Priamun

Rabel

Roland: favorite nephew of Charlemagne; a hater of Pagans. He doesn't use his weapons when the Saracens attack, trusting in Christ's supremacy over the Pagans. He was killed.

Saracen

Tedbalt

Timozel

Valdabrun

STORM LORD
By Tanith Lee

Amnorh: councillor.

Amun: charioteer.

Anakire: goddess.

Anici: merchant's siter.

Ashne'e: priestess of the goddess.

Elyr: country of poets.

Eraz: Raldnor's mother.

Krin: general.

Liun: captain.

Lomandra: queen's servant.

Orhn: prince.

Orhvan: merchant.

Orklos: merchant.

Raldnor: warrior.

Ras: assistant.

Rehdon: king of Dortha.

Thann: king of Xarar.

Val Mala: queen of Dorthar.

Xarar: neighboring country.

Xaros: merchant rogue.

Yhaheil: astrologer.

Yr Dakan: master of Orklos.

THE STORY OF BURNT NJAL
(1200s)

Aumund

Bergthora

Bork the Waxy-Toothed Blade

Fiddle Mord

Flosi

Geir the Priest

Gunnar

Hallgerda

Hauskuld

Helge

Helgi

Hildigunna

Hogni

Kari

Kolskegg

Lything

Mord

Njal

Olaf

Otkell

Rodny

Skapti

Skarphedinn

Starkad

Thangbrand

Thiostolf

Thord

Thorgeir of Lightwater

Thorgerda

Thorwald

Thrain

Unna

THE TEMPEST
(1611)
By William Shakespeare

Alanso: king and father of Ferdinand.

Antonio: Prospero's brother who plots against him.

Ariel: spirit released by Prospero.

Caliban: monstrous servant of Prospero.

Ferdinand: lover of Miranda.

Gonzalo: faithful courtier.

Miranda: Prospero's daughter.

Prospero: hero.

TRISTAN AND ISOLDE
(1210)
By Gottfried Von Strassburg

Blanchefleur: wife to Rivalin, Tristan's mother.

Brangene: companion to Isolde.

Duke Morolt: brother of Isolde.

Duke Morgan: enemy of Rivalin.

Isolde of the White Hands: wife of Tristan in name only.

Isolde the Fair: lover of Tristan.

Queen Isolde of Ireland: mother of Isolde the Fair.

Rivalin: Tristan's father.

Rual the Faithful: Tristan's foster father.

Tristan: hero.

WIZARDS' WORLDS
By Andre Norton

Alizon

Craike

Dagmar

Dairine

Elfanor

Elfreda

Elyn

Elys

Erlia

Fallon

Farne

Fritigen

Gunnora

Herdrek

Hertha

High Hallack

Horla

Inghela

Jabis

Jervon

Jonkara

Jorik

Kara

Kas

Koris

Kuno

Mafra

Malka

Nadi

Ortis

Porpae

Rinard

Rivery

Roth

Rothar

Salzarat

Sibbald

Simond

Starrex

Sulcar

Sylt

Takya

Tamisan

Tanree

Thasus

Thra

Trystan

Tursla

Uletka Rory

Unnanna

Urre

Vidruth

Volt

Wowern

Xactol

Zackuth

WOLVES OF THE DAWN
By William Sarabande

Albion

Balor

Cethlinn

Dana

Dianket

Donar

Dragda

Eala

Elathan

Falcon

Huldre

Keptah

Manannan

Mealla

Morrigan

Munremar

Nemed

Nia

Star Gazer

Uaine

BIBLIOGRAPHY

BOOKS

Abrams, M. H. *The Norton Anthology of English Literature.* New York: W. W. Norton & Co., 1973.

Adams, Douglas. *The Hitchhiker's Guide to the Galaxy.* London: Pan Books Ltd., 1981.

_____. *The Long, Dark Tea-Time of the Soul.* New York: Simon and Schuster, 1988.

Adler, Margot. *Drawing Down the Moon.* Boston: Beacon Press, 1986.

Alfred, William, trans. *Beowulf.* New York: Dutton, 1962.

Ames, Winthrop. *What Shall We Name the Baby?* New York: Pocket Books/Vistacam, 1974.

343

Andalusia the Heretic. *The Complete Discordian Moosemas Celebration Handbook.* Blue Mound, Wi.: Moonstone Press. n.d.

Anderson, William. *The Green Man: The Archetype of our Oneness with the Earth.* San Francisco: HarperCollins, 1990.

Apuleius, Lucius. *The Golden Ass.* New York: Collier Books, 1962.

Aristophanes. *Lysistrata.* New York: New American Library, 1964.

_____. *The Wasps, The Poet and the Women, and The Frogs.* New York: Penguin, 1964.

Athanassakis, Apostolos N., ed. *The Homeric Hymns.* Baltimore, Md.: John's Hopkins Press, 1976.

Avto, John. *Dictionary of Word Origins.* New York: Arcade, 1990.

Bain, Robert. *The Clans and Tartans of Scotland.* Glasgow: Collins Publishing, 1968.

Bardsley, Charles Wareing. *Curiosities of Puritan Nomenclature.* London: 1880. (Gale Research Co., facsimile reprint 1970.)

Bartlett, John. *Familiar Quotations.* New York: Little, Brown & Co., 1919.

Benjamin, Alan. *A Treasury of Baby Names.* New York: New American Library, 1991.

Boulton, Jane, ed. *Opal: The Journal of an Understanding Heart.* By Opal Whitely. Palo Alto, Calif.: Tioga Publishing Co., 1984.

Bradley, Marion Zimmer. *The Bloody Sun.* New York: Ace Science Fiction Books, 1979.

_____. *City of Sorcery.* New York: Daw Books, 1984.

_____. *The Fall of Atlantis.* New York: Baen Publishing, 1983.

_____. *The Forbidden Tower.* New York: Daw Books, 1977.

_____. *Hawkmistress.* New York: Daw Books, 1982.

_____. *The Heritage of Hastur.* New York: Daw Books, 1975.

_____. *The Mists of Avalon.* New York: Ballentine/Del Rey, 1982.

_____. *Sharra's Exile.* New York: Daw Books, 1981.

_____. *The Shattered Chain.* New York: Daw Books, 1976.

_____. *Star of Danger.* New York: Ace, 1983.

_____. *Stormqueen!* New York: Daw Books, 1978.

_____. *Thendara House.* New York: Ace, 1983.

_____. *Two to Conquer.* New York: Daw Books, 1980.

_____. *The Winds of Darkover.* New York: Ace, 1982.

_____. *The World Wreckers.* Ace Science Fiction Books, 1971.

Bradley, Marion Zimmer, and the Friends of Darkover. *Free Amazons of Darkover.* New York: Daw Books, 1985.

_____. *Sword of Chaos.* New York: Daw Books, 1982.

Bradley, Marion Zimmer. *Four Moons of Darkover.* New York: Daw Books, 1988.

Buckland, Raymond. *Scottish Witchcraft.* St. Paul, Minn.: Llewellyn Publications, 1992.

Budge, E. A. Wallis. *The Egyptian Book of the Dead: The Papyrus of Ani.* Egyptian text transliteration and translation. New York: Dover Books, 1985.

Cannon, John, and Ralph Griffiths. *The Oxford Illustrated History of the British Monarchy.* New York: Oxford University Press, 1988.

Cassell's Italian Dictionary. London: Cassell & Co., 1958.

Chadwick, Nora. *The Celts.* New York: Penguin, 1991.

Chaucer. *The Canterbury Tales.* New York: Bantam, 1964.

Coghlan, Ronan, Ida Grehan, and P. W. Joyce. *Book of Irish Names: First, Family & Place Names.* New York: Sterling Publishers, 1989.

Cottle, Basil. *Names.* London: Thames and Hudson, 1983.

Cruden, Alexander. *Cruden's Complete Concordance to the Old and New Testaments.* Grand Rapids, Mich.: Zondervan Publishing House, 1968.

Cunningham, Scott. *Magical Herbalism.* St. Paul, Minn.: Llewellyn Publications, 1982.

_____. *Cunningham's Encyclopedia of Magical Herbs.* St. Paul, Minn.: Llewellyn Publications, 1988.

Delaney, Frank. *Legends of the Celts.* London: Grafton/HarperCollins, 1991.

Delderfield, Eric R. *Kings and Queens of England and Great Britain.* New York: Facts on File, 1990.

Dickens, Charles. *Great Expectations.* New York: Scholastic Book Services, 1968.

Dinesen, Isak. *Out of Africa.* New York: Vintage Books/Random House, 1985.

Dinwiddie-Boyd, Elza. *Proud Heritage: 11,001 Names for Your African-American Baby,* New York: Avon Books, 1994.

Dolan, J. R., and Clarkson Potter. *English Ancestral Names.* New York: Crown Publishing, 1972.

Dunkling, Leslie. *English Country House Names*. 1971.

Eddings, David. *Castle of Wizardry*. New York: Del Rey/Ballantine, 1984.

_____. *Enchanters' End Game*. New York: Del Rey/Ballantine, 1984.

_____. *Magician's Gambit*. New York: Del Rey/Ballantine, 1983.

_____. *Pawn of Prophecy*. New York: Del Rey/Ballantine, 1982.

_____. *Queen of Sorcery*. New York: Del Rey/Ballantine, 1982.

Eliot, T. S. *Old Possum's Book of Practical Cats*. London: Faber & Faber, 1988.

Ellefson, Connie Lockhart. *The Melting Pot Book of Baby Names*. White Hall, Va.: Betterway Publishing, 1987.

Ellis, Peter Berresford. *Dictionary of Celtic Mythology*. London: Constable & Co., 1992.

Evslin, Bernard, Dorothy Evslin, and Ned Hoopes. *The Greek Gods*. New York: Scholastic Book Services, 1969.

Fallingstar, Cerridwen. *The Heart of the Fire*. San Geronimo, Calif.: Cauldron Publications, 1990.

Farrar, Janet and Stewart. *A Witches' Bible*. New York: Magickal Childe, 1984.

_____. *The Witches' God*. Custer, Wash.: Phoenix Publishing, 1989.

_____. *The Witches' Goddess*. Custer, Wash.: Phoenix Publishing, 1987.

Ford, Patrick K. *The Mabinogi and Other Medieval Welsh Tales*. London: University of California Press, 1977.

Gimbutas, Marija. *The Goddesses and Gods of Old Europe*. Berkeley, Calif.: University of California Press, 1990.

Godwin, Parke. *Firelord*. New York: Bantam Books, 1982.

Graves, Robert. *The White Goddess*. New York: Farrar, Straus & Giroux, 1974.

Grieve, Mrs. M. *A Modern Herbal*. New York: Dover, 1971.

Grimal, Pierre. *Larousse World Mythology*. New York: Excalibur Books, 1984.

Haley, Alex. *Roots*. New York: Bantam/Viking, 1977.

Halliday, Tim, and Dr. Kraig Adler. *The Encyclopedia of Reptiles and Amphibians*. New York: Facts on File, 1986.

Hamilton, Edith. *Mythology: Timeless Tales of Gods and Heroes*. New York: New American Library, 1969.

Hanks, Patrick, and Flavia Hodges. *A Dictionary of First Names*. New York: Oxford University Press, 1990.

_____. *A Dictionary of Surnames*. New York: Oxford University Press, 1989.

Hart, Mickey. *Drumming at the Edge of Magic*. San Francisco: Harper San Francisco, 1990.

Heinlein, Robert. *Stranger in a Strange Land*. New York: Ace Books, 1987.

Herbert, Frank. *Dune*. Philadelphia: Chosen Books, 1965.

Hope, Murry. *Practical Celtic Magic: A Working Guide to the Magical Heritage of the Celtic Races*. Wellingborough, Northamptonshire, UK: Aquarian Press, 1987.

_____. *The Psychology of Ritual*. Longmead, Shaftesbury, UK: Element Books, 1988.

Houston, Dr. Percy Hazen, and Dr. Robert Metcalf Smith. *Types of World Literature*. New York: Doubleday, Doran, & Co., 1930.

Jackson, Kenneth Hurlstone. *A Celtic Miscellany*. New York: Viking/Penguin, 1971.

Jonson, Ben. *Bartholemew Fair*. From Magill, Frank. *Cyclopedia of Literary Characters*. New York: Harper and Row, 1963.

_____. *Hymn to Diana*. From Abrams, M. H. *The Norton Anthology of English Literature*. New York: W. W. Norton & Co., 1973.

K, Amber. *True Magick: A Beginner's Guide*. St. Paul, Minn.: Llewellyn Publications, 1990.

Kaye, Marvin, and Parke Godwin. *The Masters of Solitude*. New York: Avon, 1979.

Keats, John. "Ode to Psyche." in Abrams, M. H. *The Norton Anthology of English Literature*. New York: W. W. Norton & Co., 1973.

Kolatch, Alfred J. *The Jonathan David Dictionary of First Names*. New York: J. David Publishing, 1980.

Kurtz, Katherine. *Deryni Checkmate*. New York: Ballantine/Del Rey, 1991.

_____. *Deryni Rising*. New York: Del Rey, 1982.

_____. *High Deryni*. New York: Del Rey, 1983.

Lansky, Bruce. *The Best Baby Name Book in the Whole Wide World*. New York: Meadowbrook, 1991.

Leach, Maria, ed. *Funk & Wagnall's Standard Dictionary of Folklore, Mythology and Legend*. New York: Funk & Wagnall's, 1972.

Lee, Guy, ed. *The Poems of Catullus*. New York: Oxford University Press, 1991.

LeGuin, Ursula. *A Wizard of Earthsea*. New York: Puffin Books of Viking/Penguin, 1986.

Lonnrot, Elias. *The Kalevala: An Epic Poem after Oral Tradition*. Keith Bosley, trans. New York: Oxford University Press, 1989.

Longfellow, Henry Wadsworth. *The Song of Hiawatha*. Edmonton: C. E. Tuttle Co., 1975.

Loomis, Roger Sherman, and Laura Hibbard Loomis. *Medieval Romances.* New York: New Modern Library, 1957.

Lowder, James. *Crusade.* New York: Random House, 1991.

Llywelyn, Morgan. *Lion of Ireland.* New York: Playboy Paperbacks, reprinted Houghton Mifflin Co., 1981.

_____. *The Horse Goddess.* Boston: Simon and Schuster, 1982.

Lucas, Randolph, ed. *The Illustrated Encyclopedia of Minerals and Rocks.* London: Octopus Press, 1977.

MacCana, Proinsias. *Celtic Mythology.* New York: Peter Bedrick Books, 1983.

Magill, Frank. *Cyclopedia of Literary Characters.* New York: Harper and Row, 1963.

Maro, Publius Virgilous. *The Aeneid.* New York: Library of Liberal Arts, 1965.

Martin, Lori. *The Darkling Hills.* New York: New American Library, 1986.

Matthews, Caitlin. *Elements of the Celtic Tradition.* Rockport, Mass.: Elements, 1991.

_____. *Mabon and the Mysteries of Britain: An Exploration of the Mabinogion.* London: Arkana, 1987.

McCaffrey, Anne. *Crystal Singer.* New York: Del Rey, 1982.

_____. *Dragonflight.* New York: Del Rey, 1978.

Mehrabian, Dr. Albert. *Name Game: The Decision that Lasts a Lifetime.* Bethesda, Md.: National Press Books, 1990.

Merwin, W. S., ed. *The Song of Roland.* New York: Vintage Books, 1963.

Miles, Joyce C. *House Names Around the World.* Newton Abbot, UK: David & Charles, 1972.

Monaghan, Patricia. *The Goddess Path: Myths, Invocations, and Rituals.* St. Paul, Minn.: Llewellyn Publications, 1999.

Moore, Robert, and Douglas Gillette. *King, Warrior, Magician, Lover: Rediscovering the Archtypes of the Mature Masculine.* San Francisco: HarperCollins, 1991.

Mustard, Helen, ed. *Nibelungenlied.* From Houston, Dr. Percy Hazen, and Dr. Robert Metcalf Smith. *Types of World Literature.* New York: Doubleday, Doran, & Co., 1930.

National Geographic Society. *Mysteries of the Ancient World.* Washington, D.C.: National Geographic Society, 1979.

Norton, Andre. *Wizards' Worlds.* New York: Tor Books, 1989.

Nurnberg, Maxwell, and Morris Rosenblum. *What to Name Your Baby, From Adam to Zoe.* San Francisco: HarperCollins, 1962.

O Corrain, Donnachadh, and Fidelma Maguire. *Gaelic Personal Names.* Dublin: 1981.

Paine, Albert Bigelow. *Mark Twain: A Biography.* New York: Harper & Bros., 1912.

Peterson, Roger Tory. *A Field Guide to Western Birds.* Boston: Houghton Mifflin Company, 1961.

Reaney, P. H. *The Origin of English Place Names.* London: Routledge & Kegan Paul, 1969.

Rolleston, T. W. *Celtic Myth and Legends.* New York: Dover, 1990.

Rose, Marie Arce, and Maité Junco Bebes Preciosos. *5001 Hispanic Baby Names.* New York: Avon Books, 1995.

Rowling, J. K. *Harry Potter and the Philosopher's Stone.* London: Bloomsbury Publishing, 1997.

Sarabande, William. *Wolves of the Dawn.* New York: Bantam, 1986.

Saunders, N. K., trans. *Epic of Gilgamesh.* London: Penguin Books, 1971.

Shakespeare, William. *A Midsummer Night's Dream.* New York: Penguin, 1967.

———. *Macbeth.* New York: Signet, 1987.

———. *The Tempest.* New York: Signet, 1987.

Spenser, Edmund. *The Faerie Queene.* From Abrams, M. H. *The Norton Anthology of English Literature.* New York: W. W. Norton & Co., n.d.

Squire, Charles. *Celtic Myth and Legend.* Van Nuys, Calif.: Newcastle Publishing, 1975.

Stein, Lou. *Clues to Family Names: What Do they Mean? How Did they Begin?* Bowie, Md.: Heritage Books, 1986.

Steinbeck, John. *The Acts of King Arthur and His Noble Knights.* New York: Ballantine, 1976.

Stewart, George R. *American Given Names.* New York: Oxford University Press, 1979.

Stewart, Julia. *1,001 African Names, First and Last Names from the African Continent.* New York: Kensington Publishing, 1996.

Stewart, Mary. *The Crystal Cave.* New York: Faucett Crest Books, 1970.

———. *The Hollow Hills.* Ballantine/Faucett Crest Books, New York: 1973.

———. *The Last Enchantment.* New York: Ballantine/Faucett Crest Books, 1979.

Stewart, R. J. *Celtic Gods and Celtic Goddesses.* London: Blandford Press, 1990.

Strieber, Whitley. *Cat Magic.* New York: Tom Doherty Associates, 1987.

Sujata. *Beginning to See.* San Francisco: Apple Pie Books, 1985.

Swift, Jonathan. *Gulliver's Travels.* New York: Oxford University Press, 1977.

Tennyson, Lord Alfred. *Selected Poems.* New York: Dover, 1992.

Tolkien, J. R. R. *The Lord of the Rings.* Boston: Houghton Mifflin, 1983.

———. *The Silmarillion.* London: George Allen Pub., 1977.

Turner, Nancy J. *Food Plants of British Columbia Indians.* Victoria, B.C.: British Columbia Provincial Museum. 1982.

Walker, Barbara G. *The Women's Dictionary of Symbols and Sacred Objects.* San Francisco: HarperCollins, 1988.

———. *The Women's Encyclopedia of Myths and Secrets.* San Francisco: HarperCollins, 1983.

Waring, Philippa. *A Dictionary of Omens and Superstitions.* Seacaucus, N.Y.: Chartwell Books, 1987.

Weis, Margaret, and Tracy Hickman. *Elven Star.* New York: Bantam, 1990.

Withycombe, E. G. *The Oxford Dictionary of English Christian Names.* New York: Oxford University Press, 1971.

Whitney, A. H. *Finnish.* New York: David McKay Co., 1970.

Wooton, Anthony. *Insects of the World.* New York: Facts on File Publications, 1984.

Zappa, Frank, with Peter Occhiogrosso. *The Real Frank Zappa Book.* New York: Poseidon Press, 1989.

TELEVISION AND FILMS

Dances with Wolves. Orion Home Pictures, 1990. Directed by Kevin Costner. Produced by Kevin Costner and Jim Wilson. Screenplay by Michael Blake.

Micki and Maude. Columbia Tri-Star Pictures, 1984. Directed by Blake Edwards. Produced by Tony Adams. Screenplay by Jonathan Reynolds.

The Wicker Man. British Lion Film Productions, 1971. Directed by Robin Hardy. Screenplay by Anthony Shaffer.

Star Trek: The Next Generation. Paramount, 1987 (pilot). Directed by Cory Alan. Produced by Gene Roddenberry.

SONGS

"The Morrigan." Earth Tone Studios, 1995. From the album *The Seeker.* Written and performed by Teara Jo Staples.

WEBSITES

http://heawww.harvard.edu/~jcm/space/misc/names.html (for satellite names)

Names by Their Characteristics

The following groupings list some names by the characteristics or the element they invoke. Choose a characteristic that you want to describe or invoke in the person being named, then look here for name ideas. The characteristics and their page numbers are as follows:

Gentleness 356

Happiness 357

Love 357

Lunar 357

Passion 358

Peace 358

Protection 358

Psychic 358

Recovery 359

Shadow 359

Sparkling 359

Strength 359

Success 360

Warriors 360

Water 361

Wisdom 362

Wizards 363

Youth 363

AIR NAMES

Aeolus

Aleyn

Ambar

Aria

Aurora

Boreas

Breeze

Celestial

Cirrus

Cloudy

Cumulus

Cyclone

Doldrum

Dustdevil

Eos

Ethereal

Eurus

Gale

Gusty

Hathor

Hurricane

Iris

Jumala

Lani

Leilani

Macha

Maelstrom

Makani

Mapuana

Nebula

Nimbus

Notus

Puff

Skye

Storm

Stratus

Tadewi

Thor

Thunder

Tornado

Tradewind

Tsunami

Typhoon

Ukko

Whirlwind

Wind

Zephyrus

BALANCE NAMES

Alder

Arianrhod

Asteroid

Bryony

Eostar

Equinox

Gemini

Libra

Osiris

Polaris

Robin

Season

Solstice

Turquoise

BEAUTY NAMES

Adonis

Agate

Aphrodite

Barkia

Bianca

Bonnie
Collin
Cullan
Cullin
Cully
Dagna
Duvessa
Dwight
Emerald
Farra
Farrah
Fenella
Fionan
Gannon
Gold
Golden
Guinevere
Gwendolen
Gweneth
Gwenora
Isolda
Isolde
Isolt
Izett
Jade
Jasper
Keefe
Keelia
Keelin
Keely

Keene
Kennet
Kenneth
Kennocha
Kyla
Kylia
Laurel
Mallalai
Miranda
Nix
Nokomis
Opal
Orchid
Shahla
Siran
Wynne

CLARITY NAMES

Aldebaran
Altair
Crystal
Diamond
Hermes
Iris
Jade
llma
Mica
Obsidian
Onyx
Quartz

Slate
Sorcha

EARTH NAMES

Acre
Aker
Amber
Arkose
Beryl
Chalk
Chestnut
Clay
Coast
Cybele
Daru
Desert
Earth
Eartha
Fabiana
Faunus
Flidais
Flora
Forest
Gaia
Glade
Glen
Gondwanaland
Granite
Grove
Haldis

Heartha

Hema

Inland

Island

Kaia

Kika

Laurasia

Magma

Mahkah

Meadow

Mesa

Metsa

Metsikko

Mielikki

Moraine

Moss

Ochre

Pangaea

Pichi

Planet

Quercia

Rhea

Rock

Salice

Salt

Sandy

Savanna

Shore

Silvaine

Silvanus

Silvia

Sita

Steppe

Stone

Sylvester

Sylvette

Sylvianne

Sylvie

Talus

Tapio

Terra

Terrain

Terrestrial

Tundra

Tuulikki

Tuwa

Vedis

Zia

Elders Names

Aeld

Aspen

Burtree

Crithach

Crow

December

Elder

Eldrum

Ellhorn

Elm

Falcon

February

Fir

Genna

Gennifer

Griselda

Gwyneth

Hollunder

Hylantree

Hyldor

Keenan

Keinan

Know

Meteor

Myrtle

Pethboc

Poplar

Rait

Ruis

Sage

September

Silver

Trom

Winter

Wintergreen

Wisdom

Wiseman

Wisewoman

Ysbadadden

Yule

Exotic Names

Africa
Amazon
Andorra
Anjou
Ankara
Antigua
Asia
Athabasca
Avalon
Azores
Baku
Bangkok
Bolivia
Bombay
Borah
Brea
Burma
Calcutta
Cameroon
Casablanca
Ceylon
China
Congo
Crete
Cyprus
Dacca
Delhi
Devon
Diva

Djakarta
Etna
Euphrates
Fiji
Gabon
Geneva
Genoa
Ghana
Ghea
Giza
Havana
Jandira
Jannali
Japura
Jasai
Java
Kashmir
Kilimanjaro
Kismet
Mali
Malta
Martinique
Mecca
Meru
Nauru
Nepal
Nile
Papua
Peru
Samar

Senegal
Sicily
Sikkim
Singapore
Somalia
Sumatra
Tigris
Vesuvius
Wisla
Xena
Yukon
Zambezi

Fairy Names

Aubrey
Elfin
Ella
Ellette
Elvina
Erlina
Fairy
Haltijatar
Pixie
Shay
Shea
Tatiana

Fire Names

Agate
Agni

Aidan

Anala

Arani

Ardan

Arden

Ardere

Ardin

Ardor

Aster

Aton

Basalt

Bask

Blaize

Blast

Blaze

Bowl

Brighid

Crackle

Curry

Dazzle

Didin

Didthin

Draco

Edana

Electric

Fever

Fire

Firecracker

Firefly

Flame

Flash

Galaxy

Garnet

Glow

Gold

Grainne

Kahoku

Kala

Kalama

Karan

Li

Lightning

MacGreine

Masou

Mirra

Morr

Myrrh

Opal

Paiva

Paprika

Pelee

Pyre

Pyrite

Ra

Ruby

Salamander

Satarah

Scorpio

Seb

Seker

Shamish

Solar

Spark

Sparkle

Star

Stella

Sterre

Sultry

Sundance

Sunny

Sunshine

Surya

Surya

Tama

Tannus

Tinnus

Wildfire

GENTLENESS NAMES

Affrica

Apple

Bilberry

Birch

Blueberry

Chamomile

Dalila

Damara

Galen

Goldenrod

Goldruthe

Maythen

Serena

Tara

Vanilla

Velvet

HAPPINESS NAMES

Ailsa

Alyssa

Bast

Bliss

Bluebird

Blythe

Chestnut

Chocolate

Clover

Cocoa

Delight

Desta

Faunus

Felicity

Hilary

Hillair

Hillary

Ida

Ilsa

Juniper

Lark

Magpie

Mave

Meara

Muirn

Onnellinen

Pellkita

Risa

Rosemary

Seble

Skylark

Tate

Thalia

LOVE NAMES

Adora

Amabel

Amanda

Angus

Astarte

Asthore

Charis

Coriander

Cupid

Daibhein

Ginger

Grania

Granna

Hathor

Janel

Jannel

Jannell

Kevan

Kevin

Latis

Lavender

Mint

Mistletoe

Peppermint

Spearmint

Valentine

Venus

LUNAR NAMES

Anahid

Badria

Bendis

Cerridwen

Chandra

Chantrea

Cynthia

Delia

Diana

Jacy

Konane

Kuu

Luna

Mahina

Miakoda

Migina

Mimiteh

Phoebe

Raka

Re
Selene
Selirra
Shashi
Soma
Taigi
Taini
Tanit

PASSION NAMES

Adonis
Allspice
Anise
Apollo
Arani
Ardelle
Ardis
Ardra
Barberry
Basil
Bay
Beltane
Cayenne
Cinnamon
Comet
Copper
Damara
Dionysus
Eros
Freya

Gorse
Keegan
Kundalini
Laurel
Lena
Linden
Mandrake
Min
Mountain Ash
Orchid
Pan
Parsley
Rowan
Ruby
Satry
Sweet Bay
Valentine
Witchbane
Witchen
Witchwood

PEACE NAMES

Dove
Erin
Farica
Humphrey
Irene
Pax
Peace
Tranquil

PROTECTION NAMES

Amethyst
Andromeda
Angelica
Blackthorn
Broom
Cumin
Edmee
Fern
Garda
Garner
Holly
Pepper
Raith
Ramona

PSYCHIC NAMES

Alum
Amethyst
Anise
Aquamarine
Bay
Copper
Delphi
Delphine
Gypsum
Laurel
Mana
Manda
Meda

Mica

Opal

Quartz

Sagus

Shoney

Silver

Sweet Bay

Sybil

Thyme

RECOVERY NAMES

Better

Emery

Gull

Imbolc

January

Jasper

Quicksilver

Time

SHADOW NAMES

Annikki

Arawn

Athtor

Falcon

Hades

Hecate

Kalma

Macha

Morpheus

Morrigan

Nox

Orcus

Raven

Rot

Samhain

Surma

Sycamore

SPARKLING NAMES

Asta

Astrid

Blenda

Dara

Izar

Lumen

Mamid

Palwasha

Roxanna

Snana

Stella

Stellato

Sucente

Viviane

Vivien

Vivienne

Zeno

STRENGTH NAMES

Aeld

Agate

Alioth

Antares

Arcturus

Aries

Aspen

Audrey

Brant

Breed

Brian

Briana

Brid

Bride

Bridget

Briget

Brighid

Burtree

Centaurus

Condor

Dair

Duir

Elder

Eldrum

Ellhorn

Fearghus

Flint

Galena

Granite

Hollunder

Hylantree

Hyldor

Ivy

Jupiter

Leo

Marjoram

Mars

Megan

Minerva

Oak

Pethboc

Ruis

Tamarisk

Trom

Valene

Valery

Valora

Zeus

SUCCESS NAMES

Alda

Alodie

Amelia

Ardith

Audris

August

Autumn

Cerelia

Darius

Emera

Emerald

Felix

Forbes

Ganesha

Ginger

Guri

Honeysuckle

Lammas

Lucretia

Lughnasadh

Mabon

Mercury

Midsummer

November

Nutmeg

October

Ora

Tanit

WARRIOR NAMES

Alexander

Anann

Anu

Apollo

Archibald

Ares

Artemus

Ash

Baldwin

Ballard

Baron

Barret

Bellona

Bevan

Bevis

Brenainn

Briar

Calhoun

Carlin

Casey

Cathal

Charles

Cillian

Conlan

Conway

Curran

Darren

Darrin

Donagh

Donahue

Donnovan

Donovan

Drake

Duncan

Dustin

Eagle

Eerie

Evan

Faolan

Farrell

Farry

Ferrell

Gaisgeil

Gearwe

Hardy

Hazel

Indra	Neala	**WATER NAMES**
Jarl	Neel	Aquamarine
Jarlath	Nels	Aquarius
Jarlen	Niall	Archelous
Justin	Nicholas	Atlantic
Justinian	Nolan	Bay
Kearn	Odin	Belisma
Kearney	Orion	Blackbird
Keegan	Owen	Brook
Keir	Padraic	Brooke
Kele	Padraig	Cascade
Kellen	Patric	Cascata
Kelly	Perseus	Corrente
Kennedy	Raina	Cove
Kern	Rory	Creek
Kerr	Seamus	Dagon
Kerry	Searlas	Deep
Killian	Sebastian	Dorian
Knyghten	Shemus	Dorie
Leander	Sigmund	Dorissa
Leandra	Sloan	Dory
Leola	Thor	Drizzle
Leona	Torin	Dylan
Leoni	Trahern	Ebb
Maghnus	Ulysses	Egeria
Magnus	Vassily	Flow
Mahon	Yarrow	Gannet
Marelda	Yarroway	Geyser
Myer	Yew	Gypsum
Myles		Hadrian

Hail
Harbor
Hinun
Ilmatar
Iris
Jade
Jet
Kele
Kolika
Lagoon
Lake
Lapis
Lynn
MacCuill
Manannan
Maris
Marris
Marsh
Meri
Meris
Merrick
Monsoon
Morgance
Murrough
Neptune
Nerissa
Nick
Nix

Nu
Ocean
Pisces
Pond
Rain
Rainbow
Raindrop
Rainforest
Rana
Rapid
Regenbeald
River
Rona
Saille
Sandpiper
Sea
Shoney
Snowflake
Splash
Spring
Stream
Sulla
Tamesis
Tefnut
Thaiassa
Torrente
Trenton
Ulla

Vellamo
Vesiputous
Waitilanni
Waterfall
Wave
Whirlpool
Whitewater
Willow

WISDOM NAMES

Amergin
Aspasia
Athena
August
Beech
Branwen
Chiron
Clark
Coll
Conroy
Dallan
Dallas
December
Druce
Evan
Evans
Ewan
Ewen
Fennel

Fincoll

Galen

Galena

Hazel

Hazelnut

Isidore

Jade

Kendra

Mert

Oriole

Owl

Sage

Velda

WIZARD NAMES

Fabula

Geas

Geasachd

Geasadair

Geasadioma

Gointe

Grianchrisos

Incanto

Maaginen

Magice

Magico

Mago

Magus

Maliardo

Medea

Merlin

Merlin Neo

Mistico

Mita

Moituus

Muireannach

Nahimana

Nidawi

Noita

Orenda

Orra

Orraidheachd

Orrtha

Orrthannan

Pagano

Paganus

Saga

Satinka

Sgaileach

Spin

Strega

Stregone

Stregoneria

Taliesin

Tatiana

Wakanda

Zodiak

YOUTH NAMES

Acorn

Aker

April

Ariadne

Aurora

Avril

Bayberry

Bittersweet

Bracken

Brighid

Caitlin

Calantha

Candleberry

Chloe

Chloris

Corinne

Cynthia

Daisy

Delcina

Diana

Dulce

Dulcinea

Eire

Erin

Fawn

Fawna

Fawne

Flora

Flora	Katinka	Nova
Gelsey	Kyllikki	Novia
Heather	Lahde	Spring
Hogan	Maia	Trina
Julia	Maida	Trine
Juliet	March	Vesta
Karen	May	Virgo
Kari	Mayda	Wren
Karine		

INDEX OF NAMES